BANKING [ON] BLOCKCHAIN

A Legal and Regulatory Primer

Sumeet H. Chugani **Stephen T. Gannon**

ABA
AMERICAN**BAR**ASSOCIATION
Business Law Section

Cover design by Catherine Zaccarine.

Printed in the United States of America.

28 27 26 25 24   5 4 3 2 1

ISBN: 978-1-63905-491-6

Contents

Foreword

Paul Grewal

I first came across the idea of a blockchain sometime in the early 2010s. I'm not sure the exact year, but it was when I served as a US Magistrate Judge in the federal courthouse in San Jose, California. Magistrate judges have many responsibilities, none more important than reviewing applications from federal agents for warrants to search or seize private property. The judge's task is to evaluate whether the agent had established probable cause existed to believe that what was sought to be searched or seized was evidence of a crime, contraband, or the like. As I recall that day, I was in my chambers reviewing the previous evening's applications when I came across an application to search a property for and seize a hard drive containing something built on a blockchain called … bitcoin.

Before I could even consider whether the agent had shown the required probable cause, I realized I had a problem. Not only did I not know what blockchains or bitcoin were, I had even less of an idea what laws and regulations might apply to them. And I did not even know where to look to learn. There were no books, articles, or podcasts (were podcasts even a thing yet?) to consult. Thankfully, I did have on my government-issued desktop computer access to Google, and Google quickly took me to a simple but eloquent whitepaper titled "Bitcoin: A Peer-to-Peer Electronic Case System," written by an author calling himself "Satoshi Nakamoto." From there, I was able to piece together the legal and regulatory framework required for my evaluation, as difficult as it was. Before I could see how a reference text on these questions might help others wrestling with similar questions, I got pulled into another matter and gave it no further thought.

Several years later, I had stepped off the federal bench and returned to the practice of law. I had just accepted an offer to join a young private company called Coinbase that offered a safe, regulated way to access Bitcoin and other blockchain-based digital assets. By this point in time, digital assets were well on their way to capturing the wider public's imagination. The public was taken not only by the meteoric rise in the value of certain assets but also by the promise many blockchain-based technologies offered as an alternative to traditional financial technologies and services. As for me, I was mostly taken by how much American law and regulation had taken shape around blockchains. Money transmission licenses, money services business registrations, New York bitlicense and the like were now standard fare. The SEC had launched enforcement actions targeting ICOs, and the CFTC had taken action against fraud and other misconduct. And yet there still no comprehensive reference text explaining not only how blockchains worked but also how they fit with existing and potential law and regulation, especially those applying to the banking sector.

That is, until now. With this comprehensive guide to the legal and regulatory landscape of blockchain technology, Sumeet H. Chugani and Stephen T. Gannon have filled a void that has persisted to the present day. Many fine individual resources on blockchains and law now abound, but this guide offers a single reference that covers the entire landscape of relevant legal topics. You'll be able to share in all the lessons collectively that many of us were forced to learn one by one. In a certain way, I'm jealous of the experience you're about to begin as you learn all the diverse legal lessons of this revolution. I'm also hopeful that you'll quickly see the need, as I have, for legislative and regulatory reforms that protect consumers and investors while preserving the innovative potential of blockchains to transform not only banking and other financial services but many other industries.

Paul Grewal, Chief Legal Officer, Coinbase

Acknowledgments

Sumeet H. Chugani

Banking [on] Blockchain spawned from a Summer '23 discussion with my then 10-year-old daughter, Riya Chugani. Battling Roblox attention and eyerolls, we pondered how different the universe will look as she grows—artificial intelligence, flying cars, blockchain—and other geeky, futuristic thoughts which encompass the best brain space. At the time, I was days removed from my action-packed stint at Coinbase, where I was in the trenches with the savviest, most impassioned colleagues on the planet—our mission: increase economic freedom. A mission that seems even more plausible as this book hits the shelves. And, a mission that is important as ever as 2024's global economic uncertainty presses on.

My first thank you goes to Riya, for giving me the airspace to throw thoughts and ideas against the wall during our walks to the bus stop, tennis courts, or karate class. Oddly, I know it will be those exact walks, with minutes seemingly fast-forwarded over time, that I will reminisce about later in my existence. Alongside my eldest daughter, I thank my mother, Lata Chugani, my wife, Rita Chugani, and my youngest girl, Suri Chugani, for their loving support throughout my career, and this book's creation. I also thank my mentor, my trusted advisor, and the most generous man I know, Michael Diaz, whose support changed the trajectory of my career and whose brutal honesty created a monster ready to tackle this world.

Diving into the subject matter surrounding Banking [on] Blockchain is no small feat. The law is evolving rapidly—with the underlying technology lapping both legislation and regulatory pronouncements. As formidable as this subject matter is the immense enjoyment of being swallowed by the gray areas, and predicting the future of financial services. To that end, we owe a debt of gratitude to all the chapter subject matter experts, who generously carved out time from busy schedules to geek out with us and complete Banking [on] Blockchain.

There are others who deserve praise and appreciation for bringing this book to life. Their undertaking is not from pen on paper, or images created—but from showing the love, respect, and admiration that morphs from bestowal to line-drive motivation. You know who you are.

Stephen T. Gannon

This book is bigger than those of us who were named contributors. Behind each of us is the sum total of our experiences, the paths we've taken, the people from whom we've learned and those who have supported our work. This is where we acknowledge our debts of gratitude.

****

To Sumeet H. Chugani—Whose creativity, boundless energy and unmatched determination has driven this project from its inception.

****

To Samridhi Jain—Whose organizational and editorial skills, steady hand and calm judgment, always brought us back to the middle of the fairway when Sumeet and I had hit it deep into the rough.

****

To my colleagues at Davis Wright Tremaine LLP—Whose patience with my efforts and contributions to this work were, and are, the mark of a great partnership.

****

To the staff of the American Bar Association who nurtured this book—Without their wisdom and support this project would never have gotten off its feet.

****

Finally, to my wife, Betty and my sons John and Alex—You have always been patient when I wanted to look around the next corner and see what's over the next hill. You are the greatest of all teams. Now, I wonder what's next … ?

TL;DR: The Blockchain

Sumeet H. Chugani

> Whereas most technologies tend to automate workers on the periphery doing menial tasks, blockchains automate away the center. Instead of putting the taxi driver out of a job, blockchain puts Uber out of a job and lets the taxi drivers work with the customer directly.
>
> —Vitalik Buterin (Co-founder, Ethereum)

A blockchain is a distributed database or ledger, shared among the nodes of a computer network. Blockchains store information in "blocks" which are linked together via cryptography. Different types of information can be stored on a blockchain, but its primary utility is to serve as a ledger—maintaining a secure and decentralized record of transactions for cryptocurrency systems.

The best-known blockchain, Bitcoin, is decentralized, so that no single person or group has control over the network. Instead, copies of the blockchain are stored across various parts of the network, creating a distributed record of all transactions. This data is immutable—that is, it is unable to be altered by any single user or centralized party. Because there is no ability to alter data recorded on the blockchain, the only trust needed is at the point where a user enters the data. This eliminates the need for trusted third-parties—or intermediaries.

A blockchain has similarities to a database. The key difference with a blockchain is how the data is structured, organized, and accessed. A blockchain consists of "scripts" that conduct the tasks usual for a database: accessing, saving, organizing, and storing information. A blockchain is distributed, meaning that multiple copies are saved on multiple machines, and they all must match to be valid. A blockchain collects transaction information and enters it into a block, akin to a cell and a spreadsheet. Once the block is full, its information is run through an encryption algorithm, creating a hexadecimal number, called the hash.

The hash is then entered into the following block, header and encrypted with other information in the block. This creates a series of blocks "chained" together.

The entire network works simultaneously, trying to solve a hash. Each node generates a random hash, except for the nonce ("number used once"). Each miner starts with a nonce of zero, which is appended to their randomly generated hash. If that number (0+ the randomly generated hash) isn't equal or less than the target hash, a value of one is added to the nonce, and a new block hash is generated. This process continues until one of the miners generates a valid hash, which solves the problem, wins the race and generates a reward in the form of cryptocurrency. Generating random hashes until a specific value is found is the proof of work process. It proves the miner did the work.

Blockchain decentralization is created because a blockchain allows the data in a database to be spread out among several network nodes (computers running software for the blockchain) at various locations. If one node attempts to alter a record, other nodes would prevent it. No single node within the network can alter information held within the database.

Blockchains' uses have grown considerably through creation of various cryptocurrencies, decentralized finance (DeFi) applications, non-fungible tokens (NFTs), smart contracts, and now-banking.

DECENTRALIZED DIGITAL LEDGER

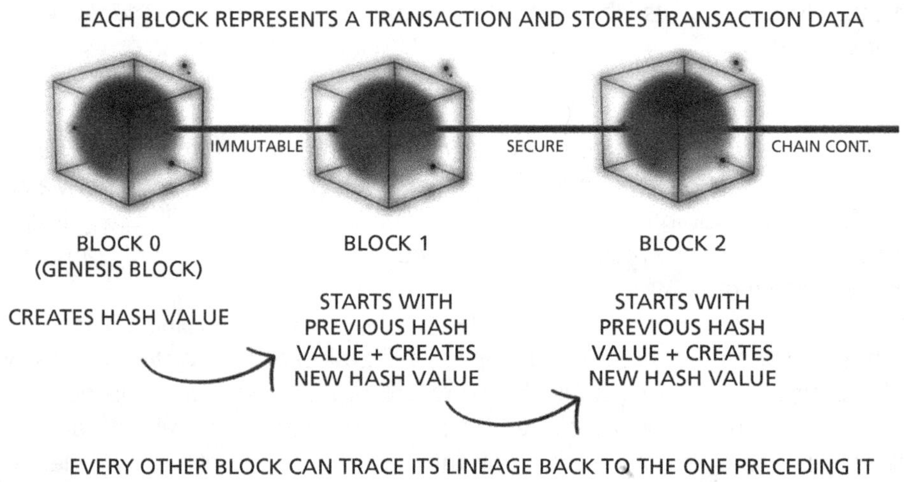

Setting the Table

Sumeet H. Chugani, Stephen T. Gannon, Ciaran McMullan

Is Banking [on] Blockchain the Future of Financial Services? ...

> Video killed the Radio Star … put the blame on VCR … in my mind and in my car, we can't rewind, we've gone too far …
>
> —The Buggles (1979)

Blockchains and digital assets are the most highly discussed and controversial technologies hitting financial services in the last 30 years. They also are the most volatile. Beginning in mid-2022, with the implosion of Terra Luna, the crypto market descended into "crypto winter." By mid-2023, that same market was recovering—and by early 2024 the market cap for digital assets touched $2 trillion and the price of Bitcoin surpassed $60,000—with BTC halving on the horizon.

Despite the robust performance, 2022 and 2023 brought into sharp focus striking business model weaknesses in early-stage blue-chip crypto firms (Terra Luna, Voyager, Celsius, BlockFi, and Three Arrows, to name a few) as well as shining light on outright fraud (FTX). Despite continued institutional investment, crypto's institutional failures such as IMB and Maersk's "TradeLens" venture can't be ignored. They are, however, a source of learning. The TradeLens project was too complex and unable to overcome dependence on globally ubiquitous bills of lading. And, the project failed to recognize the disruptive nature of blockchain innovation, as described by Clayton Christensen in The Innovator's Dilemma (Harvard Business School Press, 1997, 2000, 2016).

Blockchain and digital asset innovation can be viewed as similar to innovation in social media. Established players are ill-equipped to build the tools, technologies, and platforms to drive innovation and mass adoption. Startups are well suited for the task. Their decision-making cycles are short, internal changes required for adaptation are minimal, and new technology can be quickly assimilated. This is evident in payments, gaming, and social media and recently in crypto-specific advancements like decentralized identity and decentralized physical infrastructure networks.

Progress rarely moves in a straight line. When MTV opened its service in August 1981 alongside The Buggles' Classic, few anticipated Compact Discs (CDs), and streaming was … science fiction. Even when the future is uncertain, developers build toward real-world use cases and cross the bridge from early adopters to mainstream users. This is the financial evolutionary process, in which the strong [and the compliant] will survive and thrive.

In the midst of the build, we must understand how banks are dealing with blockchain technology and digital assets. Given that banks are centralized bodies regulated by a central government, one may pose why they need blockchain and/or digital assets at all. Below, Ciaran McMullan raises those exact questions.

One answer is security. Blockchain decentralization improves security by lowering the threat of a single point of failure or cyber-attack. A second is inclusion, by giving access to banking services in underserved or remote areas typically out of the reach of traditional centralized platforms. A third is speed of transactions, particularly globally since blockchains unlike most centralized systems, operate 24/7/365. A fourth is efficiency in the improvement of corporate operations. A fifth is the advent of tokenization into the capital markets. A sixth is to manage the generational shift to a more digital-based economy. (One survey indicates 77% of millennials are interested in cryptocurrencies and want to learn more.) A seventh is to be able to assist small and medium-sized businesses (SMBs) adopt blockchain technology with an eye toward solutions, such as Robinhood's Connect (easier customer onboarding for conversion of fiat to crypto), Corner Market (introducing blockchain benefits to small businesses) and Metis (a Layer-2 solution offering a user-friendly, no-code environment for SMB blockchain adoption). An eighth is to be prepared for the convergence of digital assets and monetary policy, often expressed in terms of the potential adoption of Central Bank Digital Currencies (CBDCs). Finally, it is simply prudent to be prepared for what is coming next. One does not want to be building battleships when your competitors are designing aircraft carriers. The recent joint request by bank trade groups asking the SEC to amend Staff Accounting Bulletin 121 to allow banks to act as custodians for Bitcoin ETFs appears to be a recognition of a willingness to adopt crypto solutions that make sense for bank business models.

There are arguments to be made for and against blockchains and digital assets. We summarize many of them in this Preface as well as in this book as a whole. We don't presume in this publication to resolve all of them. The debate rages on today by policy-makers, in courts, in legislatures, in boardrooms and, perhaps most importantly, on the Slack, Reddit, and Discord channels of digital asset developers. This book is to identify those arguments and to frame the legal issues which have and which are likely to arise. However, one cannot safely think that the issues have been mastered or even fully understood. These are cutting-edge issues, driven by evolving technology and moving regulations, that likely have already changed by the time this book's ink dries. But handling change and crafting solutions is where lawyers excel. This is just the beginning, so let's get started with a quick overview of some of the basics.

Benefits

The benefits of blockchain and digital assets are well known. Blockchains, smart contracts, and digital assets offer a full-stack payment system providing security, immutability, flexibility, and speed. Moreover, tokenized real-world assets have begun to take their place within financial services. For example, in late 2023, the municipal government in Shanghai, China [population 24 million, seventh largest in the world] released a road map to achieve blockchain breakthroughs by 2025. China intends to construct a basic service platform for the municipality which will support government affairs, cross-border trade, supply chain finance, transportation, an industrial Internet of Things, carbon management, metaverse, data element circulation and zero-knowledge proofs. And, new use cases continue to emerge. For example, stablcoins continue to be useful tools within which to conduct commerce across blockchains and their transparency has been increasing. Moreover, certain analysts believe XRP could play a role amid calls for gold-backed stable coins. In fact, the World Bank, the IMF and the World Gold Council have been openly discussing the need for a gold-backed stablecoin through which central banks might tokenize gold reserves.

Challenges

Blockchains challenges are well-known. Proof of work blockchains can be slow and difficult to scale. Different blockchains usually are not compatible with one another. Cross-chain linkages can be vulnerable to hacking. Adverse users can take the pseudo-anonymity of blockchain, complicate it with devices such as mixers, and use it as a method of transferring illicit funds. Dispute resolution frameworks have not been fully crafted including, for example, the legal standing of blockchain stored documents. Thus, overall, there is now and will be ample work for lawyers to do in analyzing and solving the various legal issues which will arise as the framework for this technology is evolving.

Talent/Liquidity/Capital

No industry sector will succeed without an ability to attract talent and generate liquidity. For now, blockchain and digital asset projects continue to attract talent and capital as past negatives are addressed. Problems of scalability, speed and security are being tackled. For example, transaction speed per second on some blockchains has now crossed the 100,000 transaction per second threshold. Entities such as Chainalysis, Elliptic, Crowd Strike and others have improved the tools to mitigate crypto sanctions evasion risk. The security of blockchains have improved and law-enforcement officials have become more effective at tracing stolen funds. Energy consumption concerns are also being addressed as proof of stake, consensus mechanisms, grow in number, and as proof of work technologies increasingly rely on the use of renewable energy and can become primary tools for removing carbon pollutants such as methane.

The recent approval of eleven spot bitcoin ETFs has significantly broadened liquidity for the industry, and improved credibility. Projects such as JP Morgan's Onyx are now scaling. Institutions such as BNY Mellon (custody); Fidelity (crypto funds); Deutsche Bank (custody, tokenized assets); Visa (payments), DTCC (clearing) and PayPal (stablecoins) all have entered the fray with their own products and projects. While the New York State Department of Financial Services (DFS) recently granted Wisdom Tree a charter to operate as a limited purpose trust company, allowing it to custody digital assets as well as issue, exchange, and manage the reserves of DFS-approved stable coins. It is unlikely that disciplined institutional players would fund blockchain and digital asset projects without an expectation of returns.

While debates remain, the markets have confirmed blockchain and digital assets are more than a mere bubble. The recent performance of the sector, on the other hand, tends to demonstrate its resilience and likely staying power. In a broader sense, the availability of spot Bitcoin ETF in the U.S. has advanced this trend and could potentially lead to the creation of more complex derivative products that rely on compliance-friendly spot ETFs, as a source of liquidity. Institutional adoption and support remains strong and one-third of institutional investors increased their crypto allocations in 2023.

Further, the reemergence of tokenization suggests that the capital efficiency of having an instantaneous settlement on repos, bonds, and other capital markets instruments is becoming more relevant. For example, in February 2024, Citibank used Layer-1 blockchain Avalanche's Spruce Subnet to explore the tokenization of private equity funds to re-architect capital markets. Citi worked with traditional financial entities WisdomTree and Wellington Management to carry out its proof-of-concept trial that was issued on Avalanche's Spruce, an Evergreen subnet designed for large financial institutions looking to use public blockchain infrastructure. tZero, Securitize, and Polymath are some of the market leaders in this space, using their platforms to transform private market securities through the use of smart contracts on the blockchain to create digital shares that can be traded on Alternative Trading Systems (ATSs).

Decentralization

The promise of decentralization continues to have powerful appeal. Banks must deploy numerous and expensive intermediaries to provide their services in an efficient, and safe and sound manner. The lower cost of immediate settlement and customer empowerment offered by blockchain projects continue to be attractive to small investors around the globe. Among the best-known use cases are remittances powered by crypto providing greater financial security to individuals living in countries with unstable financial systems. Moreover, while there is little risk in the short term of a global de-dollarization or a substantial decline in the use of the dollar as the world's reserve currency (an advantage which former French President Giscard d'Estaing referred to as the "privilege exorbitant"), it also is true that policymakers across the globe are looking closely at the weaponization of global finance as a result of the increased U.S. sanctions on Russia. This has accelerated interest in developing new cross-border payment solutions as more countries are striking bilateral agreements to reduce their dependence on the dollar. For example, perhaps ominously, both France and Brazil have started to settle commodity trades in Chinese renminbi. In addition, trials continue to be conducted with CBDC's to avoid today's cumbersome system of correspondent banks. Decentralization is not yet even a small wave, but it is an identifiable ripple in the water that appears to be gaining momentum.

Infrastructure

Besides transaction speeds, the industry is tackling weaknesses of interoperability and liquidity. For example, the Depository Trust Clearing Corporation (DTCC), along with Euroclear and ClearStream, recently released a joint industry paper (footnote to citation), highlighting how they can help develop and improve the digital asset markets of the future and play a role in the distributed ledger technology (DLT) based market. DTCC recently acquired Securrency, a crypto infrastructure, firm, providing institutional grade compliance, and interoperability. The CEO of Securrency, Nadine Chaker, commented on the acquisition: "We are excited to bring DTCC's infrastructure capabilities with Securrency's technology to embrace a future with a digitization of capital markets that is at the forefront of innovation ... [W]e will unlock opportunities to reimagine compliance, liquidity, efficiency, and interoperability in trading real world assets on the blockchain." The point, of course, is to have disparate platforms begin to interact with one another. Moreover, the continuing challenges of digital assets in connection with scalability and interoperability are being improved with Layer 2 solutions to either handle transactions off chain or in connection with other solutions such as sharding, batching, or consolidating on the main blockchain.

Regulatory Uncertainty

While the legislative and regulatory environment in the United States continues to be uncertain, there is an expectation that pending cases will be resolved, at least at the trial level, in the coming year and that those decisions will provide some guidance (even if not fully consistent) to the industry. There also is no shortage of proposed legislative solutions being offered, as we review in Chapter 1. Moreover, regulation outside the U.S., including the EU, the U.K., Singapore, Dubai, Brazil, and Canada continues to advance and add stability to what entrepreneurs can expect in the global market. The approval of spot Bitcoin ETF applications by the SEC may be the precursor to greater regulatory clarity removing much of the friction that otherwise has inhibited capital from flowing into this asset class. For example, the growth of Bullish, a digital asset exchange founded in 2021 and run by Tom Farley, former president of the NYSE. Bullish has been regulated from the beginning, just not by U.S. regulators. It secured a distributed ledger technology license from the Gibraltar Financial Services Commission in November 2021 before opening access to customers in select jurisdictions across Asia Pacific, Europe, Africa, and Latin America. It also has exploring licensing options in Hong Kong and Germany. It is audited by accounting firm, Deloitte, evidencing its commitment to transparency. It's customers go through a rigorous KYC, AML, and sanctions screening process before being on-boarded to the exchange. It also is well capitalized, often using its balance sheet to provide liquidity. Thus, despite the lack of U.S. licensing, Bullish was recently ranked fourth, by spot volume, for bitcoin by the Coin Metrics Market Data Feed. This may be the blueprint for what lies ahead—integrity, ample, mature management, transparency, and reasonable regulation.

We Are in the Starting Blocks

Much remains to broaden and deepen the adoption of blockchain and digital assets. Of course, the industry is in its infancy—approximately the same point at which air travel found itself in 1920. Over-indexing what may appear to be spectacular successes or failures (but which may only be point-in-time factoids) is mistaken. There is a path to broader adoption and success, but it remains uphill. And, it is marked with legal issues at each and every turn. The U.S. regulatory framework simply has not been written, and for some time is likely to be written by U.S. judges, and not by regulators. While this presents its challenges, other markets are showing the way to a convergence of innovation, products, benefits, and reasoned regulation that eventually will migrate to the United States. Thus, this book is, more than anything, about what the very early innings in this industry look like now and how best to advise your clients on how to navigate through an ecosystem that is developing and changing even as this is written.

Banking's integration of Blockchain will be a high mountain—with a sharp angle of ascent. This book details those challenges that appear today, how they can be overcome, and the future of Banking [on] Blockchain.

… Or, Will Blockchain and Digital Assets Be a Passing Fad?

In many environments, the strengths of blockchain and digital assets also act as barriers to broader adoption. For blockchain and digital assets to go mainstream in banking, thoughtful criticisms must be recognized, analyzed, and answered. This debate must be viewed as productive since it focuses attention on the current gaps in a blockchain-based system which require problem-solving today and in the near future.

The fundamental characteristics of a blockchain are at the center of these concerns. At the most basic level, a blockchain is a distributed copy of a simple debit/credit ledger. The most important design principle of Satoshi's blockchain was that it had to be trustless, meaning it had to securely transfer a digital asset, and users needed to trust it without the need for a central authority. Moreover, it had to be: (1) pseudo- anonymous, (2) immutable, (3) censorship resistant, (4) consensus-based, to maintain the integrity of the system, and (5) public, meaning anyone could see the history of all Bitcoin transactions since the inception of the system.

Are the Core Features of Blockchain Incongruous with Modern Banking?

Pseudo-Anonymity

Pseudo-anonymity impedes the efficient application of anti-money laundering regulations, a key requirement for any banking entity. Unlike any other medium of exchange, crypto is the only one that offers the ability to move extremely high-value amounts, extremely quickly and irreversibly. While most blockchain analytics firms track the use of illicit on-chain transactions, they often overlook the much larger problems created by obfuscation methods (such as mixers) and off-chain criminal proceeds that are laundered using crypto.

Immutability

The complexity of modern life and the speed with which technology has enabled decision-making, especially around payments and investments, dictates the ability to investigate and, where necessary, reverse transactions (such as in the case of fraud) is both critical and, in many cases, expected. Because reversing entries on a blockchain is either disallowed or extraordinarily difficult, this factor can make blockchain applications unattractive to retail customers and to regulators concerned with consumer protection.

Censorship-Resistant

While this feature can be attractive from a privacy point of view, the lack of a central authority allows any actor, good or bad, to execute transactions on the blockchain which under the AML/CFT/Sanctions environment has law enforcement and operational implications.

Consensus-Based

This characteristic of the blockchain is critical to ensuring there is no need for a centralized third party. However, the process of seeking consensus may not be attractive to retail customers who prefer the reliability of familiar systems.

Lack of Scalability

As it exists today, blockchain's append only, distributed structure is fundamentally incapable of a greater level of efficiency than a centralized, programmable database. Basic knowledge of queuing theory in mathematics illustrates the fact that the mining/consensus aspect of the technology may render it slower than a centralized system. Blockchain's highest and best use is the self-custody, ownership and transfer of a digital asset without the need for central authority. Banking and financial services, however, are increasingly high-volume businesses with a growing desire for instantaneous payment and finality. Given the characteristics of blockchain described above, significant additional work needs to be done to be able to handle high volume transactions with a short time scale finality. Those that are achieving higher speeds have done so by removing key aspects of the blockchain, such as decentralization and unhackable security. And, of course, once centralization is introduced into a blockchain environment, the argument for the blockchain itself diminishes.

Current Technology May Still Be Fit for Purpose

Centralized programmable databases/ledgers have been the basis of the banking system for decades and have proven to be efficient and robust. However, today's technology is not what hinders faster settlement, but rather the agreements, pricing and procedures utilized by participants in the process. Blockchain's solution to this particular problem is not technological, but rather is the removal of the trusted intermediaries required within our modern regulatory and financial structure via, for example, smart contracts.

Moreover, global payment systems have upped their game significantly. WISE allows for international remittances in a matter of seconds, and HSBC can instantaneously transfer high value amounts between accounts in multiple jurisdictions. At the domestic level, The Clearinghouse's Real Time Payments and the FRB's "FedNow" will soon make immediate payments ubiquitous for customers and businesses alike. Thus, it is puzzling why so much investment is being poured into overcoming the fundamental inadequacies of the "base" blockchain when fully functional alternatives exist today.

What, Then, Is Driving the Interest?

There can be no contesting the fact that significant amounts of capital [and space on the internet] have migrated into this relatively new corner of financial services. There are four things which account for this, and not all of them are good.

New Blockchains

First, new actors began to build their own blockchains with additional features and computational power above that offered by Bitcoin, Ethereum being the most well-known.

Designed by Vitalik Buterin, it goes beyond using the blockchain and its associated cryptocurrency (Ether, or ETH) as a store of value by designing the Ethereum blockchain (also known as the Ethereum Virtual Machine or EVM) to be used as a platform for development using smart contracts, as well as enabling the creation of non-native cryptocurrencies and non-fungible tokens (NFTs). Buterin's groundbreaking work encouraged others to design their own blockchains, such as Cardano and Solana. Hundreds of blockchains began to emerge, each with its own theory of value creation and investment.

The Hype Machine Began to Operate

In the late 20-teens and early 2020s blockchain and digital assets became among the most popular projects to write about on the internet. The amount of electronic ink spilled on this topic was stupendous. That intense focus and attention naturally drove interest amongst the investment class.

Venture Capital Provided Support for the Hype

As projects began to develop and promised spectacular returns, and as interest rates stayed low and liquidity remained plentiful, Venture Capital stepped behind blockchains and digital assets in a very substantial manner. In part, this was driven by the venture capital community's emphasis on (and comfort with) risk-based assets, as well as its well-known fear of missing out (FOMO, or the greater fool theory). The inadequate level of due diligence conducted with respect to projects such as Terra/Luna and FTX confirms what was at play. At the time, however, "move fast and break things" made sense.

Traditional Industry Players Added Credibility by Launching Their Own Blockchain Projects

As blockchain and digital asset products began to proliferate, they became part of the mainstream corporate innovation discussion. As a result, many of the world's largest companies decided to analyze blockchain technology and its potential to fundamentally improve their operations. Many of those companies made public announcements, hoping to ride the positive market sentiment around blockchain, which, in turn, added credibility to the sector.

Permissioned Blockchains

Many blockchain projects have launched at industrial scale. Few have landed fully intact. The vast majority of use cases being explored by the banking and financial services industry are using a *derivative* of blockchain technology called permissioned blockchains.

As mainstream players started to investigate the utility of blockchain and digital assets, they found it necessary to forfeit some of the fundamental characteristics of a blockchain in order to apply it to current corporate issues. In general, they eschewed many of blockchain's fundamental characteristics, including pseudo-anonymity, censorship resistance, public accessibility, and consensus-based approval.

While permissioned blockchains have many useful characteristics, the current variant is not the blockchain designed by Satoshi's Bitcoin innovation in 2009. In fact, permissioned blockchains are much more akin to a multi-user access, centralized and programmable database. In many cases, these permissioned blockchains are used for tokenization, such as with deposits and bonds, though they have not yet caught on at scale nor resulted in meaningfully liquid markets. Moreover, tokenization with respect to real estate and other real world assets continues to require reform of existing laws and systems for enforcing ownership—an area for legal innovation, to be sure. However, this kind of fractionalization will have to compete with prior legal innovations such as REITs. multi-member LLC, as well as product offerings from FinTech pioneers such as Robinhood and Block's CashApp.

Failed Large-Scale Corporate Projects

The success rates of large-scale commercial projects still leaves much to be desired. Recently, the *Journal of The British Blockchain Association* analyzed over 500 blockchain firms, finding that only 6.2% of projects provided evidence of a real business problem being identified, and even fewer projects (5.8%) analyzed the project architecture against alternative technologies, and only 1.5% used filtered, that is, hard evidence, to consider program outcomes.

There also are several high profile failed corporate projects where the lessons learned are available.

- Australian Stock Exchange (ASX). This project was designed to replace ASX's existing settlement system, known as CHESS. It was launched in 2015 and shut down in 2022, causing ASX to take a $200 million pre-tax write off. ASX's former CFO said: "It would have been easier to just build a new version of CHESS in some other modern language rather than blockchain."
- Lygon. Once lauded as the future of banking, this was a joint venture between various Australian banks to digitize bank guarantees using blockchain technology. It collapsed at the end of 2023.
- Maersk/IBM. This joint venture launched a new platform called TradeLens to track global trade and shipping. It was launched in 2018 and shut down in 2023. According to the *Wall Street Journal*, "the technology is complex, requires more computing power and is more expensive to run than existing databases."
- Commonwealth Bank/NDIS. This project was intended to automate benefit payments for the Australian government's National Disability Insurance Scheme (NIDS). Launched as a nationwide pilot program in 2018, it was subsequently discontinued. An independent review of the project was carried out by the National Science Agency and found "While these results for the proof of concept are positive, they could also likely be achieved by a centralized database solution."

In the end, none can argue with the laudable goal of financial democratization, which could be achieved through greater decentralization and fractionalization. The question is whether the underlying tools, that is, blockchains and digital assets, include the basic utilities needed to achieve these goals *at scale*. Thus, one needs to ask whether, once the excitement of speculation has faded, are the long term use cases for blockchains and digital assets capable of delivering value exceeding the required technological investment? After all, banks exist to return capital and profits to their investors. Thus, until that question can be answered affirmatively, the impact of blockchains and digital assets banking and financial services will remain open to challenge.

The Blockchain Hype Story—Visualized

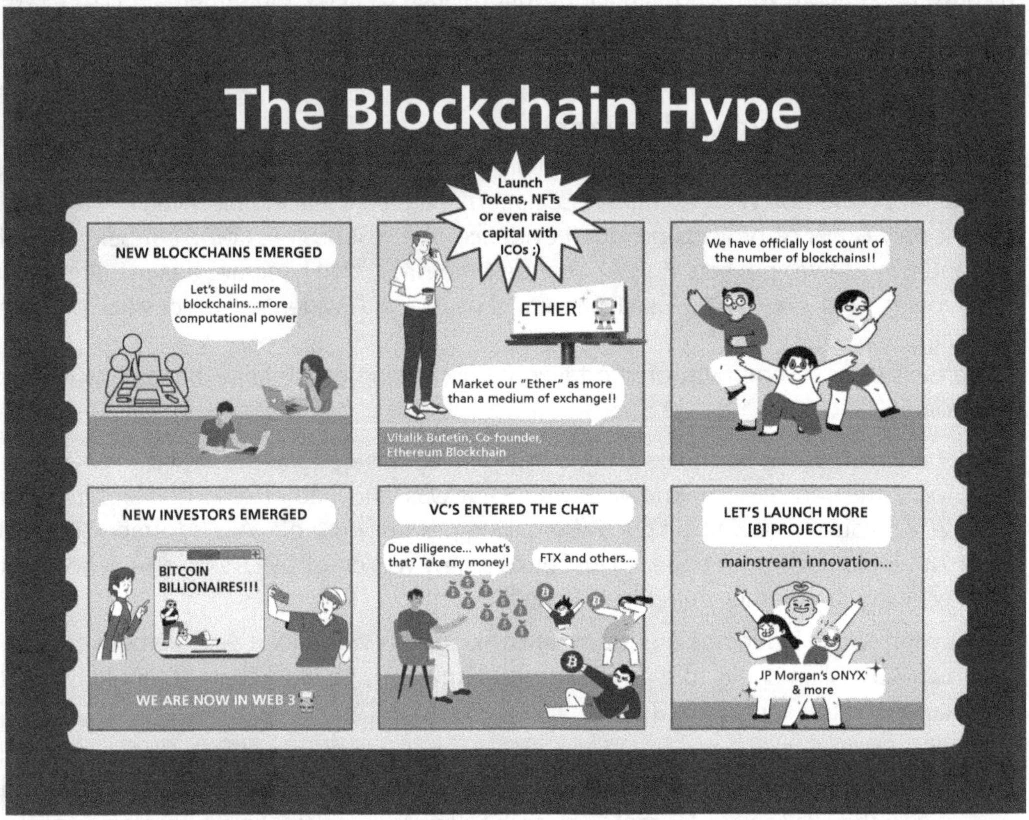

Chapter 1
Current State of Crypto Regulation

Stephen T. Gannon and Madison Breshears

Introduction

As of this writing, in the first quarter of 2024, the United States has no existing, comprehensive framework for digital asset regulation or predictable enforcement scheme, particularly in the case of securities regulation and enforcement, nor is one on offer in the near future. This state of affairs has fostered growing frustration within the industry and key market participants have grown concerned that the legislative and regulatory void allows regulators to wield enforcement authority arbitrarily, thus stymieing innovation and responsible capital formation.[1] For its part, the federal securities regulator takes the position that the industry exploits emerging technology to avoid following what the agency believes are the clearly applicable existing market and prudential standards[2] and that the industry embraces a "Wild West" attitude toward government oversight which runs to the root of the digital asset movement's history.[3] Despite the intensity of the arguments, regulation of the digital asset industry is in a state of "becoming," often leaving the industry with uncertainty and

---

1. *See e.g.*, Coinbase Global, Inc., Petition for Rulemaking – Digital Asset Securities Regulation, No. 4-789, https://www.sec.gov/files/rules/petitions/2022/petn4-789.pdf (July 21, 2022).

2. *See e.g.*, Gary Gensler, *Getting Crypto Firms to Do Their Work within the Bounds of The Law*, The Hill (Mar. 9, 2023), https://thehill.com/opinion/congress-blog/3891970-getting-crypto-firms-to-do-their-work-within-the-bounds-of-the-law/.

3. *See e.g.*, Timothy C. May, "The Crypto Anarchist Manifesto," Activism.Net (Nov. 22, 1992), https://activism.net/cypherpunk/crypto-anarchy.html (last visited Dec. 21, 2023).

fear of arbitrary enforcement. Yet, the current state of regulation can be cogently cataloged in several different and evolving dimensions. Today, at least four of those dimensions are evolved enough to study. We begin, in this chapter, with an overview of each dimension.[4]

First, there is what might be called standard regulation. That is composed of either guidance in various forms, or regulation promulgated through the notice and comment process under the Administrative Procedure Act (APA).[5] It is worth noting that guidance in this area, while not technically enforceable, is often viewed as enjoying the force of law. This is because regulated parties often consider it in their best interest to comply as though the guidance carried such a force. The risk and cost of enforcement litigation can be substantial, especially where a company faces the perception that it willfully disregarded an agency's public—if informal—statements. The securities, commodities, and banking regulators have all been active in the space.

Securities regulators have issued various forms of guidance[6] and have proposed changes to custody, accounting, and exchange rules,[7] all of which have been challenged.[8] These proposed changes are, almost uniformly, unfriendly toward the digital asset industry. Whether such a stifling approach is warranted is a distinct question and the subject of considerable debate.[9]

Banking regulators also have issued their own forms of guidance,[10] though such guidance has been less voluminous and controversial. This is no doubt due to the inherent and significant differences between U.S. banking regulations and securities regulations. Principal among many such distinctions is that securities regulation is disclosure-based, while bank regulation is fundamentally prudential and examination-based. Securities law and regulation was designed primarily to promote market transparency and mitigate fraud for the benefit of investors. On the other hand, the main focus of the prudential regulators is risk, namely, ensuring the "safety and soundness"[11] of individual U.S. banks, as well as the broader U.S. financial system. Key to understanding the rationale for this distinction is recognizing the disparate government incentives at play: while the securities laws require that information disseminated by market participants be accurate, the government does not

---

4. Later chapters will treat many of these topics in greater detail.

5. 5 U.S.C. §§ 551–559.

6. *See e.g.*, SEC, Framework for "Investment Contract" Analysis of Digital Assets (2019), https://www.sec.gov/corpfin/framework-investment-contract-analysis-digital-assets#_ednref9; *The Division of Examinations' Continued Focus on Digital Asset Securities*, Risk Alert, SEC Div. of Examinations (Feb. 26, 2021), https://www.sec.gov/files/digital-assets-risk-alert.pdf.

7. *See* SEC Staff Accounting Bulletin No. 121, 87 Fed. Reg. 21015 (Apr. 11, 2022).

8. *See e.g.*, Securities & Exch. Comm'n., B-334540, 2023 WL 7183855 (Comp. Gen. Oct. 31, 2023); *SEC v. Blockvest, LLC*, No. 18-cv-2287, 2019 WL 625163 (S.D. Cal. Feb. 14, 2019).

9. *See e.g.*, Jason Brett, *2022 Year in Review: Crypto Policy Experiences Massive Turbulence in Congress Amid TerraUSD and FTX Failures* (Dec. 23, 2022), https://www.forbes.com/sites/jasonbrett/2022/12/23/2022-year-in-review-crypto-policy-experiences-massive-turbulence-in-congress-amid-terrausd-and-ftx-failures/?sh=2d07207c5777; Paul Kiernan, *Republicans Pummel SEC's Gary Gensler over Crypto Crackdown,* Wall St J. (Apr. 18, 2023), https://www.wsj.com/articles/sec-chair-gensler-to-defend-climate-crypto-plans-before-gop-led-panel-2e3a6ade.

10. *See e.g., Digital Assets,* OCC. https://occ.gov/topics/supervision-and-examination/financial-technology/digital-assets/index-digital-assets.html (last visited Dec. 21, 2023).

11. 12 C.F.R. § 30 (1998).

guarantee it—aggrieved investors are merely afforded a private right of action to recover their losses provided disclosures are false or inadequate.[12] On the other hand, bank deposits of up to $250,000 *are guaranteed* (*i.e.*, insured) by the federal government, a fact which is reflected by the more invasive nature of the examination-based scheme, as well as a lesser focus on public disclosure.[13] Prudential regulators continually examine banks and rate them. Ratings which fall below a certain threshold can damage a bank's ability to grow which may require correction and remediation.[14]

Moreover, bank examiners have the power to prescribe Matters Requiring Attention (MRAs[15]) in supervisory examination reports which, as a practical matter, require banks to undertake certain actions to bring them into what the examiners perceived to be full compliance, consistent with the safety and soundness principles of the given banking regulator.[16] With limited exceptions, examination reports, including supervisory ratings and any outstanding MRAs, are categorized as confidential supervisory information (CSI).[17] In light of the elevated risk posed by federally insured deposits (and the broader systemic implications of bank failure generally, which raise not only concerns for the global financial system, but also—and not insignificantly—for national security), bank regulators tend to be especially risk-averse, and characteristically begrudging to adapt to—much less adopt—new financial technologies. With respect to digital assets, the approach taken by bank regulators, and the generally quiet, cautious response of banks, is therefore hardly surprising. However, it is a testament to the overall growing demand for this technology that banks have joined the conversation and expressed interest in providing digital asset services. That said, guidance from banking regulators has made clear that for a bank to be meaningfully involved in digital assets, its management of that risk would have to be of the highest order. In other words, the current banking regulators—whether intentionally or not—have signaled that

12. *See* Eva Su, Capital Markets, Securities Offerings, and Related Policy Issues, 8 (2018), https://sgp.fas.org/crs/misc/R45221.pdf.

13. *Id.* In addition, in part, because of the historic fear of bank runs, banks, (at least large ones) are often considered more systemically important than even major securities firms, most of whom are now owned by banks.

14. The best-known rating system is the OCC's CAMELS ratings, standing for: Capital adequacy, Asset quality, Management capability, Earnings, Liquidity, and Sensitivity to market risks, especially interest rate risk. For more information, see FDIC, *Uniform Financial Institutions Rating System,* 62 Fed. Reg. 752 (Jan. 6, 1997), https://www.fdic.gov/resources/regulations/federal-register-publications/ufir.pdf; see *also,* CFI Team, *CAMELS Rating System,* Corporate Fin. Inst. https://corporatefinanceinstitute.com/resources/wealth-management/camels-rating-system/ (last visited Dec. 21, 2023).

15. *See* FRB, *Supervisory Considerations for the Communication of Supervisory Findings,* SR 13-13/CA 13-10, attachment 3-4 (June 17, 2013), https://www.federalreserve.gov/supervisionreg/srletters/sr1313.htm; *See also,* Greg Baer & Jeremy Newell, *The MRA Is the Core of Supervision, but Common Standards and Practices are MIA,* Bank Pol. Inst. (Feb. 18, 2018), https://bpi.com/the-mra-is-the-core-of-supervision-but-common-standards-and-practices-are-mia/.

16. MRAs are expensive and time-consuming to resolve, and it is very much in the interest of banks to avoid them if it all possible.

17. The confidentiality of examination findings is not discretionary. Unauthorized disclosure may subject a bank to criminal penalties. *See* OCC, "Supervisory Ratings and Other Nonpublic OCC Information: Statement on Confidentiality," OCC Bulletin 2019-15 (Mar. 25, 2019), https://www.occ.treas.gov/news-issuances/bulletins/2019/bulletin-2019-15.html; *See also,* OCC, "Interagency Advisory on Confidentiality of the Supervisory Rating and Other Non-Public Supervisory Information," OCC Bulletin No. 2005-4 (Feb. 28, 2005), https://www.occ.gov/news-issuances/bulletins/2005/bulletin-2005-4a.pdf.

they will carefully scrutinize digital asset related products and business lines, which has generally discouraged banks from full-fledged involvement in digital assets.

The second dimension of digital asset regulation arises from attempts to craft legislative solutions. To date, state legislative efforts to encourage banks to adopt or accommodate digital assets or blockchain technology have been, by and large, limited by the efforts of the federal regulators to restrict crypto companies' access to the banking system, particularly the ability to send wires over either Fedwire or ACH.[18]

At the federal level, legislators have paid substantial attention to the development of a regulatory system governing the trading of digital assets, in most instances through the CFTC,[19] as well as to bills to oversee and govern the development of stablecoins,[20] and craft appropriate anti-money laundering (AML) protections.[21] Many of the existing bills are focused on a broad set of disclosure requirements about the nature of the digital asset and how they are traded.[22] Unfortunately, these efforts have stalled in connection with the highly partisan nature of a closely divided Congress, as well as other substantial budget and international priorities.[23]

The third area addressed will be developments in international regulation. Other countries have provided overseas markets with considerably more clarity with respect to digital assets. For example, Brazil has had a Bitcoin ETF since 2021.[24] Brazil also has approved several major banks for crypto trading,[25] though currently these functions appear to provide a convenient alternative for high-net-worth individuals, rather than to genuinely compete with major exchanges such as Binance or Coinbase. The development of digital asset regulation internationally is a dimension of the regulatory picture no less relevant to the future of digital assets in the United States. As regulatory uncertainty persists, developers and other digital asset participants are increasingly moving overseas, where markets continue to develop and grow causing concern in some circles within the U.S.[26]

---

18. *See e.g.,* Custodia Bank, "Order Denying Application for Membership," FRB Order No. 2023-02 (Jan. 27, 2023), https://www.federalreserve.gov/newsevents/pressreleases/files/orders20230324a1.pdf. (Custodia continues to challenge the Fed's refusal to grant it a master account to assess FRB services, including Fedwire.)

19. *See e.g.,* Financial Innovation and Technology for the 21st Century Act, H.R. 4763, 118th Cong. (2023); Lummis-Gillibrand Responsible Financial Innovation Act, S. 2281, 118th Cong. (2023); Digital Commodities Consumer Protection Act of 2022, H.R. 8950, 117th Cong. (2022).

20. *See e.g.,* Clarity for Payment Stablecoins Act of 2023, H.R. 4766, 118th Cong. (2023).

21. Digital Asset Anti-Money Laundering Act of 2023, S.2669, 118th Cong. (2023); Russian Digital Asset Sanctions Compliance Act of 2022, H.R. 7429, 117th Cong. (2022).

22. *See e.g.,* Digital Asset Market Structure and Investor Protection Act, H.R. 5745, 118th Cong (2023); Responsible Digital Asset Advertising Act of 2023, S. 1357, 118th Cong. (2023); Crypto Asset National Security Enhancement and Enforcement Act of 2023, S. 2355, 118th Cong. (2023);

23. As of this writing, commentators have stated that they do not expect Congress will be able to install a regulatory framework before 2025. *See e.g.,* Jesse Hamilton, *Crypto Won't Get Long-Awaited Rules in 2024, But Courts May Steer Its Future,* Coindesk (Dec. 18, 2023), https://www.coindesk.com/consensus-magazine/2023/12/18/crypto-wont-get-long-awaited-us-rules-in-2024-but-the-courts-may-steer-its-future/.

24. Tanzeel Akhtar, *Brazil Stock Exchange Lists First Bitcoin ETF in Latin America,* Coindesk (Jan. 23, 2021), https://www.coindesk.com/markets/2021/06/23/brazil-stock-exchange-lists-first-bitcoin-etf-in-latin-america/.

25. Paulo Alves, *Brazil's Largest Investment Bank, BTG Pactual, Launches Crypto Trading Platform*, Coindesk (Aug. 16, 2022), https://www.coindesk.com/business/2022/08/16/brazils-largest-investment-bank-btg-pactual-launches-crypto-trading-platform/; *Brazil's Largest Bank Itaú Unibanco Launches Crypto Trading Services,* Coin Market Cap (Dec. 2023), https://coinmarketcap.com/academy/article/brazils-largest-bank-itau-unibanco-launches-crypto-trading-services.

26. Jeff Wilser, *US Crypto Firms Eye Overseas Move Amid Regulatory Uncertainty,* Coindesk (Mar. 27, 2023), https://www.coindesk.com/consensus-magazine/2023/03/27/crypto-leaving-us/.

The fourth dimension is what is popularly known as "regulation by enforcement." Lacking a regulatory architecture which directly addresses digital assets, some regulators, led by the SEC, have adopted a clarity-through-enforcement approach, which—assuming the enforcement target is willing and has the means to challenge the action—leaves much of the ultimate decisions to courts, which are tasked with determining whether an agency's theories should have the force of law. For its part, the SEC has frequently brought suit against crypto firms for the unlawful sale of unregistered securities, often accompanied by claims of improper disclosure or fraud. The SEC, along with the Department of Justice, has brought a number of such cases, but far from bringing clarity, few have been particularly precedent-setting, providing scant guidance as to future conduct. In fact, most are settled outside of court, providing no binding precedential value whatsoever. At this writing, many of these cases are still at the trial level and likely will not be finally decided until well into the appellate process.

While potentially less time-consuming than traditional rulemaking or legislation, regulation by enforcement unfortunately suffers from several disadvantages which have not gone unnoticed by critics. For example, SEC Commissioner Hester Peirce has stated that the: "regulation-by-arbitrary-and-tardy-enforcement-actions approach ... is the opposite of a rational regulatory framework."[27] And at least one academic commentator has poignantly observed: "Where enforcement attempts to circumvent long standing norms of procedural fairness, informed rulemaking and deliberative analysis, the quality of policymaking can be diminished, with lower informational content, shallower expertise and limited public engagement underlying decision-making."[28] Notably, regulation by enforcement has been challenged directly by a new crypto trading platform called LEJILEX which, along with a trade association called the "Crypto Freedom Alliance of Texas" has filed a lawsuit in federal court directly challenging the SEC's regulation by enforcement policy, claiming that secondary market sales of digital assets do not constitute securities transactions and thus fall outside the scope of the SEC's jurisdiction.

Standard Regulation

In this first dimension, the SEC and the banking regulators have been the most active. In each case where either has issued guidance or proposed APA-compliant regulation, the general effect has been to render it more difficult to conduct digital asset business in the United States while purporting to protect investors and support the safety and soundness of the U.S. financial system.

The SEC

In July 2022, Coinbase, the largest crypto exchange in the U.S., petitioned the SEC under 17 CFR § 201.192 to propose and adopt rules to govern the regulation of securities that are offered and traded via digitally native methods—*i.e.*, those instruments that "are recorded

27. Comm'r Hester M. Peirce, "Outdated: Remarks before the Digital Assets at Duke Conference," (Jan. 20, 2023), https://www.sec.gov/news/speech/peirce-remarks-duke-conference-012023.

28. Chris Brummer, et al., *Regulation by Enforcement* (March 30, 2023). Univ. S. Cal. L. Rev., forthcoming, Available at SSRN: https://ssrn.com/abstract=4405036.

and transferred using distributed ledger technology."[29] Importantly, these rules would clarify which digital assets are securities. After the Coinbase petition had been pending for nearly a year, the Commission filed suit against Coinbase on June 6, 2023, alleging the company was operating as unregistered exchange through its crypto staking-as-a-service-program.[30] The case is currently pending.[31]

On December 15, 2023, SEC Chairman Gary Gensler issued a statement in support of the Commission's denial of Coinbase's petition for rulemaking.[32] In the statement, the Chairman recited a familiar theme, emphasizing that the existing definition of a security provided by the *Howey* and *Reves* tests[33] provides adequate clarity for market participants. The Chairman effectively bootstrapped this statement providing, as evidence, the SEC's successful enforcement actions against numerous crypto firms since 2019.[34] He further cited that the SEC has proposed and solicited comment on a number of rules applicable to digital asset securities including Regulation Best Execution, Safeguarding Advisory Client Assets, Regulation Systems Compliance and Integrity, and Amendments Regarding the Definition of "Exchange" (all of which have been criticized or challenged).[35]

Interestingly, the chair also pointed to the SEC's 2021 Special Purpose Broker Dealers (SPBD) Release as evidence of the SEC's successful efforts in regulating the space. Although the SPBD release provided a limited safe harbor regarding certain crypto asset activities,[36] as of this writing in January 2024, only *one* broker-dealer (Promethium Ember Capital) is currently registered under the safe harbor. Many began to raise questions about the startup

---

29. "Digitally native securities are recorded and transferred using distributed ledger technology and do not rely on centralized entities or certificated forms of ownership that characterize traditional financial instruments." Coinbase Petition, *supra* note 27 at 1.

30. Press Rel., *SEC Charges Coinbase for Operating as an Unregistered Securities Exchange, Broker, and Clearing Agency,* SEC (June 6, 2023), https://www.sec.gov/news/press-release/2023-102.

31. *SEC v. Coinbase, Inc.* et al., Case No. 1:23-CV-04738 (S.D.N.Y. 2024).

32. G. Gensler, *Statement on Denial of a Rulemaking Petition Submitted on behalf of Coinbase Global, Inc.*, (Dec. 15, 2023).

33. *SEC v. W.J. Howey Co.,* 328 U.S. 293 (1946); Reves *v. Ernst & Young*, 494 U.S. 56, 60-61 (1990).

34. Statement of Chair Gary Gensler, *supra* note 27, (citing e.g., SEC v. Blockvest, LLC, No. 18-cv-2287, 2019 WL 625163, at *4-*9 (S.D. Cal. Feb. 14, 2019); SEC v. Nat. Diamonds Inv. Co., 19-cv-80633, 2019 WL 13277296, at *8-*10 (S.D. Fla. May 28, 2019); SEC v. Telegram Grp. Inc., 448 F. Supp. 3d 352, 368-79 (S.D.N.Y. 2020), appeal dismissed, No. 20-1076, 2020 WL 3467671 (2d Cir. May 22, 2020); SEC v. Kik Interactive Inc., 492 F. Supp. 3d 169, 177-80 (S.D.N.Y. 2020); SEC v. NAC Found., LLC, 512 F. Supp. 3d 988, 995-97 (N.D. Cal. 2021); SEC v. LBRY, Inc., 639 F. Supp. 3d 211, 216-21 (D.N.H. 2022), appeal dismissed, No. 23-1743 (1st Cir. Oct. 23, 2023); SEC v. Terraform Labs Pte. Ltd., No. 23-cv-1346, 2023 WL 4858299, at *10-*15 (S.D.N.Y. July 31, 2023)). (Unfortunately, many of these cases were settled or were decided on unique facts which provide little forward guidance to the industry.)

35. *Id.* at n. 14 Regulation Best Execution, 88 Fed. Reg. 5440, 5448-49, 5540-42 (proposed Jan. 27, 2023) (proposed rules requiring broker-dealers to seek best execution of customer orders, including for crypto asset securities); Safeguarding Advisory Client Assets, 88 Fed. Reg. 14672, 14676, 14688-94, 14700, 14706, 14710, 14715, 14726 (proposed Mar. 9, 2023) (proposed rules addressing investment advisers' obligations regarding the custody and safeguarding of clients' assets, including security and non-security crypto assets); Regulation Systems Compliance and Integrity, 88 Fed. Reg. 23146, 23166-68 (proposed Apr. 14, 2023) (discussing proposed amendments to the application of technology infrastructure rules for markets and intermediaries, including relevant systems pertaining to crypto asset securities); Supplemental Information and Reopening of Comment Period for Amendments Regarding the Definition of "Exchange," 88 Fed. Reg. 29448 (proposed May 5, 2023) (soliciting comments on the application of the proposed amended definition to trading systems for crypto asset securities, among other issues).

36. Custody of Digital Asset Securities by Special Purpose Broker-Dealers, 86 Fed. Reg. 11627, 11628 (Feb. 26, 2021) (Special Purpose Broker-Dealers Release).

crypto firm after co-CEO Aaron Kaplan testified at a hearing before the House Financial Services Committee in June 2023.[37] Kaplan's testimony, which cast other crypto-industry executives calling for clarity as "simply not willing to comply," and praised the SEC, drew significant attention. Subsequent reporting would uncover details about Prometheum's business that prompted calls for an investigation into Prometheum's SPBD approval by members of the House Financial Services Committee[38] and the crypto-advocacy group Blockchain Association,[39] both suggesting that Prometheum secured a sweetheart deal with the regulator in exchange for the company's testimony. At the time of this writing, Prometheum has secured coveted approvals from the self-regulatory organization governing broker-dealers, FINRA (the Financial Industry Regulatory Authority).[40] And they have announced they will soon launch its first product, a custody service for ETH. Prometheum plans to later offer clearing and settlement services for ETH and eventually other crypto assets. (Notably as well, contrary to the CFTC and most of the market, Prometheum holds the view that ETH is an investment contract and therefore is a security.) The long road from Prometheum's approval as an Alternative Trading System (ATS) in July 2021 to its planned initial product launch in the Spring of 2024 is instructive as to the regulatory pace associated with registration.

The SEC's 2023 denial of Coinbase's Petition for Rulemaking, over a year after its July 2022 petition and the revelations about its sole approved licensee under its SPBD rule, is an illustrative starting point. The bitter conflict between the SEC and the flagship U.S.-based digital-asset exchange, and the pace of approval for one registered entity, is reflective of the kinds of cumbersome challenges that have ground progress on crypto securities regulation to a crawl in the United States. Meanwhile, both the industry mired in uncertainty, and an agency that appears to be focused on misconduct (as opposed to rule-making)[41] appear to

---

37. *Id. See* Jesse Coghlan, *Who the Hell' Is Prometheum and What Did It Say to Congress about SEC Compliance?,* CoinTelegraph (Jun. 15, 2023), https://cointelegraph.com/news/who-is-prometheum-what-testify-congress-about-crypto-sec.

38. Letter to Chair Gary Gensler on Behalf of Members of the House Financial Services Committee (Aug. 9, 2023), https://financialservices.house.gov/uploadedfiles/2023-08-09_fsc_gop_letter_to_sec_re_prometheum.pdf.

39. Press Rel., *Blockchain Association Calls for Investigation into SEC Approval of Promethium Ember Capital as Special Purpose Broker-Dealer,* Blockchain Association (July 12, 2023), https://theblockchainassociation.org/blockchainassociation-calls-for-investigation-into-sec-approval-of-prometheum-ember-capital-as-special-purpose-broker-dealer/; *see also,* Turner Wright, *Blockchain Association Calls for Investigation into Prometheum over Alleged "Sweetheart" SEC Deal,* CoinTelegraph (Jul. 12, 2023), https://cointelegraph.com/news/blockchain-association-calls-for-investigation-prometheum-sweetheart-sec-deal.

40. Jalpa Bhavsar, *Prometheum Gets FINRA Approval for Clearing Services,* The Crypto Times (Dec. 22, 2023), https://www.cryptotimes.io/prometheum-gets-finra-approval-for-clearing-services/78.

41. At a September 2023 conference to commemorate the 15th anniversary of the collapse of Lehmann Brothers in September 2008, Chairman Gensler stated, referring to the digital asset markets: "I've never seen a field so rife with misconduct, and people trying to run outside of the law." The same month, during testimony at a hearing before the Senate Banking Committee, the Chairman remarked, "We've seen this story before. It's reminiscent of what we had in the 1920s before the federal securities laws were put in place." *See* Ruholamin Haqshanas, *SEC Chair Gensler: Crypto Industry Plagued by Misconduct and Legal Challenges,* CryptoNews (Sep. 14, 2023), https://cryptonews.com/news/sec-chair-gensler-crypto-industry-plagued-by-misconduct-legal-challenges.htm. (What the Chairman's statements overlook is the small percentage of fraudulent activity compared to the market as a whole. It pales in comparison to, for example, the penny stock frauds of the 1980s.)

be equally dissatisfied with the status quo. A brief summary of the SEC's recent activity with respect to rulemaking follows:

Proposed Crypto Asset Custody Rules

First, the SEC proposed amendments to Rule 203, the Custody Rule, which requires that registered investment advisors (RIAs) only engage with qualified custodians as the custodians of their clients' assets. According to the OCC's January 2002 Comptroller's *Handbook on Custody Services*: "Services provided by a bank custodian are typically the settlement, safekeeping, and reporting of customers' marketable securities and cash." Digital asset custody relates to various methods of storing and protecting digital assets on behalf of their owners, and in that sense, is similar to the custody of traditional financial assets. However, crypto owners acquire their digital assets in transactions recorded on a blockchain, through which the owners are issued cryptographic public and private keys to prove their ownership, and which keys must be used when transferring such assets. Those keys must be protected to ensure the owners' assets are safe, because if they are lost or stolen the digital assets may be unrecoverable. Thus, digital asset custody revolves around the various methods of storing the public and private keys of crypto owners. The topic of digital asset custody is dealt with in more detail in Chapter 4, *infra*.[42] Because most investment advisors contract with custodians to provide such services, being able to engage with a qualified custodian is central to the RIA business model. Among other things, the proposed rule would:

- Extend the custody rules' coverage beyond client funds and securities to client assets, which would include all crypto assets.
- Specify that a qualified custodian cannot maintain a client asset for purposes of the rule if it does not have possession or control of that asset, which is redefined in the proposal as "holding assets such that the qualified custodian is required to participate in any change in beneficial ownership of those assets."
- Require RIAs to secure through agreement a variety of assurances from the custodian, including indemnification against losses, and the clear identification and segregation of client assets from the custodians' assets and liabilities.

The challenge, of course, is how a custodian could prove exclusive control of a crypto asset given the fact that the asset is transferable by anyone in possession of a private key. The proposal sets a high bar for demonstrating such exclusive possession or control over crypto assets, and it is not certain whether any qualified custodian could meet the exclusive possession or control test.

The rule was originally proposed in February 2023 with its initial comment period expiring in May 2023. However, given the level of public interest and the high number of comments in the proposed rule, the Commission reopened the comment period until the end of October 2023 to allow persons additional time to "analyze the issues and prepare comments in

42. SEC, *Proposed Rule: Safeguarding Advisory Client Assets,* 88 Fed. Reg. 14672 (Mar. 9, 2023); Office of the Comptroller of Currency, *Custody Services*, Comptroller's Handbook (Jan. 2002), https://www.occ.gov/publications-and-resources/publications/comptrollers-handbook/files/custody-services/index-custody-services.html.

light of the final rules and amendments."[43] As of this writing, the final rule has not been proposed. However, once it is proposed, litigation is expected from various market participants.

Staff Accounting Bulletin 121

Staff Accounting Bulletin 121 (SAB 121)[44] creates another hurdle for large institutions seeking to offer crypto services at scale. This theoretically non-binding guidance raises concerns about prohibitive costs due to the unfavorable accounting treatment of crypto custody. SAB 121 identifies unique technological, legal, and regulatory risks associated with on platform crypto storage, which could expose banks to greater financial loss. Accordingly, SAB 121 states that the institution should record the crypto asset as both a liability and a corresponding asset on the balance sheet, both measured at the fair market value of the held crypto. This increased capital requirement could significantly impact banks' liquidity, potentially making digital asset custody a cost-prohibitive offering for large institutions. (See chapter on Bank Capital, infra.)

SEC Commissioner Hester Peirce expressed her views on SAB 121, pointing out that unlike other Staff Accounting Bulletins, SAB 121 provides interpretive guidance specifically for a very narrow group of public companies (those seeking to custody virtual assets), and details the specific disclosure the staff expects to receive.[45] After it was issued, a number of associations and elected officials called for greater clarity from the SEC on SAB 121's expected impact on financial institutions as well as a comprehensive notice and comment rulemaking amendment.[46] Interestingly, the presence of banking organizations in crypto asset markets could ultimately be beneficial for investors, financial markets, and the broader general public. The risks outlined in SAB 121 are largely mitigated due to the fact that banks are already heavily supervised and adhere to comprehensive regulation and related industry practices.

Notably, the Basel Committee on Banking Supervision has already adopted rules on the capital treatment of crypto asset exposure.[47] Its final crypto capital rule (*SCO 60: Crypto Asset Exposures*) generally exempts crypto-custodial assets from heightened capital requirements applicable to crypto exposures under the rule. By contrast, the capital treatment of crypto custodial assets for U.S. bank custodians that are SEC registrants is far less certain, creating an uneven playing field for U.S. banks and their consumers.

---

43. Press Release, SEC, SEC Reopens Comment Period for Enhanced Safeguarding Rule for Registered Investment Advisors Proposal (Aug. 23, 2023) (on file with SEC).
44. SEC, *Staff Accounting Bulletin No. 121*, 87 Fed. Reg. 21015 (Apr. 11, 2022).
45. *See* Comm'r Hester Peirce, Response to Staff Accounting Bulletin No. 121 (Mar. 31, 2022), https://www.sec.gov/news/statement/peirce-response-sab-121-033122.
46. *See e.g.,* Celisa Morin and Will Atherton, *A SAB State of Affairs: SEC Guidance Deters U.S. Financial Institutions from Providing Crypto-Asset Custody,* ReedSmith (Jul. 25, 2023), https://www.reedsmith.com/en/perspectives/2023/07/a-sab-state-sec-guidance-us-financial-institutions-crypto asset-custody; Press Release, Rep. Mike Flood, Congressman Mike Flood Leads the Uniform Treatment of Custodial Assets Act with Bipartisan Support (Sep. 27, 2023) (on file with Congressman Mike Flood campaign); Letter from Sen. Cynthia M. Lummis (R-WY) and Rep. Patrick McHenry (R-NC), to Hon. Michael Barr, Vice Chair Supervision, Fed. Rsrv. Sys., Michael Hsu, Acting Comptroller, OCC, Hon. Marty Gruenberg, Chairman of the Board, Fed. Deposit Ins. Corp., and Hon. Todd Harper, Chairman of the Board, Nat'l. Credit Union Admin., (Mar. 2, 2023) (on file with Sen. Cynthia Lumis).
47. BCBS, *Prudential Treatment of Cryptoasset Exposures,* BIS.Org (Dec. 16, 2022), https://www.bis.org/bcbs/publ/d545.htm.

SAB 121 ran into further difficulty when on October 31, 2023, the Government Accountability Office (GAO) ruled that SAB 121 was a rule (rather than mere guidance) and therefore must be submitted to Congress under the Congressional Review Act (CRA).[48] The GAO decision also suggests that rules like SAB 121, should be governed by the notice and comment processes of the APA. At a minimum, if a rule is not submitted to Congress under the CRA, it is of no force or effect. In February 2024, Senator Cynthia Lummis (R-WY), Rep. Wiley Nickel (D-NC) and Rep. Mike Flood (R-NE) introduced a bipartisan, bicameral Congressional Review Act resolution to overturn SAB 121.

Unfortunately, however, the SEC appears to be ignoring these requirements and pushing forward with attempting to persuade the industry to comply with SAB 121.[49] Ultimately, this is likely to lead to additional uncertainty and litigation.

Proposed Amendments to Key Definitions in the Exchange Act

The third formal effort is the SEC's proposed amendments to the Exchange Act, redefining the terms "exchange" and "dealer." [50] In January 2022, the SEC proposed amendments to Rule 3b-16 and the term "exchange."[51] These amendments make the criteria for being an exchange significantly broader and would have a direct impact on decentralized finance (DeFi).[52] Under the SEC's proposed amendment, any organization, association, or group of persons that passively make available a communication protocol under which buyers and sellers with trading interests can interact and agree on the terms of the trade is an "exchange."

In March 2022, the SEC also proposed rules that would expand the Exchange Act definition of "dealer" which could lead to dealer registration requirements for automated market-makers and other liquidity providers in the cryptocurrency and DeFi space.[53] If adopted, a significant number of companies and software developers in the crypto DeFi space would become subject to the SEC broker-dealer framework, including registration with the SEC and mandatory FINRA membership. The scope of the proposed rule's definition of "dealer" is extremely broad and would capture most proprietary trading firms as well as digital asset entities, specifically automated market makers (AMMs) as well as other liquidity providers

48. See GAO, SEC – Applicability of the Congressional Review Act to Staff Accounting Bulletin No. 121, B-334540 (Oct. 31, 2023), https://www.gao.gov/products/b-334540.

49. See Soyoung Ho, *Gensler Defends SEC Staff Accounting Bulletin on Crypto after GAO Report Deems It a Rule*, Reuters (Dec. 13, 2023), https://tax.thomsonreuters.com/news/gensler-defends-sec-staff-accounting-bulletin-on-crypto-after-gao-report-deems-it-a-rule/.

50. SEC, *Further Definition of "As a Part of a Regular Business" in the Definition of Dealer and Government Securities Dealer,* Proposed Rule, 87 Fed. Reg. 23054 (May 27, 2022); SEC, *Amendments Regarding the Definition of "Exchange" and Alternative Trading Systems (ATSs) That Trade U.S. Treasury and Agency Securities, National Market System (NMS) Stocks, and Other Securities,* Proposed Rule, 87 Fed. Reg. 15496 (Apr. 18, 2022).

51. 87 Fed. Reg. 15496.

52. According to the January 2024 report of the CFTC's Technical Advisory Committee, DeFi is "characterized by highly automated financial networks that have no single point of failure, do[es] not rely on a single source of information, and [is] not governed by a central authority that is capable of altering or censoring this information in order to perform tasks central to delivery of one or more financial services." Report of the Subcommittee on Digital Assets and Blockchain Technology, Technology Advisory Committee (TAC) of the U.S. Commodity Futures Trading Commission, p. 6.

53. 87 Fed. Reg. 23054.

in the cryptocurrency and DeFi space. Moreover, the proposed expansion of that definition should be read in connection with the Commission's recent proposal to broaden the definition of "exchange" in Exchange Act Rule 3b-16, which would include additional market participants such as "communications protocol systems" and also would extend to organizations which provide trading facilities or set trading rules which are made available for others to use, thus capturing most decentralized exchanges (DEXs). Being classified as a "dealer" or an "exchange" would require registration with SEC and with FINRA, as well as a wide variety of disclosure rules.

Both of these proposals have attracted substantial opposition and to date neither proposal has been finalized.

Approval of Spot Bitcoin ETF

At the time of this writing, the SEC has recently announced its long-anticipated approval of the first spot market Bitcoin exchange traded funds/products (ETFs/ETPs).[54] The approval marked a significant milestone for the industry after a tumultuous years-long journey since the first application for a Bitcoin ETF was filed with the SEC in July 2013 by Gemini co-founders Cameron and Tyler Winkevoss.[55] In the years that followed, between 2018 and 2023, the SEC denied more than 20 exchange rule filings for spot bitcoin ETPs.[56] These denials occurred despite the fact that the SEC had previously approved a Bitcoin futures ETF, while at the same time claiming that the risks associated with a spot Bitcoin ETF are materially different.

The SEC's stance seemed unwavering until Grayscale Investments, the world's largest digital currency asset manager, launched a suit against the SEC in 2022 after its proposal to convert its Grayscale Bitcoin Trust (GBTC) to a spot Bitcoin ETF was denied by the agency.[57] In August 2023, the United States Circuit Court of Appeals for the District of Columbia ruled in favor of the fund, characterizing the SEC's denial as arbitrary and capricious.[58] When the SEC decided not to appeal the ruling, and subsequently, a number of other ETF applications were filed, it had been widely speculated that an approval was imminent at the turn of the new year.

The situation took an unexpected turn, however, when, shortly after the market close on January 9, 2024, the SEC's official X (formerly Twitter) account posted an announcement that it had approved bitcoin ETFs to begin trading. Less than half an hour later the post was deleted, after Gary Gensler's official account retracted the post, stating that the SEC's had been hacked, and that bitcoin ETFs had not been approved.[59] However, the next day, the SEC,

---

54. *See* Chair Gary Gensler, *Statement on the Approval of Spot Bitcoin Exchange-Traded Products,* SEC.Gov (Jan. 10, 2024), https://www.sec.gov/news/statement/gensler-statement-spot-bitcoin-011023 (hereinafter "Statement of Chairman Gensler").
55. *See* Ezra Reguerra, *Spot Bitcoin ETF Approval Recap: A 10-year Journey Concludes in Historic Win for Crypto,* CoinTelegraph (Jan. 11, 2024), https://cointelegraph.com/news/historic-win-crypto-spot-bitcoin-etf.
56. Statement of Chairman Gensler, *supra,* note 48.
57. *See* "GBTC Lawsuit," Grayscale (visited Jan. 9, 2024), https://www.grayscale.com/company/gbtc-lawsuit.
58. Grayscale Invs., LLC v. Sec. & Exch. Comm'n, 82 F.4th 1239 (D.C. Cir. 2023).
59. *See* Matthew Fox, *SEC Says Twitter Account Was Compromised, It's Not Approved a Bitcoin ETF,* Markets Insider (Jan. 10, 2024), https://www.msn.com/en-us/money/other/sec-says-twitter-account-was-compromised-it-s-not-approved-a-bitcoin-etf/ar-AA1mIfs0.

in fact, formally approved the listing and permitted the trading of a number of spot bitcoin ETP's. For good measure, however, the Chairman made clear that the SEC's approval does not signal an endorsement of Bitcoin or other cryptocurrencies.[60] The X post-signaling approval and sudden reversal caused a rapid price surge and subsequent drop in the price of Bitcoin, leading some commentators and lawmakers to accuse the agency of engaging in the same market manipulation they regularly charge companies with.[61] In addition to an FBI investigation already opened into the matter, members of Congress have also demanded answers.[62] Despite the chaos, during the first week after the official approval, U.S. inflows into Digital Asset ETPs were $1.18 billion (shy of the $1.5 billion record set by the rollout of the first Bitcoin futures products in 2021), and quickly broke trading volume records, at $17.5 billion.[63]

Banking Regulators

Since 2021, banking regulators have generally discouraged bank involvement in digital assets and blockchain technology.[64] This trend primarily manifests through increased scrutiny and risk assessments associated with crypto-related activities, limiting or cutting off important sources of liquidity for the future and ongoing development of projects in the emerging sector. The issuance of statements focusing on the danger of digital assets and the introduction of a variety of operational and credit risk mitigation controls associated with digital assets have typically caused many banks to stay away from digital assets and digital asset services to avoid the costs of increased scrutiny from a regulator.

Industry commentators have dubbed these efforts "Operation Chokepoint, 2.0"—after Operation Chokepoint, a controversial initiative undertaken by the Obama administration that ultimately faced legal challenges for allegedly restricting access to banking services for certain categories of banking customers that included, among others, payday lenders and gun dealers.[65]

---

60. *Supra,* note 48. (Notably, this dispute over spot Bitcoin ETFs seems to deviate from the SEC's policy from its founding of disclosure-based regulation. The SEC appears to have decided that, on their merits, digital assets should not be allowed into the American markets, and the Commission is prepared to vigorously challenge their adoption or advancement. Particularly as it may relate to climate change rules, which change in philosophy should be watched closely by other industries which may manufacture or be associated with currently unpopular products such as fossil fuels, tobacco, firearms, livestock breeding, sales and processing, digital asset miners, and, potentially, artificial intelligence companies (voracious consumers of energy).)

61. See, Joel Khalili, *Lawmakers Are Out for Blood after a Hack of the SEC's X Account Causes Bitcoin Chaos,* Wired (Jan. 10, 2024), https://www.wired.com/story/sec-x-account-hack-investigation/.

62. *See* Benzinga, *SEC Confirms FBI Investigation into Its Twitter Account Hack after False Bitcoin ETF Announcement,* Bus. Insider (Jan. 10, 2024), https://markets.businessinsider.com/news/etf/sec-confirms-fbi-investigation-into-its-twitter-account-hack-after-false-bitcoin-etf-announcement-1032958530; Julia Shapero & Rebecca Klar, *Senators Call for Probe Into SEC Account Hack,* The Hill (Jan. 12, 2024), https://thehill.com/newsletters/technology/4406219-senators-call-for-probe-into-sec-account-hack/.

63. *See* James Butterfill, *Volume 165: Digital Asset Fund Flows Weekly Report,* CoinShares Blog (Jan., 15, 2024), https://blog.coinshares.com/volume-165-digital-asset-fund-flows-weekly-report-32a1e5e9e197.

64. *See* e.g., Federal Reserve, SR 21-19 (Dec. 10, 2021); OCC, Bull. 2021-57 (Nov. 23, 2021), https://occ.gov/news-issuances/bulletins/2021/bulletin-2021-57.html; OCC, Interp. Ltr. 1172 (Sept. 21, 2020), https://www.occ.gov/topics/charters-and-licensing/interpretations-and-actions/2020/int1172.pdf.

65. *See* David Z. Morris, *The Reality Behind the Crypto Banking Crackdown: "Operation Choke Point 2.0" Is Here,* CoinDesk (Sep. 28, 2023), https://www.coindesk.com/consensus-magazine/2023/03/22/the-reality-behind-the-crypto-banking-crackdown-operation-choke-point-20-is-here/.

The U.S. Treasury Department's Office of the Comptroller of the Currency

On November 18, 2021, the Office of the Comptroller of the Currency (OCC) (within the U.S. Treasury Department) issued an Interpretive Letter, IL 1179, insisting that banks which had not yet engaged in digital asset related activity, provide advance written notification and receive supervisory non-objection prior to engaging in the industry.[66] While the OCC presumably perceives this as an olive branch, inviting engagement between banks and their examiners in service of a safe and sound financial system, it has been perceived negatively by industry especially given the belief that few bank examiners have been trained regarding digital asset functionality, operations, or risk.

IL 1179 requires that a bank engaged with digital assets demonstrate "to the satisfaction of [the OCC's] supervisory office"[67] that it has appropriate controls in place to manage digital asset risks. Those controls would address risks related to:

- Liquidity;
- Strategy;
- Compliance (including BSA, AML, OAC, and consumer protection laws); and
- Operational risk generally, including specifically risks related to:
  - New and evolving technologies;
  - Hacking;
  - Fraud and theft; and
  - Third-party risk management.

IL 1179 further states that the OCC "will also evaluate any other supervisory considerations, relevant to the particular proposal."[68] The signal to the industry is clear: Bank regulators will seemingly use available tools to ensure that banks properly manage every and all manner of risk related to digital assets and in a way that does not appear to have been applied to other financial technologies.

The Federal Deposit Insurance Corporation

The Federal Deposit Insurance Corporation (FDIC) followed several months later on April 7, 2022, with a Financial Institution Letter, FIL-16-2022.[69] While using different language, the two documents are largely aligned in their heightened focus on potential risks associated with banks engaging in crypto-related activities. Despite this similarity, the FDIC notably acknowledged the dynamic nature of the crypto landscape and the limited understanding of its associated risks, stating: "crypto assets and crypto-related activities are rapidly evolving, and the risks of this area are not well understood...."[70] Similar to the OCC's IL 1179, FIL-16-2022 established a cautious approach toward bank involvement in the crypto

66. OCC, Interp. Ltr. 1179 (Nov. 18, 2021), https://occ.gov/topics/charters-and-licensing/interpretations-and-actions/2021/int1179.pdf.
67. *Id.* at 1.
68. *Id.* at 4.
69. FDIC, "Notification of Engaging in Crypto-Related Activities," FIL-16-2022 (Apr. 7, 2022), https://www.fdic.gov/news/financial-institution-letters/2022/fil22016.html.
70. *Id.*

sphere, potentially raising significant hurdles for entry. The additional weight of FDIC concerns, given its role as an insurer for many banks, adds another layer of scrutiny. Beyond the safety and soundness concerns highlighted earlier, the FDIC further identified specific risks associated with:

- Fundamental ownership interest (including whether virtual assets can be clearly validated and confirmed);
- IT risk exposure, including the sufficiency of existing IT frameworks;
- Credit risk exposure;
- Counterparty risk exposure;
- General concern about "whether it is possible for insured depository institutions to manage those risks and exposures;"
- Accounting auditing, and financial reporting treatment of crypto assets;
- Liquidity risk exposure; and
- General financial stability.

The Federal Reserve

Following the FDIC release, on August 16, 2022, the Federal Reserve Board of Governors (the Fed or FRB) released Supervisory and Regulation Letter SR 22-6 regarding engagement and crypto asset-related activities by Federal Reserve-supervised banking organizations.[71] While less detailed than the OCC or FDIC releases, it provided a similar notice that the Fed will look carefully at any of its supervised banks engaging in or seeking to engage in crypto asset-related activities.

Interagency Guidance

Finally, at the beginning of 2023, all three agencies issued a joint statement on crypto asset risks to banking organizations, signaling that prudential regulators are united in their cautious approach to crypto-related activities and exposures within U.S. banks.[72]

The agencies noted that they would "continue to take a careful, conscientious approach"[73] regarding existing or proposed crypto involvement, suggesting a potentially high bar for approval. While acknowledging that banks are not explicitly prohibited from serving "any customer," the statement underscored industry concerns that the provision of services to digital asset users, in the regulators' own words, "could be inconsistent with safe and sound banking practices" due to perceived or actual risks.

It is noteworthy that this regulatory stance has been implemented through pronouncements and statements, without formal legislation or rulemaking under the APA. This has

71. FRB, Engagement in crypto asset-Related Activities by Federal Reserve-Supervised Banking Organizations, SR-22-6/CA 22-6 (Aug. 16, 2022), https://www.federalreserve.gov/supervisionreg/srletters/SR2206.htm.

72. Press Release, Federal Reserve System, Federal Deposit Insurance Corporation, and Office of the Comptroller of Currency, Joint Statement on crypto asset Risks to Banking Organizations (Jan. 3, 2023) (on file with the Federal Reserve)

73. *Id.*

raised further concerns about transparency and predictability for banks navigating the crypto space.[74]

International Counterpoints and Potential Future Directions

Banks in other countries have begun to pick up the slack. For example, in Brazil, Nubank launched crypto trading in 2022, adding access to Polkadot (DOT), Avalanche (AVAX), Stella Lumens (XLM), Arbitrium (ARB), and Optimism (OP) in November 2023.[75] Nubank also has partnered with stablecoin issuer Circle to extend USDC exposure to Brazilian Nubank customers. Brazil's securities regulator approved Brazil's first Bitcoin ETF in 2021.[76] Moreover, rather than trying to compete with centralized exchanges, Brazilian banks are primarily focused on adding digital assets as an extra option for existing clients.[77] Brazil could serve as a proof of concept for the integration of traditional and decentralized finance, that could provide valuable insights for the global economy.

Joining Brazil's Nubank and Itau Unibanco, is Switzerland's St. Galler Kantonbank (SGKB), among the largest banks in the country, which announced its partnership with SEBA Bank, a global bank specializing in crypto.[78] As of November 2023, SGKB offers clients access to trading and custody services for Bitcoin (BTC) and Ether (ETH).

In September 2023, Germany's Deutsche Bank said it was set to establish digital asset custody and tokenization services.[79] The flagship financial institution announced its plans to provide the services through a strategic partnership with Taurus, a Swiss startup that provides digital asset trade, issue, and custody infrastructure.[80] Instead of the time-consuming and expensive process of developing in-house solutions, foreign banks appear to be leveraging white-labeled products to bring digital asset products and services to market. This preference for readily available tools may lead to the construction of reliable pathways toward greater integration within the DeFi ecosystem, significantly outpacing progress observed in the United States.

The CFTC

The CFTC has taken a distinct approach to digital assets, prioritizing disclosure, and robust monitoring over outright bans within the commodities market. In August of 2021, CFTC Commissioner Dawn D. Stump issued a statement purporting to clarify the CFTC's regulatory

---

74. *See* Chapter 7: Risk Management and Governance.
75. *See* Ritika Sharma, *Nubank to Enable Ethereum and Bitcoin Trading to Their Clients,* The Coin Republic (May 12, 2022), https://www.thecoinrepublic.com/2022/05/12/nubank-to-enable-ethereum-and-bitcoin-trading-to-their-clients/.
76. *See* Tanzeel Akhtar, *Brazil Stock Exchange Lists First Bitcoin ETF in Latin America,* CoinDesk (Sep. 14, 2021), https://www.coindesk.com/markets/2021/06/23/brazil-stock-exchange-lists-first-bitcoin-etf-in-latin-america/.
77. *Supra,* n. 24.
78. *See* Helen Partz, *Top Swiss Bank Launches Bitcoin and Ether Trading with SEBA,* CoinTelegraph (Nov. 2, 2023), https://cointelegraph.com/news/swiss-bank-bitcoin-ether-trading-seba.
79. *See* Ian Allison, *Deutsche Bank to Delve Into Crypto Custody, Tokenization with Taurus*, CoinDesk (Sep. 14, 2023), https://www.coindesk.com/business/2023/09/14/deutsche-bank-to-delve-into-crypto-custody-tokenization-with-taurus/#:~:text=Deutsche%20Bank%20is%20working%20with%20Taurus%2C%20a%20Swiss,custody%20license%20from%20the%20country%E2%80%99s%20financial%20watchdog%2C%20BaFin.
80. *See* Peter Sonner, *Deutsche Bank Launches Digital Asset Custody & Tokenization with Taurus,* beinsure. (Sep. 24, 2023), https://beinsure.com/news/deutsche-bank-digital-asset-custody/.

authority with respect to digital assets.[81] Dismissing the SEC and (generally speaking) the industry's preoccupation with classifying a digital asset as either a security or a commodity, Commissioner Stump stated that the question of whether the CFTC has power to regulate hinges on whether the digital asset in question involves a derivatives product, such as a future, swap, or option contract. Notably, the statement pointed out, even *if* a digital asset were to be classified as a commodity, the CFTC may not have authority to regulate it.[82] As the statement also points out, the CFTC's enforcement authority is broader than its regulatory authority, encompassing both derivatives markets as well as spot market (or cash transactions) in digital assets where fraud would impact the derivatives market.[83]

Despite Commissioner Stump's statement (which carried the required disclaimer that did not necessarily represent those of the CFTC or her fellow Commissioners), its meaning seemed all but forgotten when, in a 2022 interview on CNBC, Chairman Rostin Benham stated (in passing) that Bitcoin and Ether are, indeed, commodities.[84] If true that Ether and Bitcoin are commodities (and not securities), this would mean that the CFTC held jurisdiction over nearly 70% of the 1.7 trillion dollar digital asset market.[85] While many in Congress appear to be optimistic about the CFTC's capabilities as a principal regulator of digital assets,[86] it is worth noting the agency is dwarfed by its sister market regulator, the SEC. For comparison, in 2022, the CFTC had a budget of $332 million, and less than 800 full-time employees, while the SEC's budget that year stood at nearly $2 billion, with a full-time staff of more than four thousand.[87]

Executive Action

Finally, while not standard regulation, the Biden Administration released an Executive Order 14067, Ensuring Responsible Development of Digital Assets, (the EO) in early 2022 outlining an approach to address risks stemming from the growth of digital assets and blockchain technology.[88] The EO focused on six priorities: (1) consumer and investor protection; (2) financial stability; (3) illicit finance; (4) U.S. leadership in the global financial system; (5) financial inclusion; and (6) responsible innovation. The EO called for research,

---

81. *See* Press Release, Dawn D. Stump, Statement of Commissioner Dawn D. Stump on the CFTC's regulatory authority applicable to digital assets (Aug. 23, 2021) (on file with CFTC).

82. *Id.* The statement points out, for example, that "[c]attle are commodities, and the CFTC regulates futures contracts on cattle – but, the CFTC is not out regulating cash cattle markets, such as sale barns or video auctions."

83. *Id.*

84. *See Bitcoin, Ethereum are Commodities, Says CFTC Chair Rostin Behnam,* CFTC (May 16, 2022), https://www.cnbc.com/video/2022/05/16/bitcoin-ethereum-are-commodities-says-cftc-chair-rostin-behnam.html; *See also,* Kevin Helms, *CFTC Chairman Confirms Bitcoin, Ether Are Commodities,* Bitcoin.com (May 22, 2022), https://news.bitcoin.com/cftc-chairman-confirms-bitcoin-ether-are-commodities/.

85. *See* https://coinmarketcap.com/ (accessed Jan. 10, 2024).

86. *See e.g.,* Alexander C. Drylewski, et al., *New Senate Crypto Bill Would Limit SEC Regulatory Role in Favor of CFTC,* Skadden (July 20, 2023), https://www.skadden.com/insights/publications/2023/07/new-senate-crypto-bill-would-limit-sec-regulatory-role.

87. *See* Freddy Brewster, *Crypto Swindler Sam Bankman Fried Has Scored a Big Win From Behind Bars,* Jacobin (Jan. 3, 2024), https://jacobin.com/2024/01/sam-bankman-fried-cryptocurrency-deregulation-bitnomial-cftc; Recently, this gap has narrowed, but only slightly, with the CFTC's budget for fiscal year 2024 raised to $863,612,829, and the SEC's lowered slightly to $1,749,354,861. *See Agency Profiles, "CFTC," and "SEC,"* USASpending.Gov (Jan. 8, 2024), https://www.usaspending.gov/agency.

88. Exec. Order No. 14067, *Ensuring Responsible Development of Digital Assets*, 87 Fed. Reg. 14143 (Mar. 9, 2022), https://www.federalregister.gov/documents/2022/09/20/2022-20279/ensuring-responsible-development-of-digital-assets-request-for-comment.

reports, and plans on these issues and also called for regulatory coordination.[89] In addition, on March 20, 2023, the White House published its 2023 Economic Report of the President, which included an entire chapter on digital assets, much of which took a critical stance, casting doubt on the claimed benefits and highlighting the potential harms, like market volatility, illicit and terrorist financing, and environmental impact.[90]

Through a united front across agencies, the White House has implemented a major policy shift toward digital assets, without relying on a single law. This so-called "whole-of-government" approach has effectively cordoned off traditional banking from crypto, making it harder for the industry to raise capital. This approach has been heavily criticized as an overreach of executive power, and in general, the "whole of government" approach has not fared well in the courts.[91] These steps again appear to reflect a strong hostility by the Biden Administration toward blockchain and cryptocurrency as an accepted part of the financial system. While understanding that banning cryptocurrencies entirely would require legislative authority for which it lacks the votes, this Administration's "whole of government" approach, without thoughtful limitation and application, has the potential to pit the current administrative state against inclusion of cryptocurrencies and blockchain as a viable part of the banking system.

Measures from Executive Order 14067 [March 9, 2022]

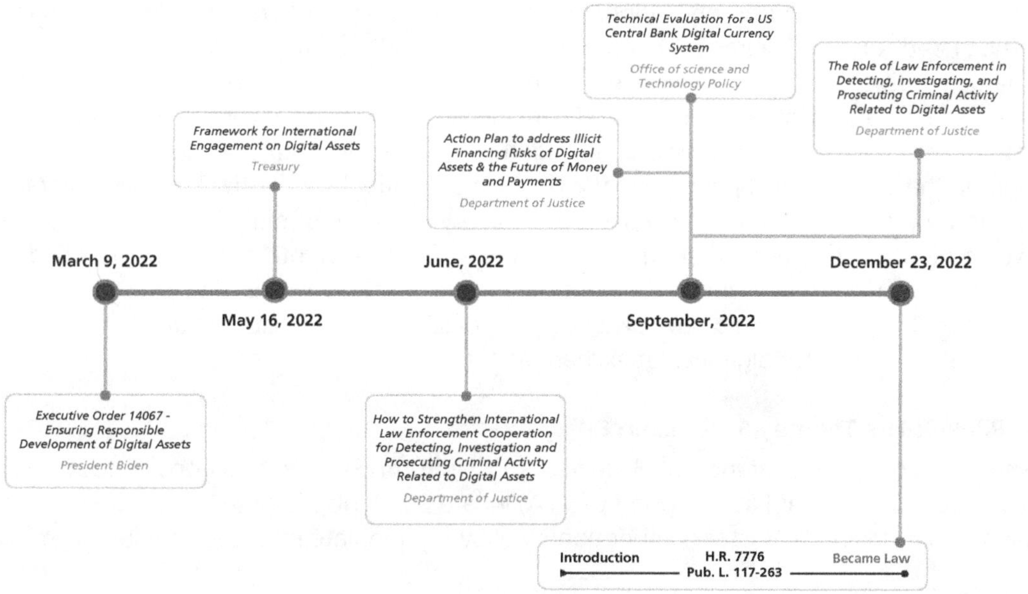

89. *Id.*

90. *See* Economic Report of the President, Chapter Eight – "Digital Assets: Relearning Economic Principles," 237 (March 2023), https://www.whitehouse.gov/wp-content/uploads/2023/03/ERP-2023.pdf; *See also,* Nickhilesh De, *White House Takes Aim at Crypto in Scathing Economic Report,* CoinDesk (Mar. 21, 2023), https://www.coindesk.com/policy/2023/03/21/white-house-takes-aim-at-crypto-in-scathing-economic-report/.

91. Dave Yost, *Biden Tempts Judicial Fate With "Whole of Government" Plans,* Wall St. J. (Jan. 3, 2024), https://www.wsj.com/articles/biden-tempts-judicial-fate-with-whole-of-government-plans-2a1ad927.

Legislation

Legislation is the father of regulation and is (or rather is supposed to be) looked to as the original source of authority, as well as an ongoing guide. Consequently, no comprehensive discourse on regulatory matters can be complete without discussing proposed legislation. Despite persistent efforts since 2018, Congress has yet to enact a crypto regulatory framework. Dozens of proposed bills tackled broad concerns and specific issues like stablecoins and AML, but none reached the finish line. Here are the leading contenders with recent traction.

H.R. 4451—"Securities Clarity Act"

In July of 2021, Representatives Tom Emmer (R-MN) and Darren Soto (D-FL) introduced the bipartisan Securities Clarity Act (H.R. 4451)[92] which sought to address the confusion created by the current patchwork of laws which fails to distinguish digital assets from the investment contracts they might be part of. The bill also acknowledged that some cryptocurrencies could start as securities but later become something else, like a commodity, as the project evolves.

S. 4356—The Responsible Financial Innovation Act

The Responsible Financial Innovation Act (RFIA) sponsored by Senators Cynthia Lummis (R-WY) and Kirsten Gillibrand (D-NY) would have provided regulatory clarity for agencies charged with supervising digital assets, a regulatory framework for stablecoins, and integrated digital assets into existing tax and banking law.[93] An updated version of the RFIA was introduced in July 2023. This version included provisions that increased consumer protections in the event of the bankruptcy of a digital asset entity.[94] Under the Lummis-Gillibrand framework, the CFTC would have been the primary regulator of digital assets. The agency would be granted spot market jurisdiction over all fungible crypto assets not classified as securities in addition to its jurisdiction over any digital asset derivatives and leveraged transactions.[95] The agency would have also been responsible for administering an oversight and registration regime for digital asset exchanges.[96]

H.R.5340: The Toomey Stablecoin Bill

The Stablecoin Transparency of Reserves and Uniform Safe Transactions (TRUST) Act, introduced by Senator Patrick Toomey (R-PA) in late 2022, also known as the Toomey Stablecoin Bill, sought to foster competition by allowing regulated entities to issue payment

---

92. *Securities Clarity Act*, H.R. 4451, 117th Cong (2022).
93. Lummis-Gillibrand Responsible Financial Innovation Act, S. 4356, 117th Cong. (2022); *See* Press Release, Lummis-Gillibrand Introduce Legislation to Create Regulatory Framework for Digital Assets (June 7, 2022) (on file with Sen. Lummis).
94. Lummis-Gillibrand Responsible Financial Innovation Act, S. 2281, 118th Cong. (2023).
95. *See id.*; *See also, Government Strategies Update*, "U.S. Congressional Leaders Introduce Two Landmark Bills to Create a Digital Assets Regulatory Scheme," Sidley (July 15, 2023), https://www.sidley.com/en/insights/newsupdates/2023/07/us-congressional-leaders-introduce-two-landmark-bills-to-create-a-digital-assets-regulatory-scheme/.
96. *Id.*

stablecoins.[97] The bill would have (a) created a regulatory framework for stablecoins and issuers, (b) enhanced transparency by establishing disclosure requirements and attestations [by whom?], (c) offered three options for the issuance of payment stablecoins, (d) distinguished stablecoins from securities, and (e) applied privacy protections to stablecoins.[98]

H.R. 4766: Clarity for Payment Stablecoins Act of 2023

In early 2023, on the House side, Representative Patrick McHenry (R-NC) introduced the Clarity for Payment Stablecoins Act of 2023,[99] which would have set out criteria for who can issue stablecoins and what rules would govern redeemability and collateral. In particular, permitted issuers would need to have be a subsidiary of an insured depository institution, or an otherwise qualified non-bank stablecoin issuer, that was subject to federal or state regulation.[100] The bill also set reserve requirements for stablecoin issuers (a one-to-one backing), based on assets defined by the bill.[101]

S.5030: Digital Commodities Consumer Protection Act of 2022

The Digital Commodities Consumer Protection Act (DCCPA), sponsored by Senator Debbie Stabenow (D-MI), and co-sponsored by a bipartisan group of six additional senators,[102] was introduced in the fall of 2022. This bill, mirroring many other digital asset proposals seen from Congress, entrusted the CFTC with regulating so-called "digital commodity platforms" and "digital commodity" trading.[103] A "digital commodity" was defined in the bill as a fungible digital form of personal property that can be possessed and transferred from person to person without reliance on an intermediary.[104]

S.5030: Digital Trading Clarity Act

Shortly after the DCCPA, Senator Bill Haggerty (R-TN) introduced the Digital Trading Clarity Act of 2022. The Bill proposed a safe harbor for digital asset exchanges, allowing them protection from certain SEC enforcement actions.[105] The two-year safe harbor would apply

---

97. *Stablecoin TRUST Act of 2022*, S. 5340, 117th Cong. *See* Press Release, U.S. Sen. Comm. Bank. Housing. & Urb. Affairs, Toomey introduces legislation to guide future stablecoin regulation (Dec. 21, 2022) (on file with U.S. Sen. Bank. Housing & Urb. Affairs).

98. *Id. See also*, "Section-by-Section Summary," (Dec. 21, 2022), https://www.banking.senate.gov/imo/media/doc/stablecoin_trust_act_section-by-section.pdf.

99. *Clarity for Payment Stablecoins Act of 2023*, H.R. 4766, 118th Cong (Jul. 20, 2023), https://www.congress.gov/bill/118th-congress/house-bill/4766.

100. *Id.*

101. *Id.*

102. (Co-Sponsors: Sen. Cory Booker (D-NJ), Sen. John Boozman (D-NJ), Sen. John Thune (R-IA), Sen. Kirsten Gillibrand (D-NY), Sen. Ben Ray Lujan (D-NM)); *Digital Commodities Consumer Protection Act of 2022*, S. 4760, 117th Cong (2022) https://www.congress.gov/bill/117th-congress/senate-bill/4760.

103. S. 4760, 117th Cong (2022) https://www.congress.gov/bill/117th-congress/senate-bill/4760.

104. *Id. See also* Chu Chen, *Digital Commodities Consumer Protection Act of 2022: A Controversial Effort Caught in the Crossfire of the FTX Collapse*, Jolt Digest (Dec. 12, 2022), https://jolt.law.harvard.edu/digest/digital-commodities-consumer-protection-act-of-2022-a-controversial-effort-caught-in-the-crossfire-of-the-ftx-collapse-1.

105. *Digital Trading Clarity Act of 2022*, S.5030, 117th Cong. (2022) https://www.congress.gov/bill/117th-congress/senate-bill/5030?s=1&r=1; Press Release, Sen. Bill Hagerty, Hagerty introduces legislation to provide crucial regulatory clarity for digital assets (Sep. 29, 2022) (on file with office of Sen. Bill Hagerty).

if, subject to a determination by the SEC or a federal court, a digital asset would not have been a security [so long as it was.] listed through an intermediary that met certain custody, disclosure, and other customer safety requirements.

H.R.4763: Financial Innovation and Technology for the 21st Century Act

In July 2023, Representatives Patrick McHenry (R-NC) and Glenn Thompson (R-PA) introduced into the House of Representatives the Financial Innovation and Technology for the 21st Century Act.[106] This bill—which has passed initial committee review—proposes a comprehensive framework to fill regulatory gaps and provide clarity and would clearly define the roles of the CFTC and SEC in overseeing digital assets. It still requires a full House vote and faces potential hurdles in the Senate.

Bank Secrecy Act (BSA)-AML Crypto-Legislation

There are also significant efforts to enhance AML provisions and protections as it relates to digital assets. This means ensuring compliance with the Bank Secrecy Act, overseen by the Treasury's Financial Crimes Enforcement Network (FinCEN). Two companion bills were introduced in the House and Senate, both under the title, Financial Technology Protection Act of 2023 (H.R. 2969 /S.1340).[107] Both bills propose the establishment of an independent Financial Technology Working Group to combat terrorism and illicit financing in digital assets.[108]

As part of the National Defense Authorization Act, a provision was added requiring the U.S. Treasury Department's Office of Foreign Asset Control (OFAC) to begin risk-based examinations of money services businesses regarding digital assets, and for reports on anonymity-enhanced cryptocurrencies and tools.

This was followed by the reintroduction of a bill by Senators Elizabeth Warren (D-MA), Roger Marshall (R-KS), Joe Manchin (D-WV), and Lindsey Graham (R-SC) called the Digital Asset Anti-Money Laundering Act of 2023.[109] Other bills have been introduced on the same subject and are currently under consideration.

---

106. *Financial Innovation and Technology for the 21st Century Act,* H.R. 4763, 118th Cong (2023) https://www.congress.gov/bill/118th-congress/house-bill/4763; *Overview of H.R. 4763, Financial Innovation and Technology for the 21st Century Act* (August 16, 2023), https://crsreports.congress.gov/product/pdf/IN/IN12223.

107. *See Financial Technology Protection Act,* H.R. 2969, 118th Cong. (2023) https://www.congress.gov/bill/118th-congress/house-bill/2969?q=%7B%22search%22%3A%22H.R.+2969%22%7D&s=2&r=1; *Financial Technology Protection Act,* S. 1340, 118th Cong. (2023) https://www.congress.gov/bill/118th-congress/senate-bill/1340?q=%7B%22search%22%3A%22S.1340%22%7D&s=1&r=1.

108. *See* Kirsten Errick, *Lawmakers Introduce Bill to Tackle Criminal and Terrorist Crypto Activities,* NextGov (May 1, 2023), https://www.nextgov.com/emerging-tech/2023/05/lawmakers-introduce-bill-tackle-criminal-and-terrorist-crypto-activities/385811/.

109. *Digital Asset Anti-Money Laundering Act of 2023,* S.2669, 118th Cong. (2023) https://www.congress.gov/bill/118th-congress/senate-bill/2669/all-info.

Stages of Crypto-related Bills

	Bill Introduced	Passed Body of Origin	Passed Second Body	Sent for Signature	Became Law
S. 3801 A bill to amend the Federal Reserve Act to prohibit the Federal Reserve banks from offering certain products or services directly to an individual, to prohibit the use of central bank digital currency for monetary policy, and for other purposes. Latest Action: 02/26/2024 - Read twice and referred to the Committee on Banking, Housing, and Urban Affairs.	02/26/2024	-	-	-	-
Pub. L. 118-31 National Defence Authorisation Act for Fiscal Year 2024 Latest Action: 12/22/2023 - Became Public Law No: 118-31	04/18/2023	07/14/2023	07/27/2023	12/14/2023	12/22/2023
S. 3441 A bill to prevent Foreign Terrorist Organizations and their financial enablers, whether in currency or digital assets, from accessing financial and other institutions of the United States, and for other purposes. Latest Action: 02/08/2024 - Committee on Banking, Housing, and Urban Affairs. Hearings held.	12/07/2023	04/27/2023	-	-	-
H.R. 6588 International Financial Institution Counter Terrorism Accountability Act. Latest Action: 12/05/2023 - Referred to the House Committee on Financial Services.	12/05/2023	-	-	-	-
H.R. 6589 Prevent the Financing of Terrorism Through the Drug Trade Act Latest Action: 12/05/2023 - Referred to the Committee on Financial Services, and in addition to the Committee on Foreign Affairs, for a period to be subsequently determined by the Speaker, in each case for consideration of such provisions as fall within the jurisdiction of the committee concerned.	12/05/2023	-	-	-	-
S. 3384 Combating Cross-border Financial Crime Act of 2023 Latest Action: 11/30/2023 - Read twice and referred to the Committee on Banking, Housing, and Urban Affairs.	11/30/2023	-	-	-	-
H.R. 6505 FREED Act Latest Action: 11/29/2023 - Referred to the Committee on Financial Services, and in addition to the Committees on Foreign Affairs, the Judiciary, and Oversight and Accountability, for a period to be subsequently determined by the Speaker, in each case for consideration of such provisions as fall within the jurisdiction of the committee concerned.	11/29/2023	-	-	-	-
S. Res. 460 A resolution supporting the United States dollar as the reserve currency of the world and combating the economic influence of the People's Republic of China. Latest Action: 11/13/2023 - Referred to the Committee on Foreign Relations. (text: CR 55479)	11/13/2023	-	-	-	-

	Bill Introduced	Passed Body of Origin	Passed Second Body	Sent for Signature	Became Law
S. 3248 Chinese CBDC Prohibition Act of 2023 latest Action: 11/08/2023 - Read twice and referred to the Committee on Banking, Housing, and Urban Affairs.	11/08/2023	-	-	-	-
H.R. 6307 CLARITY Act of 2023 Latest Action: 11/08/2023 - Read twice and referred to the Committee on Banking, Housing, and Urban Affairs.	11/08/2023	-	-	-	-
S. 3229 A bill to prohibit Federal agencies from restricting the use of convertible virtual currency by a person to purchase goods or services for the person's own use, and for other purposes. Latest Action: 11/06/2023 - Read twice and referred to the Committee on Banking, Housing, and Urban Affairs.	11/06/2023	-	-	-	-
H. Res. 599 Urging the European Union to designate Hizballah in its entirety as a terrorist organization. Latest Action: 11/01/2023 - Motion to reconsider laid on the table Agreed to without objection.	07/18/2023	11/01/2023	-	-	-
H.R. 5966 Off-Chain Digital Commodity Transaction Reporting Act of 2023 Latest Action: 01/18/2024 - Referred to the Subcommittee on Commodity Markets, Digital Assets, and Rural Development.	10/17/2023	-	-	-	-
H.R. 5745 Digital Asset Market Structure and Investor Protection Act Latest Action: 01/17/2024 - Referred to the Subcommittee on Commodity Markets, Digital Assets, and Rural Development.	09/27/2023	-	-	-	-
S. 2860 SAFER Banking Act Latest Action: 12/06/2023 - Committee on Banking, Housing, and Urban Affairs. Hearings held.	09/20/2023	-	-	-	-
H.R. 389 PORTFOLIO Act Latest Action: 01/17/2023 - Referred to the Committee on Oversight and Accountability, and in addition to the Committees on the Judiciary, House Administration, and ways and Means, for a period to be subsequently determined by the Speaker, in each case for consideration of such provisions as fall within the jurisdiction of the committee concerned.	01/17/2023	-	-	-	-
H.R. 370 FinCEN Modernization Act of 2023 latest Action: 01/17/2023 - Referred to the House Committee on Financial Services.	01/17/2023	-	-	-	-

* * *

In short, despite extensive and earnest legislative efforts, the digital asset regulatory landscape in the United States remains characterized by a significant lack of consensus. In the absence of such a framework, regulators appear to be faced with something of a Hobbesian choice: await definitive congressional authorization, or proactively take on the mantle of regulation, as the SEC has chosen. This decision is complicated by the ever-shifting sands of political considerations, making it difficult to discern the precise motivations underpinning regulatory actions.[110]

110. Unfortunately, the picture at the moment continues to become cloudier as SEC rulemaking continues to be challenged, such as the March 2024 challenge by a series of trade groups to the SEC's new "dealer rule," in addition to several challenges to the SEC's climate change rule. Indeed, industry challenges to rule making processes are not limited to the SEC. The CEO of the American Bankers Association was quoted on March 20, 2024 as saying the trade group had no choice but to file several lawsuits against federal regulators arguing that the agencies had overstepped their authority on regulations such as a revamp of the Community Reinvestment Act and tighter limits on credit card late fees.

Consequently, much of the legal landscape surrounding digital assets remains subject to ambiguity, with both the definition and regulatory purview of digital assets oscillating between different administrative agencies and the judicial branch. For the moment, there is no reason to suspect administrative agencies will change their current course of rulemaking, enforcement actions, and litigation which has the effect of slowing the integration of blockchain and digital assets within the American financial system. Nevertheless, there is every reason to think that this is a passing phenomenon, a transitory phase in the inevitable development of a framework which will allow the existence and growth of blockchain and digital assets within the U.S. banking system.

Overview of the Number of Bills per State

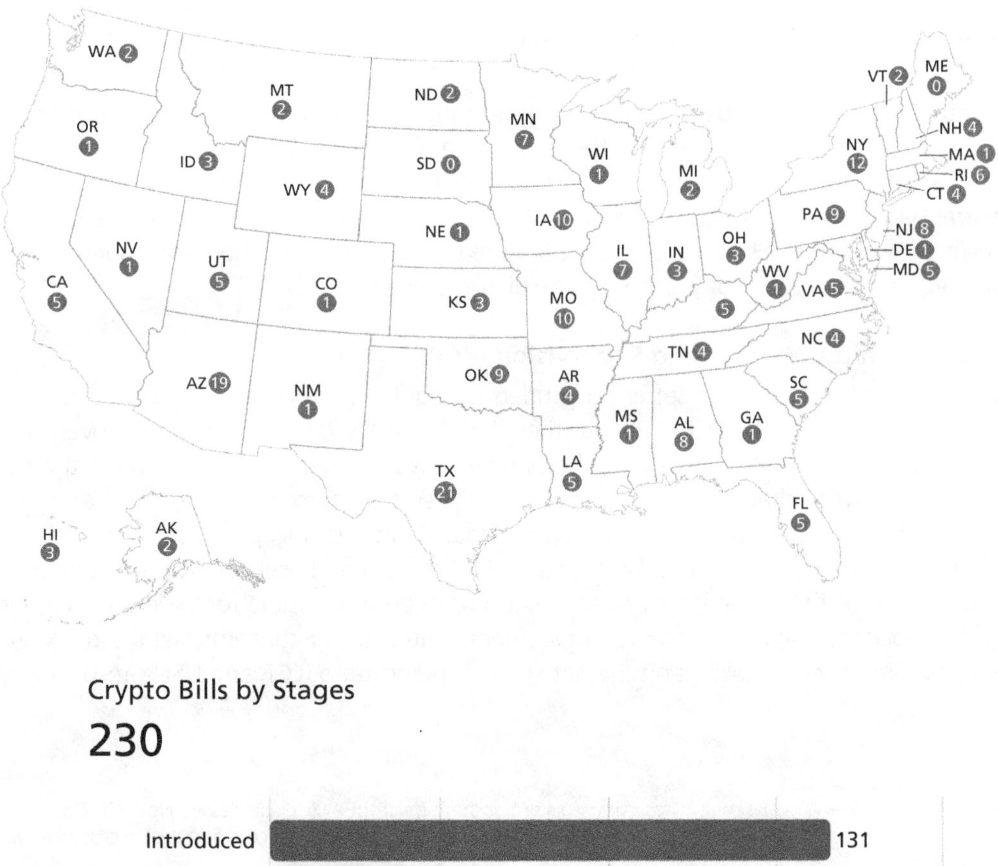

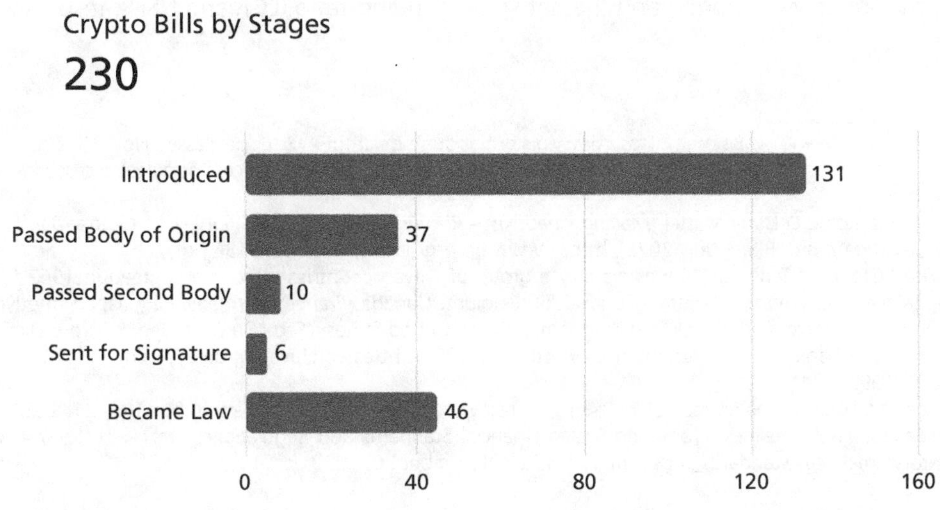

International Regulation

The third dimension of digital asset regulation is international regulation. This is of some importance because, unlike other stores of value, digital assets are traded 24 hours a day, seven days a week, and 365 days a year—globally. They also settle instantaneously, and the settlement is immutable. Accordingly, funds which are not accessible in the United States will tend to move overseas. Moreover, the development of projects is likely to flourish in areas where the regulatory environment is more open and accepting of digital assets. Unlike in the United States, certain regulators overseas have been more focused on constructing regulatory frameworks in which digital assets can develop, evolve, and address evolving customer needs, subject to appropriate guardrails. There is a series of international organizations overseas which have led this effort with a considerable amount of analysis and experimentation.

Bank for International Settlements (BIS)

Founded in 1930, the BIS is an international organization owned by 63 central banks from countries across the globe, collectively representing approximately 95 percent of global GDP.[111] BIS serves as a forum for the Basel Committee on Banking Supervision (BCBS), established in 1974, operating as a platform for international collaboration.[112] Like other central banks, BIS regularly publishes findings and reports. In 2022, BIS released a survey which showed that 93 percent of central banks participating in their study were actively involved in pilot testing for a central bank digital currency (CBDC).[113]

Basel Committee on Banking Supervision (BCBS)

The primary global standard setter for prudential regulation of banks, the Basel Committee on Banking Supervision (BCBS) was formed 1974. Initially comprised of the Governors of each of the G10[114] central banks, its first meeting was held in 1975. Ever since, the committee has played a key role in the global financial system, since expanding its membership to 45 institutions from 28 jurisdictions worldwide.[115] Since its inception, the committee has spoken, through its consecutive Accords (Basel I, Basel II, and Basel III),[116] upon foundational matters such as the definition of capital, and has been responsible for assigning standards for its associated risk-based reserve requirements, introducing concepts like the bank leverage-, the liquidity coverage-, and the net stable funding-ratio (LCR and NSFR, respectively).

---

111. *About BIS-Overview,* Bis.org , https://www.bis.org/about/index.htm?l=2 (last accessed Nov. 20, 2023).
112. *The Basel Process – Overview*, Bis.org , https://www.bis.org/about/basel_process.htm (last accessed Nov. 20, 2023).
113. Anneke Kosse & Llaria Mattei, *Making Headway – Results of the 2022 BIS Survey on Central Bank Digital Currencies and Crypto*, BIS, 1 (July 2023), https://www.bis.org/publ/bppdf/bispap136.pdf.
114. The "Group of Ten" (G-10) was actually a group of eleven countries which had agreed in 1962 to lend money to the International Monetary Fund (IMF): Belgium, Canada, France, Germany, Italy, Japan, the Netherlands, Sweden, Switzerland, the United Kingdom, and the United States. (*See* "Group of Ten," Oxford Dictionary of Finance and Banking, 207 (Jonathan Law, 4th Ed., 2008), https://archive.org/details/isbn_9780199229741/isbn_9780199229741.
115. *See Basel Committee Membership,* Bis.org, https://www.bis.org/bcbs/membership.htm (July 21, 2022).
116. *See History*, "Timelines: Promoting Sound Financial Standards and Regulations," Bis.org, https://www.bis.org/history/timeline/4-standards_regs.htm (last visited November 20, 2023).

BCBS initiated its exploration of regulatory measures for bank exposure to crypto assets in 2019.[117] Initial steps included the publication of a newsletter in March 2019,[118] highlighting the associated risks and outlining minimum supervisory expectations for banks engaging with crypto assets.[119] Subsequently, in December 2019, the committee released a discussion paper seeking broader stakeholder perspectives on the prudential treatment of crypto assets.[120] This marked the beginning of the BCBS's efforts to carve out a global standard for regulating crypto assets in the banking sector.

In June 2021, BCBS embarked on an inevitably more divisive regulatory endeavor, initiating a public consultation on the prudential treatment of banks' crypto asset exposures.[121] Preliminary proposals categorized crypto assets into two groups: those eligible for modified treatment under the existing Basel Framework and those, like Bitcoin, believed to be high risk and subject to a more conservative approach.[122]

Building upon the first consultation, BCBS issued a revised set of proposals in June 2022, providing greater detail on the proposed standard and introducing new elements, such as an infrastructure risk add-on to address the emerging risks associated with distributed ledger technologies.[123]

Later that year, on December 16, 2022, the committee finalized an amended version of their comprehensive framework, dubbed the Crypto Standard.[124] Most notably, under the finalized standard, crypto assets are classified into two groups. Group 1 includes tokenized traditional assets and stablecoins, and would be subject to existing risk-weighted capital requirements under the Basel Framework.[125] Group 2 crypto assets includes those which fail to meet the requirements for any of those in Group 1, and are subject to new, more rigorous standards, these include any and all unbacked crypto assets.[126] The December 2022 Crypto Standard has been officially added as a chapter of the consolidated Basel Framework (SCO60), with an implementation date set for January 2025.[127]

---

117. While its fairly common today to hear terms like crypto assets, cryptocurrency, and even digital assets used interchangeably, even among mindful regulators, it was clear the Committee's choice of words had been highly intentional. An article in the *ABA's Banking Journal* remarked on the reference to virtual currencies like bitcoin as crypto assets "which it did not describe as cryptocurrencies, since they [quoting the Discussion Paper] 'do not reliably provide the standard functions of money and can be unsafe to rely on as a medium of exchange or store of value." *Basel Committee Taking a Look at crypto assets, Virtual Currencies,* ABA Bank. J. (Dec. 12, 2019), https://bankingjournal.aba.com/2019/12/basel-committee-taking-a-look-at-crypto assets-virtual-currencies/.

118. BCBS, *Statement on crypto assets,* Newsletter, Bis.org (Mar. 13, 2019), https://www.bis.org/publ/bcbs_nl21.htm.

119. *Id.*

120. BCBS, Discussion Paper: Designing a Prudential Treatment for crypto assets (Dec. 2019), https://www.bis.org/bcbs/publ/d490.pdf.

121. Press Rel., BCBS, Basel Comm. Consults on Prudential Treatment of Cryptoasset Exposures (June 10, 2021), https://www.bis.org/press/p210610.htm.

122. BCBS, Consultative Doc.: Prudential Treatment of Cryptoasset Exposures (June 2021), https://www.bis.org/bcbs/publ/d519.pdf.

123. BCBS, Consultative Doc.: Second Consultation on Prudential Treatment of Cryptoasset Exposures (June 2022) https://www.bis.org/bcbs/publ/d533.pdf.

124. Press Release, BCBS, Prudential Treatment of Cryptoasset Exposures (Dec. 16, 2022) (on file with BCBS).

125. *See* BCBS. Supervision, Prudential treatment of cryptoasset exposures, 1 (Dec. 2022), https://www.bis.org/bcbs/publ/d545.pdf.

126. *Id.*

127. *Id.*

Most recently, BCBS issued a consultative document titled Disclosure of Cryptoasset Exposures on October 17, 2023, for public review.[128] This document establishes the prudential requirements for banks' crypto-asset exposures and provides a set of standardized disclosure templates which are detailed in a new chapter of the consolidated Basel Framework.[129] The implementation date for these requirements is set for January 2025.[130]

Committee on Payments and Market Infrastructure (CPMI)

The Committee on Payments and Market Infrastructures (CPMI) is an international standard-setting body dedicated to enhancing the safety and efficiency of payment, clearing, settlement, and related arrangements.[131] The CPMI serves as a central forum for central bank collaboration on relevant oversight, policy, and operational matters, including the provision of central bank services.[132]

CPMI has been involved most visibly in the area of central bank digital currencies (CBDCs) in coordination with the Federal Reserve, the International Monetary Fund (IMF) and the BIS, in providing its expertise and opinion to G20 nations with respect to the risks and potential benefits of CBDCs in facilitating cross-border payments.[133] According to a speech by Michelle Neal, Executive Vice President of the Federal Reserve Bank of New York in November 2022, a high priority for CMPI was the study and coordination of efforts to develop "24/365 RTGS systems—like FedNow—globally." RTGS stands for Real Time Gross Settlement and is a funds transfer system allowing for the instantaneous transfer of money and/or securities. It is the continuous process of settling payments on an individual order basis without the netting of debits and credits (as is done with a batch system) across the books of a central bank. Real time settlement means that a payment transaction is not subject to any waiting and is settled as soon as it is processed. The new FedNow service is a recent example of RTGS, and, according to the FedNow website, it "enables individuals and businesses to send and receive payments within seconds at any time of the day, or on any day of the year, so that the receiver ... can use the funds immediately."[134]

The International Organization of Securities Commissions (IOSCO)

The IOSCO is an international body that brings together the world's securities regulators and is recognized as a global standard setter for the securities sector. It develops, implements, and promotes adherence to internationally recognized standards for securities regulation. It works closely with the G20 and the Financial Stability Board (FSB) on the global regulatory reform agenda.

---

128. BCBS, Consultative Document: Disclosure of Cryptoasset Exposures (Oct. 17, 2023), https://www.bis.org/bcbs/publ/d556.pdf.
129. *Id.*
130. *Id.*
131. BIS, *CMPI – Overview,* Bis.org https://www.bis.org/cpmi/about/overview.htm (last accessed Nov. 22, 2023).
132. *Id.*
133. *See* Central Bank Digital Currencies for Cross-Border Payments, Joint Report to G20 (July 2021), https://www.bis.org/publ/othp38.pdf.
134. *See* Michelle Neal, Executive Vice President and Head of Markets, Federal Reserve Bank of New York, Advances in Digital Currency Experimentation, Remarks at the Singapore Fintech Festival, (Nov. 4, 2022), *in* Fed. Rsrv. Bank N.Y., Press Center available at https://www.newyorkfed.org/newsevents/speeches/2022/nea221104.

On November 16, 2023, IOSCO released its Final Report of policy recommendations for crypto and digital asset markets.[135] The recommendations were designed to support consistency with respect to the regulatory frameworks and oversight in IOSCO member jurisdictions and to address concerns related to market integrity and investor protection. The recommendations were developed under the stewardship of the IOSCO Board's Fintech Task Force (FTF) in accordance with IOSCO's Crypto Asset Roadmap, published in June 2022.[136]

The Report describes eighteen recommendations in connection with (i) the application of IOSCO's objectives and principles for securities regulation and (ii) supporting IOSCO standards, recommendations, and good practices with respect to crypto asset activities. The recommendations cover six key areas:

1. Conflicts of interest arising from vertical integration of activities and functions.
2. Market manipulation, insider trading, and fraud.
3. Cross-border risks and regulatory cooperation.
4. Custody and client asset protection.
5. Operational and technological risk.
6. Retail access, suitability, and distribution.

According to IOSCO, the recommendations amount to a functional, economic approach to mitigate against risks, rather than attempting to develop a one size fits all prescriptive taxonomy. Accordingly, the IOSCO approach was developed to be outcome-focused and principle-based across each key area as noted above. Moreover, the specific chapters treat more granular subjects, such as governance and disclosure of conflicts; order, handling, and trade disclosures; listing of crypto assets and primary market activities; custody of client monies and assets; retail distribution; and stablecoins.

In December 2023, IOSCO also issued a Final Report with policy recommendations which followed (and concluded) IOSCO's March 2022 DeFi Report.[137] The Final Report noted that the use of blockchain technologies "may have the potential to foster financial innovation, increase, efficiencies, and improve access to financial products, services and activities ... includ[ing] those related to primary market issuance, secondary market trading, asset servicing, and life cycle management." There is a particular focus on lending and borrowing, two of the primary DeFi activities. The objective of the Final Report is to describe the state of DeFi and its common products and services, demonstrating why they do not materially differ from products and services offered in traditional financial markets and why DeFi has the potential to present significant investor and market risks. Along with the Final Report itself, IOSCO also included a DeFi Consultation Report.[138]

---

135. Policy Recommendations for Crypto and Digital Asset Markets, Final Report (November 16, 2023), https://www.iosco.org/library/pubdocs/pdf/IOSCOPD747.pdf.
136. IOSCO crypto asset Roadmap for 2022-2023 (July 7, 2022), https://www.iosco.org/library/pubdocs/pdf/IOSCOPD705.pdf.
137. Final Report with Policy Recommendations for Decentralized Finance (DeFi) (December 2023), https://www.iosco.org/library/pubdocs/pdf/IOSCOPD754.pdf.
138. Policy Recommendations for Decentralized Finance (DeFi) Consultation Report (Sept. 2023), https://www.iosco.org/library/pubdocs/pdf/IOSCOPD744.pdf.

The IOSCO reports are both comprehensive and reflect a point of view that crypto assets and DeFi should promptly be brought into regulated environments, either through such projects adapting to existing regulations or by the adoption of new regulations which fit the underlying technology.

Financial Action Task Force (FATF)

The Financial Action Task Force (FATF) is an international, intergovernmental organization established in 1989 by members of the G7 to serve as the global watchdog against money laundering and terrorist financing. It develops and promotes global standard adoption and implementation.[139] The FATF has been active in the crypto space since 2018 and has continued to update its guidance.[140]

In February 2023, FATF implemented an action plan to update its recommendations related to crypto assets, specifically to address vulnerabilities exploited by hackers through ransomware attacks.[141] In addition, on November 16, 2023, the Task Force released amendments to its crypto-related recommendations which it believes will provide law enforcement, financial intelligence units, and prosecutors better tools for asset recovery, including recovering digital assets, from criminals.[142]

Financial Stability Board (FSB)

The Financial Stability Board (FSB) is an international institution dedicated to identifying and monitoring risks to the global financial system and issuing recommendations to global policymakers.[143] The FSB has been active in publishing its research and recommendations related to crypto and blockchain. The FSB has contributed not only to the study of the digital assets themselves, but to the market phenomenon that has accompanied them. The high-level research and policy recommendations contained in the many reports issued by FSB are beyond the scope of this overview, but several of their useful resources and reports have been included in the footnotes for optional further reading.[144]

---

139. *See* U.S. Dept. of Treasury, *Financial Action Task Force*, https://home.treasury.gov/policy-issues/terrorism-and-illicit-finance/financial-action-task-force (accessed Nov. 30, 2023).

140. *See* Ian Allison, *FATF Crypto Guidance Looks to Bring Industry in Line with Banks*, Coindesk (May 11, 2023, 1:00 p.m. EDT), https://www.coindesk.com/policy/2021/10/28/fatf-crypto-guidance-looks-to-bring-industry-in-line-with-banks/.

141. *See* Jordan Finneseth, *FATF Action Plan Aims for 'Timely Global Implementation' of Crypto Norms*, Kitko News (Feb. 24, 2023), https://www.kitco.com/news/2023-02-24/FAFT-action-plan-aims-for-timely-global-implementation-of-crypto-norms.html; *See also, Outcomes of FATF Plenary, 22-24 February 2023*, FATF: "Disrupting the Financial Flows from Ransomware" https://www.fatf-gafi.org/en/publications/Fatfgeneral/outcomes-fatf-plenary-february-2023.html (last accessed Nov. 25, 2023).

142. *See* FATF, *Amendments to the FATF Standards to Strengthen Global Asset Recovery* (Nov. 16, 2023), https://www.fatf-gafi.org/en/publications/Fatfrecommendations/amendment-FATF-standards-global-asset-recovery.html.

143. FSB, *About the FSB*, https://www.fsb.org/about/ (last accessed Nov. 25, 2023).

144. *crypto assets Regulators Directory*, FSB (April 5, 2019), https://www.fsb.org/2019/04/crypto assets-regulators-directory/; *Regulation, Supervision, and Oversight of "Global Stablecoin" Arrangements*, FSB (Oct. 13, 2020), https://www.fsb.org/wp-content/uploads/P131020-3.pdf; Assessment of Risks to Financial Stability from crypto assets, FSB (Feb. 16, 2022), https://www.fsb.org/2022/02/assessment-of-risks-to-financial-stability-from-crypto assets/; FSB, Regulation, Supervision and Oversight of crypto asset Activities and Markets – Consultative Document (Oct. 11, 2022), https://www.fsb.org/2022/10/regulation-supervision-and-oversight-of-crypto asset-activities-and-markets-consultative-report/; FSB, Review of the FSB High-Level Recommendations of Regulation, Supervision and Oversight of

The FSB has been especially active in the last year, publishing numerous substantive reports related to blockchain and digital assets technology. For example:

On February 16, 2023, the FSB published its report[145] on the financial stability risks posed by DeFi.[146] The report discussed the growth of DeFi, where it converges and diverges from traditional finances (TradFi), and vulnerabilities involving DeFi that could pose a risk to financial stability under future circumstances. The FSB's report suggests that DeFi, while mostly confined within the digital asset market and thus posing insubstantial risks to the greater financial system, poses inherent vulnerabilities that will need to be addressed if its popularity continues to grow.[147] The FSB reported that traditional vulnerabilities such as operational risk and liquidity and maturity mismatch are particularly amplified in the space because of DeFi's potentially opaque and manipulable governance protocols, reliance on novel technology like self-executing contracts and oracles, and cross-chain thefts.[148] Based on these findings, the FSB indicated it will carry out additional work to analyze the growth and implications of the DeFi markets to determine whether the international regulation needs to be enhanced to account for these unique risks.

In July 2023, the FSB released two significant reports[149] including its final recommendations for regulating, supervising, and overseeing global stablecoin (GSC) arrangements,[150] and its final report on high-level recommendations for regulating, supervising, and overseeing crypto asset activities and markets. The stablecoin report's primary recommendations include the establishment of prudential requirements such as capital and liquidity reserve requirements, clarifying depositor redemption rights, ensuring the stability of GSC values through robust governance frameworks, and building the necessary supervisory

"Global Stablecoin" Arrangements – Consultative Report (Oct. 11, 2022), https://www.fsb.org/2022/10/review-of-the-fsb-high-level-recommendations-of-the-regulation-supervision-and-oversight-of-global-stablecoin-arrangements-consultative-report/.

145. FSB, The Financial Stability Risks of Decentralized Finance (Feb. 16, 2023), https://www.fsb.org/wp-content/uploads/P160223.pdf.

146. DeFi is a broad term used to describe the growing market for financial services products and services employing blockchain and digital assets technology. DeFi can be primarily characterized by decentralization (facilitated by distributed ledger technology) and disintermediation (permitting the consumption and provision of financial products and services directly from their source without the need for a third-party intermediary, like a banker or broker-dealer). Services such as lending and borrowing have become especially popular, and controversial, in the DeFi market, and regulators, as well as traditional financial institutions, are unsurprisingly keeping close watch on these developments.

147. *Supra,* n. 32 at 1.

148. The report argues that dependence on this technology, while designed to ensure transparency and reliability, could lead to crises in the event of disruptions (like theft or congestion) due to the immutable and decentralized nature of DeFi transactions. *Supra,* n. 32 at 1.

149. *High-level Recommendations for the Regulation, Supervision and Oversight of Global Stablecoin Arrangements*: Final report, FSB https://www.fsb.org/2023/07/high-level-recommendations-for-the-regulation-supervision-and-oversight-of-global-stablecoin-arrangements-final-report/; *High-level Recommendations for the Regulation, Supervision and Oversight of crypto asset Activities and Markets: Final report*, FSB https://www.fsb.org/2023/07/high-level-recommendations-for-the-regulation-supervision-and-oversight-of-crypto asset-activities-and-markets-final-report/.

150. The FSB has defined Global Stablecoin Arrangements (GSCs) as stablecoins that are designed to maintain a stable value relative to an asset or pool of assets, usually fiat currency. Distinct from Central Bank Digital Currencies (CBDC), they are not necessarily tied to the currency of any one jurisdiction. Examples include Tether, USD Coin (USDC), and Paxos (PAX). It does not include in this definition algorithmic stablecoins. *See High-level Recommendations for the Regulation, Supervision and Oversight of Global Stablecoin Arrangements*: Final report, FSB https://www.fsb.org/2023/07/high-level-recommendations-for-the-regulation-supervision-and-oversight-of-global-stablecoin-arrangements-final-report/.

infrastructure to oversee GSC arrangements. The regulation, supervision, and oversight report focused primarily on consumer protection, prudential standards, and market integrity recommendations. The final report also emphasized the need for regulators to establish a licensing framework for the registration of crypto asset service providers; install clearer standards for market conduct to combat insider trading, market manipulation, and conflicts of interest; and form enhanced consumer protection measures to account for the unique challenges.[151] The report also calls for the installation of prudential standards for leverage and liquidity, and the establishment of a clear framework for custody, and asset valuation to improve disclosure and transparency.[152]

EU v. UK: Markets in Crypto Assets Regulation (MiCA) and the UK Treasury (HMT) Proposals

MiCA, the Markets in Crypto Assets regulation stands as a proposed regulation by the European Commission. It forms a key element within the broader Digital Finance Strategy package and represents the first legislative initiative at the European level addressing crypto assets.[153] Within the UK, discussions surrounding the regulation of crypto assets often reference MiCA, drawing comparisons between the UK's approach[154] and that of the European Union. Interestingly, the UK's proposed regulatory framework shares many similarities with MiCA.[155] Both frameworks aim to regulate stablecoins, including non-fiat backed varieties like asset-referenced tokens, exchange tokens with identifiable issuers, and utility tokens.[156] Additionally, both frameworks encompass activities such as custody, exchange venue operation, and issuance.[157]

Stablecoins and Central Bank Digital Currencies (CBDCs)

Stablecoins are cryptocurrencies pegged to real-world assets like currencies (*e.g.*, USD) or commodities (*e.g.*, gold), they aim to provide an option suitable for everyday transactions (something which the high volatility of more popular stablecoins like Bitcoin and Ethereum have made impracticable for most).[158] This stability is achieved through collateralized reserves or algorithmic control mechanisms that manage the coin's supply.[159]

---

151. See High-level Recommendations for the Regulation, Supervision and Oversight of crypto asset Activities and Markets: Final report, FSB https://www.fsb.org/2023/07/high-level-recommendations-for-the-regulation-supervision-and-oversight-of-crypto-asset-activities-and-markets-final-report/.

152. *Id.*

153. *See Regulating Crypto Assets in Europe: Practical Guide to MiCA*, Norton Rose Fulbright (Sep. 2022), https://www.nortonrosefulbright.com/en/knowledge/publications/2cec201e/regulating-crypto assets-in-europe-practical-guide-to-mica.

154. *See Regulating Cryptoassets: Comparing MiCA and the HMT Proposals,* Norton Rose Fulbright (March 2023), https://www.gov.uk/government/consultations/future-financial-services-regulatory-regime-for-cryptoassets; *See also, Future Financial Services Regulatory Regime for Cryptoassets*, UK.gov (Oct. 30, 2023), https://www.gov.uk/government/consultations/future-financial-services-regulatory-regime-for-cryptoassets.

155. *A Closer Look at the Proposed UK Cryptoassets Regulatory Regime*, Skadden (March 29, 2023), https://www.skadden.com/insights/publications/2023/03/a-closer-look-at-the-proposed-uk-cryptoassets-regulatory-regime.

156. *Id.*

157. *Id.*

158. See Adam Hayes, *Stablecoins: Definition, How They Work, and Types*, Investopedia (July 6, 2023), https://www.investopedia.com/terms/s/stablecoin.asp.

159. *Id.*

By contrast, Central Bank Digital Currencies (CBDCs) are digital forms of fiat currencies issued directly by central banks.[160] Functionally, a CBDC would be the digital equivalent of cash, legal tender in your wallet.

CBDCs are gaining significant traction worldwide, with over 114 countries, representing 95% of global GDP, actively exploring or developing them.[161] 60 countries are currently in advanced stages of development, while over 20 central banks have launched pilot programs. Brazil, Japan, and Russia are among the early adopters testing the technology in real-world scenarios.[162] Eleven nations have already fully launched their CBDCs, and 20 more are expected to follow suit in the subsequent year.[163] Countries with strong but non-dominant currencies have the highest incentives to launch CBDCs to gain technological first-mover advantage.[164] In December 2023, Hong Kong announced that it was beginning an official consultation period for a new regulatory framework for stablecoin issuers operating within the city.[165] According to the consultation paper,[166] stablecoin issuers operating within Hong Kong will, among other things, need to be licensed with the Hong Kong Monetary Authority (HKMA), and will be required to maintain full-backing for all of their circulating stablecoins, and provide regular public disclosures of their reserve assets.[167] With this recent news from Hong Kong, it is perhaps unsurprising that China leads the charge in CBDC adoption, recording over $3.6 billion in monthly digital yuan transactions, but micronations like Palau are also exploring how digital currencies can unlock sustainability goals and financial inclusion.[168]

According to the Atlantic Council, as of 2023, 19 of the 20 G20 country members are in advanced stages of CBDC development.[169] While the U.S. has made slower progress in developing a retail CBDC, other members like the UK and Japan are actively prototyping their digital currencies and engaging in public consultations to address privacy and financial stability concerns.[170] Notably, the U.S. is forging ahead with the development of a wholesale CBDC, intended for interbank settlements.[171]

---

160. *See* What is Central Bank Digital Currency (CBDC), McKinsey (March 1, 2023), https://www.mckinsey.com/featured-insights/mckinsey-explainers/what-is-central-bank-digital-currency-cbdc.

161. *See CBDCs: A New Chapter in Global Banking,* Ripple (Sep. 19, 2023), https://ripple.com/insights/cbdcs-a-new-chapter-in-global-banking/.

162. Alisha Chhangani, *Snapshot: Which Countries Have Made the Most Progress on CBDCs so far in 2023,* Atlantic Council (March 21, 2023), https://www.atlanticcouncil.org/blogs/econographics/which-countries-have-made-the-most-progress-in-cbdcs-so-far-in-2023/.

163. *Supra*, note 48.

164. *Id.*

165. *See* Katherine Ross & Jack Kubinec, *Hong Kong to Create Regulatory Regime for Stablecoin Issuers,* Blockworks (Dec. 27, 2023), https://blockworks.co/news/hong-kong-stablecoin-regulation.

166. See HKMA, Legislative Proposal to Implement the Regulatory Regime for Stablecoin Issuers in Hong Kong, Consultation Paper (Dec. 2023), https://www.hkma.gov.hk/media/eng/doc/key-information/press-release/2023/20231227e4a1.pdf.

167. *See* Ross et al., *supra,* note 152.

168. *Id.*

169. *Central Bank Digital Currency Tracker,* Atlantic Council, https://www.atlanticcouncil.org/cbdctracker/ (accessed Dec. 3, 2023).

170. *Id.*

171. *Id. See also,* Josh Lipsky and Ananya Kumar, *It's Official: The United States is Developing a Bank-to-Bank Digital Currency,* Atlantic Council (Dec. 15, 2022), https://www.atlanticcouncil.org/blogs/new-atlanticist/its-official-the-united-states-is-developing-a-bank-to-bank-digital-currency/; Ernest Hoffman, *NY Fed Launches 12-week CBDC Pilot Program with Major Banks,* Kitko (Nov. 15, 2022), https://www.kitco.com/news/2022-11-15/NY-Fed-launches-12-week-CBDC-pilot-program-with-major-banks.html.

Regulation by (SEC) Enforcement

Much of the current U.S. regulatory activity regarding blockchain and digital assets is to be found in a series of SEC enforcement actions filed since late 2020.[172] Most of these actions revolve around the question of whether digital assets are securities and, if so, what characteristics they must have in order to be considered as securities.[173] Because the legislative process is currently at an impasse, this litigation is currently at the center of the regulatory environment regarding digital assets. In the United States, the question of whether digital assets are securities revolves around a test fashioned by the Supreme Court in 1946 in *SEC v. Howey*.[174] According to the *Howey* test, an asset is a security if:

1. It is an investment of money,
2. In a common enterprise,
3. With an expectation of profits,
4. Derived solely from the efforts of others.[175]

If an asset meets these four criteria, it will be considered an "investment contract," a catch-all category which qualifies as a security under the Securities Act of 1933. This is the crux of all the ongoing SEC litigation because, if an asset is qualified as a security, it typically needs to be registered and must be traded on a national securities exchange.

Regulation by enforcement has been frequently and broadly criticized. A forthcoming law review article by the same name writes: "Policymaking through enforcement ... can be interpreted as more of a 'destructive' act. Successful agency litigation stops conduct by a regulated industry through a cease-and-desist order, for example, a censure, license suspension, and fines."[176] SEC Commissioner Hester Peirce put it this way in her January 2023 remarks before the Digital Assets at Duke Conference:

> The SEC needs to conduct better, more precise, and more transparent legal analysis. The SEC's approach to regulating crypto looks like [this]: We tell people to come down to the office to talk to us about their projects, plug the information they give us into our proprietary security-identifying algorithms, and then send the people home with a court date. Hardly a reasonable way forward, and one that results in what one lawyer has dubbed "regulation by anxiety."

Operating in such an opaque environment is very stressful for law-abiding people.[177] From the agency's perspective, regulation by enforcement provides flexibility in determining what it believes to be violative conduct on a case-by-case basis. However, there are also public trade-offs involved, not least of which is a lack of clarity and difficulty faced by regulated

172. *See Crypto Assets and Cyber Enforcement Actions,* SEC.Gov (accessed Jan. 14, 2024).
173. *See e.g.,* Susan I. Gault-Brown, *The SEC's Position on Digital Assets,* Harvard L.S. Forum on Corp. Gov. (Sat. Apr. 27, 2019), https://corpgov.law.harvard.edu/2019/04/27/analysis-of-secs-current-position-on-digital-assets/.
174. S.E.C. v. W.J. Howey Co., 328 U.S. 293 (1946).
175. *Id.* The word "solely" has been effectively carved out of the *Howey* test by subsequent case law.
176. *See* Brummer et al., *supra,* note 27, at 8.
177. See Comm'r Peirce Remarks at Duke, *supra,* note 26.

entities to plan for the future, as well as the real consequences which could await those who try. For example, in their July 2021 Statement regarding the *Coinschedule* matter,[178] SEC Commissioners Peirce and Roisman expressed disappointment "that the Commission's settlement with Coinschedule did not explain which digital assets touted by Coinschedule were securities, an omission which is symptomatic of [the Commission's] reluctance to provide additional guidance about how to determine whether a token is being sold as a part of a securities offering or which tokens are securities ...." As a result, they conclude, "[m] arket participants ... cannot get a clear answer, backed by a clear Commission-level statement, that something is a securities offering."[179]

As noted by Professor Carol Goforth from the University of Arkansas School of Law, the SEC has declined to initiate any formal rulemaking regarding crypto assets, "instead relying on non-binding statements by individual officials and complicated frameworks that may or may not apply in any given situation."[180] The absence of normal notice and comment procedures required by formal rulemaking has given the Commission significant flexibility, but the tradeoff is that "[c]rypto entrepreneurs must operate in the face of uncertainty with the knowledge that their actions may be challenged by the Commission years after the fact. Crypto entrepreneurs must choose between the risk that they or their businesses may later face substantial penalties, or they must forego operating in the U.S."[181] The SEC began its regulation by enforcement efforts in earnest in 2020 when it sued Ripple in connection with Ripple's development and marketing of the digital asset XRP.[182] XRP had existed for years and had been tremendously successful (although the SEC's litigation resulted in the destruction of approximately 50% of its market value).[183] After extensive discovery and the exchange of numerous expert reports, the court decided on cross motions for summary judgment in mid-2023. Ultimately, the court decided that the original marketing of XRP which could be implied to have been part of its capital raising purposes was a security and therefore should have been registered. However, sales of XRP subsequent to that time were not securities because they were anonymous, and therefore purchasers could not have understood that its value was somehow related to the efforts of others, thus falling short of meeting all the elements of the *Howey* test. Ripple and most of the digital asset industry interpreted this ruling as a win for the industry and the SEC attempted an immediate interlocutory appeal to the Second Circuit which was denied by the District Court. As this is written, the District Court is deciding on the remedies phase. Regardless of the details of

---

178. Statement by Comm'r Hester Peirce & Elad L. Roisman, "In the Matter of Coinschedule," SEC.Gov (July 14, 2021), https://www.sec.gov/news/public-statement/peirce-roisman-coinschedule.

179. *Id.*

180. Carol R. Goforth, *Regulation by Enforcement: Problems with the SEC's Approach to Cryptoasset Regulation*, at 42 (Apr. 27, 2022). Maryland Law Review, forthcoming (Available at SSRN: https://papers.ssrn.com/sol3/papers.cfm?abstract_id=4084033).

181. *Id.* at 43.

182. *SEC v. Ripple Labs Inc.*, No. 20-CV-10832. *See* Joseph A. Castelluccio et al., *Defining Digital Asset Securities: U.S. District Court Issues Summary Judgement Rulings in SEC v. Ripple Labs,* Mayer Brown (July 24, 2022), https://www.mayerbrown.com/en/perspectives-events/publications/2023/07/defining-digital-asset-securities-us-district-court-issues-summary-judgment-rulings-in-sec-v-ripple-labs.

183. Scott Mascianica et al., *SEC v. Ripple: When a Security Is Not a Security,* Holland & Knight (July 20, 2023), https://www.hklaw.com/en/insights/publications/2023/07/sec-v-ripple-when-a-security-is-not-a-security.

that decision, it will no doubt be appealed to the Second Circuit Court of Appeals with an appeal to the U.S. Supreme Court likely to follow.

As an aside, the Ripple matter is a reasonable illustration of the destructive power of regulation by enforcement as a result of the sheer expense related to litigation and the substantial amount of time which inevitably is devoted to such a defense. On the date the SEC filed suit, XRP's market value dropped 25%. Moreover, to date, Ripple has estimated it has spent over $100 million in defense of this litigation.[184] Future costs of defense are likely to be in the scores of millions of dollars. Given the pace at which courts operate and the complexities of the issues at hand, it is unlikely that a final decision from the Supreme Court would be possible before mid-2025. Obviously, only the most financially strong institutions can bear these kinds of costs, distractions, and delays. The SEC is quite aware of this and therefore often is able to secure settlements from less well-financed defendants who are willing to settle simply to avoid financial ruin. Fighting can often lead to disastrous results. For example, the SEC was able to prevail in a motion for summary judgment against LBRY resulting in the destruction of that project and the financial ruin of its developers and investors, all in the absence of any evidence that LBRY had harmed any investor. The litigation drove away customers, exhausted LBRY's financial resources, and made it simply unable to afford an appeal. Whether this is an appropriate method of regulation under the rule of law is for the reader to decide. The SEC also prevailed in motions for summary judgment against digital entrepreneurs Kik and Telegram.[185] However, those matters are unique on their own facts and while the SEC also was able to put those projects out of business (without an appeal) they have not been perceived as particularly helpful in matters pending before other District Courts. Other settled matters such as against Kraken, Bittrex, and against individuals who were involved in insider trading while employed at Coinbase are similarly unhelpful in terms of their precedent setting effect. Notably, Kraken and Bittrex moved either all of their business, or a substantial portion of it, overseas as a result of their respective settlements.[186] As of this writing, no Circuit Court has ruled on the issue of what is a security and what is not in the digital asset space.

The SEC has also brought similar litigation against Coinbase claiming that it has allowed digital assets which are in fact securities to be traded on its digital asset exchange and that therefore that exchange should have been registered as a national securities exchange with

184. *See Id.* As noted by Ripple's General Counsel: "The process is the punishment."

185. *See* David I. Miller, et al., *Another Significant Cryptocurrency Decision: SEC v. Kik Interactive Inc. and Token Offerings Under the Securities Laws,* Nat'l Law Rev. (Oct. 16, 2020), https://www.natlawreview.com/article/another-significant-cryptocurrency-decision-sec-v-kik-interactive-inc-and-token#:~:text=In%20granting%20the%20SEC%E2%80%99s%20summary%20judgment%20motion%2C%20Judge,the%20public%20sale%2C%20all%20necessitating%20a%20registration%20statement.

186. *See* Press Release, SEC, SEC Charges Crypto Asset Trading Platform Bittrex and its Former CEO for Operating an Unregistered Exchange, Broker, and Clearing Agency (Apr. 17, 2023) (on file with SEC.GOV); Bittrex Global (@BittrexGlobal), X (Nov. 20, 2023), https://x.com/BittrexGlobal/status/1726652430673121310?s=20; Press Release, SEC, SEC Charges Kraken for Operating as an Unregistered Securities Exchange, Broker, Dealer, and Clearing Agency (Nov. 20, 2023) (on file with sec.gov); *See* Mitchell Clark, *Kraken Pays a $30 Million Fine and Shuts Down Crypto Staking in the US,* The Verge (Feb. 9, 2023), https://www.theverge.com/2023/2/9/23593183/kraken-staking-sec-settlement-penalties-crypto-interest.

the SEC.[187] Similar litigation has been brought against Binance along with the claim that Binance's stablecoin is a security that should have been registered.[188] The current regulatory landscape, particularly as it relates to securities regulation, features SEC enforcement actions that would appear to lack a clear and consistent framework, pose significant risks for digital asset projects. This "case-by-case" approach, targeting large and small enterprises without discernible criteria at the discretion of an administrative agency, casts a cloud of uncertainty over the entire industry, discouraging investment and impeding long-term growth due to the potential for arbitrary intervention.

Crypto Lifecycle and the Four Dimensions of Crypto Regulations–Parallel Analogy

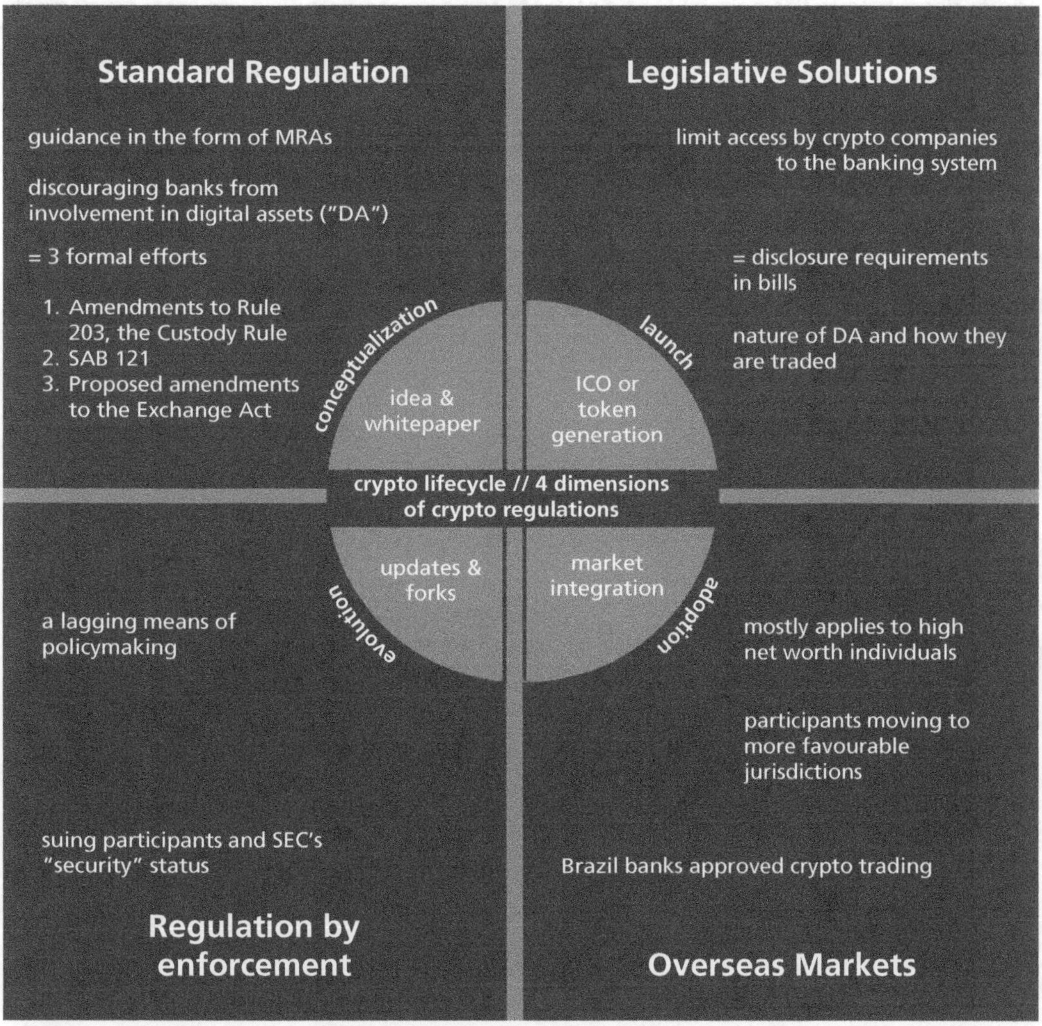

187. *See SEC v. Coinbase*, *supra* note 31; Press Release, SEC, SEC Charges Coinbase for Operating as an Unregistered Securities Exchange, Broker, and Clearing Agency, SEC.Gov (June 6, 2023) (on file with sec.gov).

188. Press Release, SEC, SEC Files 13 Charges Against Binance Entities and Founder Changpeng Zhao (June 5, 2023) (on file with sec.gov).

Conclusion

The current state of crypto asset regulation might be broadly analogized to attempting to reach port in the midst of a stormy sea. Winds and waves will shift, and crosscurrents will push the vessel off course. It is not inconceivable that the waves will swamp the vessel, that a hidden shoal or set of rocks will sink it, or that it will simply lose power and drift before it reaches harbor.

Nevertheless, crypto entrepreneurs are resilient. The challenges are many, but for them the effort is worthwhile. The regulatory environment is not friendly, but one reasonably can expect a certain moderation as products such as ETFs become more mainstream and as courts, academics, trade associations, Congress, and non-U.S. legislative and regulatory bodies demonstrate the possibility of a rational and safe regulatory crypto asset framework. For the moment, however, the large forces shaping the U.S. framework will play out in the courts, keeping the overall picture blurred and uncertain, as each case advances at its own pace and based on its own facts. The uniformity of crypto regulation in the U.S. is simply not on the near horizon, and the horizon itself often is clouded and murky.

That said, one also can expect the industry to benefit from ongoing analysis and writing, such as this volume, which addresses many of the legal challenges surrounding digital assets as well as the potential for solving those challenges.

Until then, however, the regulatory landscape will be difficult to map and uncertain of a safe path. Ultimately, a system of safe, secure, and well-regulated digital assets is a goal worthy of the investment and one that, eventually, will be achieved.

Chapter 2
Capital Ratios and Liquidity

Chen Xu

Capital Requirements for Banks Engaged in Crypto Activities

Bank capital is a central pillar of bank prudential requirements globally, often serving as a deciding factor in determining whether a given activity is viable for a bank. Current U.S. bank capital requirements, however, are not well-calibrated for crypto asset activities. Together with overarching concerns regarding the permissibility of crypto asset activities,[1] ambiguities in capital treatment have made it difficult for U.S. banking organizations to expand their crypto asset product and service offerings to meet market demands. Section I provides the relevant background on bank capital requirements and explains how bank capital requirements operate in connection with accounting standards. Section II provides an overview of the U.S. regulatory capital framework as relevant for crypto assets and highlights uncertainties in its treatment of crypto assets. Finally, Section III discusses the Basel Committee on Banking Supervision's recently adopted framework for bank crypto exposures that may serve as a blueprint for crypto asset capital regulation in the United States.

Why Is Bank Capital Important and How Does It Work?

For bank regulators, the term capital roughly refers to a bank's net worth, i.e., the excess of its assets over its liabilities. This conception of capital is useful for a bank regulator, given that the core business of banking involves transforming short-term liabilities (deposits) into long-term assets (loans). Whereas commercial enterprises tend to rely on a mix of debt

1. Press Release, Fed. Rsrv. Sys., Fed. Deposit Insurance Corp., and OCC, Joint Statement on crypto asset Risks to Banking Organizations (Jan. 3, 2023) (on file with Fed. Rsrv. Sys.).

and equity to fund their business operations, banks must rely primarily on debt in order to discharge their obligations as credit intermediaries. Yet the primary role of debt in the business of banking heightens the role of equity as a prudential safeguard because equity serves as a buffer to protect a bank's creditors (most notably its depositors) from potential asset losses.

To illustrate this principle, Figure 1 is a stylized depiction of a bank's balance sheet, with assets on the left side, and liabilities and equity on the right-hand side, ordered based on subordination.

Figure 1

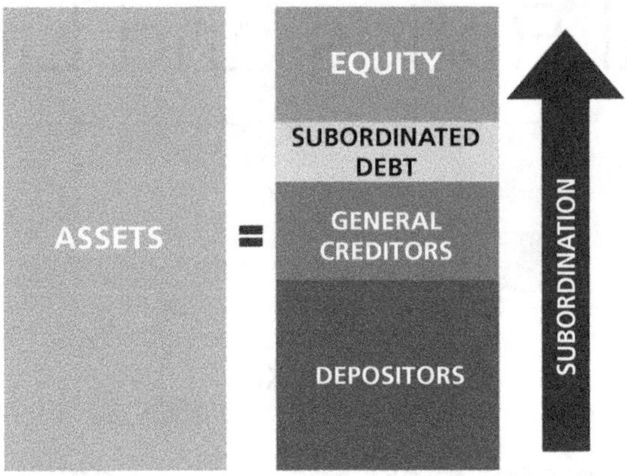

As described in Figure 1, equity represents the extent to which a bank's assets exceed its liabilities. Any losses on the asset side of the balance sheet must be balanced by a corresponding reduction of equity and liabilities. By virtue of its subordination, equity holders absorb losses before subordinated debt holders, and so on.

A bank that does not have sufficient capital to absorb losses (i.e., that must allocate losses to creditors) becomes insolvent. An illustration of this can be found in Figure 2.

Figure 2

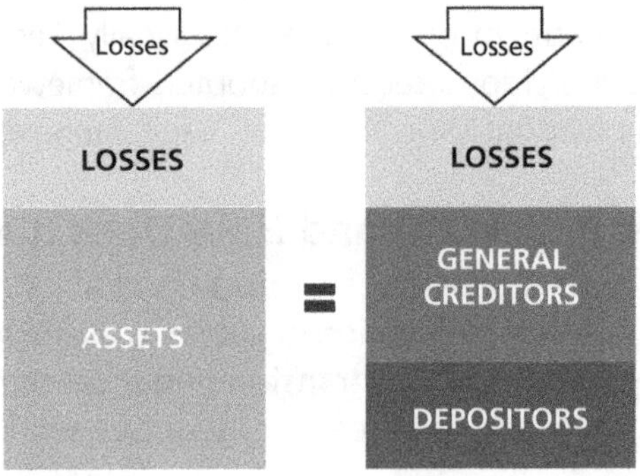

Given this loss absorbing role and the significant negative externalities associated with bank failure, bank regulators seek to mandate minimum amounts of bank regulatory capital.

The most common measure of capital adequacy is a bank capital ratio, expressed as the ratio of qualifying capital to some measure of a bank's assets. A minimum capital ratio requirement ensures that banks always fund a certain percentage of assets via equity, rather than using liabilities (deposits), lowering the risk that creditors ultimately bear the risk of any losses.

Qualifying capital generally includes balance sheet items that are available to absorb losses (i.e., are written down) prior to general creditors. These frequently include retained earnings, common stock and associated surplus, non-cumulative perpetual preferred stock, and subordinated debt. The measure of assets in the denominator of the ratio can vary depending on the type of ratio. In a risk-based capital ratio, the most commonly used measure, the denominator includes assets and certain off-balance sheet items that are adjusted by risk-weighting them based on their perceived riskiness. Riskier items receive a higher risk weight and thus require more offsetting qualifying capital (in the numerator) in order to maintain the same ratio. Less risky items may not require any capital at all, including U.S. Treasury securities.

An illustration of a risk-based capital ratio can be found in the following figure:

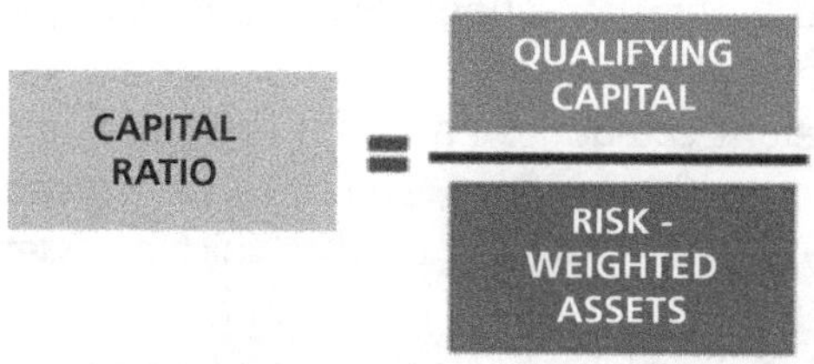

All else being equal, the more qualifying capital a bank has issued or retained, the higher the bank's ratio will be. Similarly, all else being equal, the more assets that a bank has on its balance sheet, the lower the bank's ratio will be.

By construction, increasing capital requirements imply more equity funding and less debt funding, meaning less maturity transformation of deposits into loans. Thus, while capital requirements may decrease the risk of bank failure, bank regulators must balance those benefits against these opportunity costs—excessively high bank capital requirements can make it more difficult for banking organizations to serve their function as credit intermediaries.

The implications for banks' business planning, and for bank crypto asset activities are two-fold.

First, bank capital requirements create a scarce resource (regulatory capital) that must be allocated among a bank's balance sheet (and certain off-balance sheet) activities. Activities that do not offer a sufficient return on regulatory capital may see increased prices or banks exiting those business lines. To the extent capital requirements for crypto asset activities are set high, banks may be reluctant to offer those services at a reasonable cost—this may prove to be a challenge for lower return businesses such as clearing and custody.

Second, bank capital requirements rely heavily on balance sheet accounting concepts. With few exceptions,[2] activities that do not result in an asset being recorded on-balance

2. Exceptions include off-balance sheet items that are tied to credit risk, e.g., letters of credit, financial guarantees, derivatives, etc.

sheet currently (and generally) do not give rise to capital requirements.[3] Thus crypto-activities that are entirely off-balance sheet such as providing transactional services generally are not subject to bank capital requirements, while banks' holding of crypto assets as principal would result in bank capital requirements. Distinctions between whether an item is classified as on-balance vs. off-balance can be subtle. For example, cash deposits almost always result in both an asset and a liability on a bank's balance sheet, even if held in a custodial or fiduciary capacity. In contrast, non-cash assets held by a bank in custody are typically not included on the bank's balance sheet. As we discuss further in this chapter, subtleties and ambiguities in the accounting classification of activities can have significant capital implications.

Current U.S. Regulatory Capital Framework for Crypto Assets

Currently, the U.S. bank regulatory capital framework is based on the 2010 Basel III framework (Basel III), adopted by the Basel Committee on Banking Supervision (BCBS) shortly following the 2008–2009 global financial crisis. Under Basel III, qualifying capital consists of three tiers—common equity tier 1, additional tier 1, and tier 2, with common equity tier 1 serving as the preferred form of capital. In the denominator, the U.S. implementation of Basel III divides assets into different categories based on risk stripe, including general credit risk, cleared transactions, unsettled transactions, securitization exposures, equity exposures and market risk.[4] Based on the category or risk stripe into which an asset or activity falls, the framework prescribes different methodologies for quantifying the resulting capital requirements.

As previously mentioned, Basel III was not designed with crypto asset activities in mind, and presents challenges for banking organizations as they try to fit new activities (which have different risk profiles) into a potentially outmoded taxonomy for risk.

In some cases, crypto assets and activities fall neatly into existing categories. This generally would be the case for a traditional asset that has simply been tokenized. To the extent that the tokenization process confers upon the banking organization the same legal rights as ownership of the traditional asset without introducing additional credit risks, then the same capital treatment could (and should) apply. With respect to these types of crypto assets and activities, the current bank capital framework does not present a significant obstacle for growth and expansion (rather the primary concerns appear to be supervisory concerns regarding whether banking organizations fully understand the risks involved in engaging in these activities).

Oftentimes, however, crypto assets often appear to fall into multiple asset designations. Moreover, even where a crypto asset can fit neatly into an asset class, the methodologies for calculating capital requirements for those assets may not accurately reflect the risk inherent in those activities. For example, a loan of a crypto asset by a banking organization subject to a smart contract that automatically returns the crypto asset to the banking organization at maturity would appear to be recorded as a loan for financial reporting purposes,

3. This may change under the Basel Committee's 2017 revisions to their Basel III framework, which contemplates an operational risk capital requirement assessed based on revenue and expense, rather than assets.

4. The very largest banking organizations are also subject to internal models-based capital requirements, referred to as the advanced approaches.

but does not carry credit risk in the traditional sense. If anything, the bank's primary risk is the operational risk that the smart contract somehow does not deliver the loaned asset back to the bank at maturity, rather than the risk that the borrower does not satisfy its promise as a result of financial difficulty. Assigning credit risk weights to the loan under the existing framework would thus appear to significantly overstate credit risks associated with that activity and potentially understate nascent technological/operational risks. Ambiguities of this type can pose significant challenges for banking organizations that seek to meet increased market demand for crypto assets and activities. Unless these ambiguities are resolved, either by revision of the existing framework or clarification from bank regulators, capital requirements would remain a key obstacle to expansion.

Ambiguities can also arise from uncertainty in the accounting treatment of crypto assets (and related activities). A salient example is the uncertainty regarding the accounting classification of crypto assets held in custody. On April 11, 2022, the U.S. Securities Exchange Commission (SEC) issued Staff Accounting Bulletin No. 121 (SAB 121) to address the unique risks and uncertainties posed by bank custody of crypto assets not present in arrangements to safeguard other assets, including technological, legal, and regulatory risks and uncertainties.[5]

In addition to requiring certain disclosures regarding the risks of custody-ing crypto assets, SAB 121 stated that a crypto asset custodian should present a liability on its balance sheet to reflect its obligation to safeguard the crypto assets. In particular, because such custodians face "significant risks" in holding crypto assets for users, "it would be appropriate to measure the liability at initial recognition, and then at each reporting date, using the fair value of the crypto assets." This marks a significant departure from existing accounting practice for custody activities.

As mentioned above, currently non-cash assets held by a custodian are not recorded on the custodian's balance sheet because the custodian is simply holding the asset on behalf of its customer and does not ultimately bear the risk of loss (other than as a result of operational failure). Thus, non-cash custody activities historically have not been subject to any capital requirements. The lack of meaningful regulatory capitalization is critical for the custody business, which tends to be a high volume, low margin business. Requiring bank custodians to record crypto assets held in custody on their balance sheet results in significant capital requirements for custody, which can make crypto asset custody difficult to scale.

Looming Framework for the Prudential Treatment of Crypto Asset Exposures

Recognizing the shortcomings of the current bank capital framework for crypto asset exposures and the significant growth in the market driving demand for banking services, the Group of Central Bank Governors and Heads of Supervision (the oversight body of BCBS), endorsed the BCBS's finalized prudential standards for the treatment of crypto assets (the Standards).[6] The establishment of the Standards is a key milestone on the path to develop uniform, comprehensive, and tailored regulation of bank crypto exposure.

---

5. 17 CFR Part 211.121.
6. BCBS, Prudential treatment of crypto asset exposures (Dec. 16, 2022), available at https://www.bis.org/bcbs/publ/d545.htm. Cites below are to the Standards, unless otherwise mentioned.

The Standards define crypto assets as "private digital assets that depend primarily on cryptography and distributed ledger or similar technology."[7] Notably, this definition excludes "digital representations of fiat currencies," such as central bank digital currencies (CBDCs).[8]

Categories of Crypto Assets

- In line with previous consultations, the Standards classify crypto assets into two broad categories.

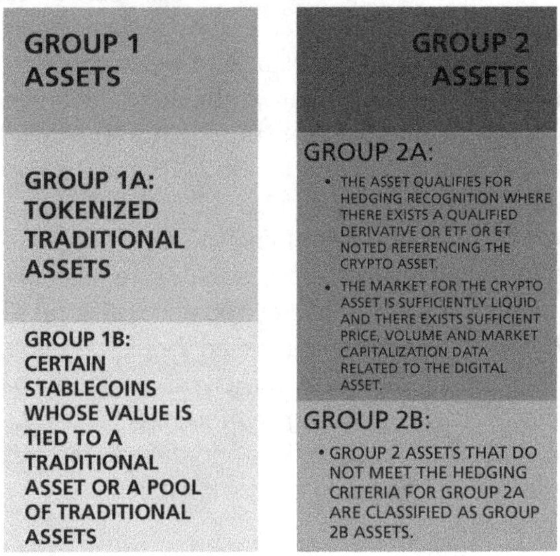

Capital Requirements: Digital Assets

- Credit Risk.
    - Capital requirements related to credit risk arising from Group 1a digital asset exposure will be in line with capital requirements associated with the relevant traditional asset.[9] However, banks should consider whether these adequately capture risk related to liquidity for the digital asset.[10]
    - For Group 1b assets, banks must determine the credit risk-weighted assets (RWA) associated with the reference asset, either by using the RWA related to directly holding the reference asset or for a pool of reference assets, use the approach required for a bank's equity investment in funds.[11] In addition, a bank must calculate credit RWA to account for the risk that the digital asset redeemer defaults and, if the bank intermediates between redeemers and digital asset holders, the

---

7. 60.131(1).
8. 60.131(2).
9. 60.27.
10. 60.29.
11. See BCBS, "Equity Investments in Funds," *CRE Calculation of RWA for Credit Risk* (Jan. 1, 2023), https://www.bis.org/basel_framework/chapter/CRE/60.htm.

bank must consider the exposure related to commitments to purchase digital assets from holders.[12]

- Market Risk.
  - For Group 1 exposures, a bank can use the Simplified Standardized Approach (SSA), Standardized Approach (SA), or Internal Models Approach (IMA) to calculate market risk capital requirement, subject to certain specifications.[13]
  - For Group 2a exposures, a bank can use modified versions of the SSA and SA standards.[14]
  - For Group 2b exposures, a bank must apply a conservative 1250% risk weight to the greater of the absolute values of the aggregate long and short positions in the digital asset. To the extent this treatment does not fully capture the risk of a Group 2b exposure, supervisors may consider an add-on capital charge.[15]
- Credit Valuation Adjustment (CVA) Risk. With respect to exposures to digital asset derivatives and securities financing transactions (SFT):[16]
  - Group 1 derivative and SFT exposures will be subject to the same market risk rules as for the relevant traditional asset.
  - Capital requirements for Group 2a derivative and SFT exposures must be calculated using the basic approach (BA-CVA).[17]
  - Group 2b derivative and SFT exposures will continue to be subject to the conservative treatment for Group 2b assets discussed above.
- Counterparty Credit Risk ("CCR").
  - Group 1 derivative exposures will be treated in line with the relevant traditional asset, subject to sufficient data being available.
  - Capital requirements for Group 2a derivatives will be calculated using the Standardized Approach for Counterparty Credit Risk (SA-CCR) with certain modifications.[18]
  - Capital requirements for Group 2b derivatives will be calculated based an exposure amount defined as the replacement cost of the asset plus 50% of the gross notional amount, multiplied by 1.4.[19]
- Operational and liquidity risk; leverage ratio requirements. Operational and liquidity risk should be calculated based on existing BCBS rules but should reflect additional

12. 60.33–60.36.
13. 60.40–60.42. *See* BCBS, *Minimum Capital Requirements for Market Risk*, MAR20, MAR 30 and MAR 40 (Jan. 2019), https://www.bis.org/bcbs/publ/d457.pdf.
14. 60.56. *See* BCBS, *Minimum Capital Requirements for Market Risk*, MAR 20 and MAR 40 (Jan. 2019),https://www.bis.org/bcbs/publ/d457.pdf.
15. 60.84, 60.86.
16. 60.88
17. *See* BCBS, "Credit Valuation Adjustment Framework," *Calculation of RWA for Market Risk*, MAR 50.1-50.26 (Jan. 2023), https://www.bis.org/basel_framework/chapter/MAR/50.htm.
18. *See* BCBS, "Standardized Approach to Counterparty Credit Risk," *Calculation of RWA for Credit Risk* (Jan. 2023), https://www.bis.org/basel_framework/chapter/CRE/52.htm.
19. 60.99, 1.4 is the alpha factor in CRE 52.1, *see id.*

risks associated with digital assets.[20] Leverage ratio exposure should be calculated based on the relevant account treatment for the digital assets. A bank must also include digital assets it has agreed to purchase for holders to redeem[21]

- Capital add-on for infrastructure risk. The Standards provide supervisors with the flexibility to add-on to a bank's Group 1 digital asset exposure capital requirement to reflect risk related to digital asset infrastructure.[22]

20. 60.100–60.101.
21. 60.113–60.114.
22. 60.53.

Chapter 3
Consumer Protection Issues under the Federal Consumer Financial Laws

Andrew W. Grant, Josh Garcia, and Jenny Leung[1]

As consumer use of virtual assets and blockchain technology[2] becomes more pervasive, banks may eye offering products to capitalize on this demand. That said, banks must ensure the products comply with *existing* consumer protection laws. The United States does not yet have bespoke federal consumer financial protection laws for virtual assets or blockchain technology.

What does this mean for banks keen to innovate? In essence, banks must assess the compatibility between the Federal consumer financial laws[3] and products or services that rely on blockchain technology. Some requirements are standards-based (e.g., the prohibition against unfair, deceptive, or abusive acts or practices), while others are prescriptive (e.g., disclosing the annual percentage rate in open- or closed-end credit transactions).

---

1. Andrew W. Grant is a partner at Runway LLP. Josh Garcia is a partner and Jenny Leung is an associate at Ketsal PLLC. The views in this chapter are their own and do not necessarily represent the views of Runway LLP or Ketsal PLLC.
2. For ease for this chapter, we refer to virtual assets throughout. This term refers to *any* product or service that a bank may offer that relies on, uses, or otherwise incorporates blockchain technology, even if such product or service may use a different name, either now or in the future.
3. 12 U.S.C. § 5481(14). "Federal consumer financial laws" include the "enumerated consumer laws" (such as the laws discussed within), the prohibition against unfair, deceptive, or abusive acts or practices, and any other rules the CFPB is authorized to prescribe.

Transposing such requirements—especially those with prescriptive requirements—to products that rely on decentralized technology may pose compliance challenges.

Complicating matters—and where this chapter hopes to provide illumination—is the lack of guidance from the Consumer Financial Protection Bureau (CFPB or the Bureau) or the prudential regulators on harmonizing the use of virtual assets with Federal consumer financial laws. While the CFPB began expressing concerns about virtual assets about a decade ago,[4] it has been more vocal regarding its concerns over virtual assets in the past few years.[5] The Bureau recently asserted in a proposed rulemaking that it considers "funds" to include virtual assets.[6] Prudential regulator guidance has focused almost exclusively on a bank's ability to engage in *any* virtual asset or blockchain-based activity rather than on how to achieve compliance.

This chapter addresses select compliance considerations and potential complications that arise under the following Federal consumer financial laws: (1) the Electronic Funds Transfer Act (EFTA) and Regulation E; (2) the prohibition against unfair, deceptive, or abusive acts or practices (UDAAP); (3) the Truth in Lending Act (TILA) and Regulation Z; (4) the Equal Credit Opportunity Act (ECOA) and Regulation B; and (5) the Fair Credit Reporting Act (FCRA) and Regulation V.

This chapter's issue spotting is not exhaustive but illustrative. Further, some products or services may cover multiple Federal consumer financial laws; violating one may breach another. Finally, we do not assess *whether* the CFPB or prudential regulators have authority under the above laws to regulate bank activity involving virtual assets or the underlying blockchain technology; instead, we presume such authority exists.[7] Use cases and the Bureau's legal scope often do not align tidily. We expect further targeted guidance or rulemaking to be promulgated in the coming years.

EFTA and Regulation E

The EFTA and its implementing regulation, Regulation E, present the most logical starting point for reviewing existing Federal consumer protection law and their application to blockchain technology. But, the EFTA is also a problematic law for regulating virtual assets, unless the CFPB prescribes regulations directly regulating such assets under Regulation E. The "primary objective [of the EFTA and Regulation E are] the protection of individual consumers engaging in electronic fund transfers and remittance transfers."[8] To do so, the EFTA

---

4. See, e.g., Consumer Fin. Prot. Bureau, CONSUMER ADVISORY, *Risks to consumers posted by virtual currencies* (Aug. 2014), https://files.consumerfinance.gov/f/201408_cfpb_consumer-advisory_virtual-currencies.pdf.

5. See, e.g., Consumer Fin. Prot. Bureau, *Complaint Bulletin: An analysis of consumer complaints related to crypto assets*, November 2022, available at https://files.consumerfinance.gov/f/documents/cfpb_complaint-bulletin_crypto assets_2022-11.pdf; Consumer Fin. Prot. Bureau, PRESS RELEASE, *Statement of CFPB Director Chopra on Stablecoin Report* (Nov. 1, 2021), https://www.consumerfinance.gov/about-us/newsroom/statement-cfpb-director-chopra-stablecoin-report/ ("[S]tablecoins may also be used for and in connection with consumer deposits, stored value instruments, retail and other consumer payments mechanisms, and in consumer credit arrangements").

6. 88 Fed. Reg. 80,197, 80, 202 (Nov. 17, 2023).

7. For example, while the CFPB recently stated that "funds" includes "digital assets that have monetary value and are readily useable for financial purposes, including as a medium of exchange," parties could challenge that conclusion—if finalized—arguing that the CFPB is exceeding its authority to interpret "funds" in this manner.

8. 12 C.F.R. § 1005.1(b); see also 15 U.S.C. § 1693(b).

and Regulation E generally govern any "electronic fund transfer"[9] authorizing a "financial institution" to debit or credit a "consumer's account."[10]

For this section, we assume (1) at least some virtual assets are "funds" (as the CFPB recently proposed[11] and at least one court has concluded[12]); (2) banks that hold or custody such virtual assets on a consumer's behalf may be doing so in an "account;" and (3) the transfer of such virtual assets to or from an "account" is an "electronic fund transfer" (EFT).[13]

Below, we address *some* consumer protection and compliance issues stemming from these assumptions. Notably, whenever a regulator sought to expand Regulation E's jurisdiction, that regulator engaged in formal rulemaking designed to address the expansion.[14] As of the date this article was published, the CFPB has not proposed to do so for virtual assets. However, because of the potential complexities involved with meeting Regulation E's obligations for virtual assets, doing so would be consistent with past regulatory practice.

Accounts and Virtual Assets

Regulation E defines an "account" to mean, in part, a "consumer asset account ... held directly or *indirectly* by a financial institution...."[15] If virtual assets are funds, then if a bank holds virtual assets directly for the consumer, the bank would likely be doing so in an account. For example, this may occur if the bank uses an internal ledger rather than a blockchain ledger and pools consumer's virtual assets into a single blockchain network address to be controlled by the bank (Omnibus Account). In this scenario, the bank may need to comply with relevant EFTA and Regulation E obligations, such as initial account disclosures, periodic statements, liability for unauthorized transfers, and error resolution.

Two other scenarios complicate the application of Regulation E. First, a bank may provide wallet software that allows consumers to create and maintain private keys associated with their own blockchain network address. Second, a bank may provide wallet software that allows consumers to distribute private key or signature creation across multiple parties, with varying amounts of control or discretion flowing back to the consumer, the other parties, and/or the bank. In either scenario, it is unclear whether the bank would be considered to be indirectly holding a consumer asset account (Segregated Accounts).

Liability for Unauthorized Transfers

Regulation E addresses when—and how much—a consumer is liable for an unauthorized EFT. This section addresses some compliance difficulties if virtual assets are involved.

9. 12 C.F.R. § 1005.3(b).

10. *Id. at* §§ 1005.3(a), 1005.2(b).

11. 88 Fed. Reg. 80,197, 80, 202 (Nov. 17, 2023).

12. *Rider v. Uphold HQ Inc.*, 657 F. Supp. 3d 491 (S.D.N.Y. 2023).

13. This means, in part, we are assuming the primary purpose for the transfer of "funds" will not be for the purchase or sale of a security that is excluded from Regulation E's definition of an "electronic fund transfer." 12 C.F.R. § 1005.3(c)(4).

14. See, e.g., 59 Fed. Reg. 10,678 (Mar. 7, 1994) (The Federal Reserve Board amended Regulation E to address government benefit cards); 71 Fed. Reg. 51,437 (Aug. 30, 2006) (The Federal Reserve Board amended Regulation E to include payroll card accounts); and 81 Fed. Reg. 83,934 (Nov. 22, 2016) (The CFPB amended Regulation E to cover specified prepaid accounts).

15. 12 C.F.R. § 1005.2(b)(1). For this analysis, we are not addressing scenarios where the account holding virtual assets is a prepaid account, but note that depending on the account's structure, the account may be categorized as such.

In short, a consumer's liability for an unauthorized electronic fund transfer is determined by whether it involved a lost or stolen access device and whether timely notice was given.[16] For accounts holding virtual assets, it is unclear what an access device would be. Determining what that term means for virtual assets may require looking at the means the consumer used to access the account to initiate the EFT. For Segregated Accounts, that could mean the private key necessary to initiate a transaction. *If* Segregated Accounts are deemed accounts under Regulation E, a hack of someone's Segregated Account in which the hacker gains access to a consumer's private key, i.e., access device, may result in substantial liability to the bank. While loss or theft of access devices for Omnibus Accounts likewise presents a risk to banks, banks may be better able to mitigate these risks versus those for Segregated Accounts. Absent clear guidance from regulators on what constitutes an account for purposes of virtual assets may mean that banks do not want to expose themselves to such financial risk and will not offer Segregated Account products to consumers.

Further, the amount of liability is described in dollars—no more than $50 in some cases and $500 in others. Regulation E is unclear on *how* the bank must reimburse the consumer. The rule could be interpreted to require payment in the dollar value of the virtual asset at the time of the unauthorized EFT, or it may require payment in the virtual asset itself. It is unclear. If banks offer accounts for virtual assets that are not purportedly pegged to a stable value, either conclusion could result in financial gain or loss to the consumer—and correspondingly could magnify the bank's loss—if the virtual asset shifted substantially in price.

Disclosures

Regulation E requires that banks make specified disclosures at the time a consumer contracts for an EFT service or before the first EFT involving the consumer's account is made.[17] While quite a few of these disclosures will not pose potential compliance issues if virtual asset accounts require them, a few could.

For example, banks are required to disclose "[a]ny fees imposed by the financial institution for [EFTs] or for the right to make transfers."[18] Users often pay gas fees to interact with the blockchain underlying the virtual asset. Because these fees are assessed on users by the underlying blockchain, banks are not directly imposing these fees on consumers. But the Official Commentary discusses requiring the account-holding institution to disclose fees paid "to the operator of a shared or interchange ATM system ... [if] they are imposed on the consumer by the account-holding institution."[19] The CFPB could consider gas fees equivalent to interchange system fees because, for example, in a proof of stake system, gas fees are paid to validators and the bank would then impose such fees on the consumer. If it does, how would a bank disclose a variable fee in the initial disclosures, especially one that can vary significantly depending on the nature of the transaction requested or skyrocket in the event of network congestion. Alternatively, a bank could absorb the risk of fluctuations in the gas fees and charge a fixed gas fee.

16. 12 C.F.R. § 1005.6(b).
17. 12 C.F.R. § 1005.7(a).
18. 12 C.F.R. § 1005.7(b)(5).
19. Regulation E Official Commentary, 1005.7(b)(5)-3.

Brief Conclusion

The EFTA and Regulation E provide a logical source for the CFPB or prudential regulators to regulate bank products involving virtual assets that act as asset accounts. And virtual assets present additional unique features with no corollary in fiat, such as a fork of the underlying blockchain, multisignature wallets, or an airdrop of virtual assets. Depending on the nature of these activities, some may constitute an EFT even though such events are outside the control of the bank and consumer, and potentially be subject to various components of the EFTA and Regulation E.

Additionally—and not discussed above—Regulation E regulates remittance transfers, another source for compliance complexities and an additional vector for regulation of services involving virtual assets.

UDAAP

The Dodd–Frank Act empowered the CFPB's authority to take actions to prevent UDAAPs in transactions for a "consumer financial product or service."[20] The latter definition is critical—it extends the CFPB's authority across eleven categories of consumer financial products. This means that even if a bank provides a product or service involving virtual assets that does not implicate an "enumerated consumer law," the CFPB or the prudential regulators will still have jurisdiction if the bank provides a "consumer financial product or service."

There are at least five categories[21] potentially broad enough to include virtual asset activity if provided by a bank (subject to potential exceptions or exclusions):

- extending credit and servicing loans;
- engaging in deposit-taking activities or exchanging funds, or otherwise acting as a custodian of funds;
- selling, providing, or issuing, stored value or payment instruments;
- providing payments or other financial data processing products or services; or
- providing financial advisory services.

Because the CFPB has provided limited guidance on UDAAP regarding virtual assets, looking at past CFPB bulletins or circulars regarding UDAAP in other contexts, plus the CFPB's bulletin analyzing consumer complaints regarding virtual assets (Virtual Assets Complaints Analysis) is a prudent step for any bank seeking to offer virtual asset products or services to its consumer customers. Below are a few possible areas where the CFPB could use its UDAAP authority in connection with a bank's offering of virtual asset products.

Undisclosed Fees

In the Virtual Assets Complaints Analysis, the CFPB flagged undisclosed or unexpected costs as a category in which the CFPB received numerous complaints. This aligns with the CFPB's

20. 12 U.S.C. § 5531(a). Note that the CFPB also has rulemaking authority allowing it to identify and prevent UDAAPs. The CFPB has not issued any such rules regarding virtual assets or other products that may use blockchain technology.
21. 12 U.S.C. § 5481(15).

longstanding unease over hidden or unexpected consumer costs. In the Virtual Assets Complaints Analysis, the CFPB included complaints regarding misleading claims of free conversion from one virtual asset to another and discrepancies between listed prices and the amounts the consumer received when selling the virtual asset.

While these are only examples, banks should be upfront about not only the fees that consumers may incur but also where banks may be unable to provide accurate estimates of fees at the outset of the consumer relationship (e.g., gas fees the consumer may incur if the bank broadcasts transactions to the relevant blockchain rather than settling transactions via an omnibus internal account). The CFPB may consider a failure to do so unfair because it caused or is likely to cause substantial injury that consumers cannot reasonably avoid and no countervailing benefits outweigh the injury. Further, the CFPB may consider such failure to be abusive if the failure materially interfered with a consumer's ability to understand the product's terms and conditions.

Material Misrepresentations in Contracts

In the CFPB's bulletin regarding Unfair and Deceptive Acts or Practices That Impede Consumer Reviews,[22] the CFPB emphasized that material contractual representations unsupported by applicable law can be deceptive. Specifically, including unenforceable material terms is deceptive because consumers are misled "into believing the contract term is enforceable." Careful attention to drafting agreements between consumers and banks is imperative to ensure that they do not contain any potentially deceptive material contractual representations.

Acting as a Custodian

A financial product or service also includes acting as a custodian of funds. If a bank was to store a consumer's private keys as part of its services, it may be providing a financial product or service. If the bank does not maintain adequate data protection or security to maintain the security and confidentiality of the consumer's private keys, the bank may be subject to unfairness claims because such failure may cause significant harm to consumers via the loss of a consumer's virtual assets. The practice may be unfair, in part, because the consumer will not reasonably be able to avoid this harm because "[t]hey do not control the creation or implementation of an entity's security measures."[23]

Misrepresenting FDIC Insurance

While the FDIC has aggressively addressed misrepresentations regarding deposit insurance by crypto companies,[24] the CFPB has also stated that misusing the FDIC's name or logo to

---

22. Consumer Fin. Prot. Bureau, BULLETIN 2022-05, *Unfair and deceptive acts or practices that impede consumer reviews* (Mar. 22, 2022), https://files.consumerfinance.gov/f/documents/cfpb_bulletin-2022-05_unfair-deceptive-acts-practices-impede-consumer-reviews.pdf.

23. Consumer Fin. Prot. Bureau, CIRCULAR 2022-04, *Insufficient data protection or security for sensitive consumer information* (Aug. 11, 2022), https://www.consumerfinance.gov/compliance/circulars/circular-2022-04-insufficient-data-protection-or-security-for-sensitive-consumer-information/.

24. See, e.g., FDIC, FIL-35-2022, *Advisory to FDIC-insured institutions regarding deposit insurance and dealings with crypto companies* (July 29, 2022).

make representations regarding deposit insurance likely constitutes a deceptive act or practice.[25] FDIC-insured banks cannot misstate whether virtual assets they hold on a customer's behalf are eligible for FDIC insurance. Therefore, banks need to be careful when describing the nature of a customer's virtual assets, and need to ensure their third-party service providers take equal care to the extent they manage communications with the banks' customers.

Brief Conclusion

Overall, the CFPB has broad authority to enforce UDAAP violations. And virtual assets also present novel issues that banks will need to prepare for, such as how to handle airdrops or forks to Omnibus Accounts to ensure that consumers are not disadvantaged such that a UDAAP claim could arise. While the CFPB's broad UDAAP authority is not new to banks, it seems likely that the CFPB will scrutinize any consumer complaints arising from a bank providing virtual asset services to its consumer customers.

UDAAP Authority Checklist for CFPB

Undisclosed Fees

Banks should be upfront about:

- fees consumers may incur
- if they are unable to provide estimates of other fees arising from the relationship. Ex: "gas fees" if transactions are broadcasted on a blockchain.

Material Misrepresentations in Contracts

CFPB called unenforceable terms in contracts "deceptive" as consumers are misled "into believing the contract term is enforceable."

Attention to drafting agreements between consumers and bank is imperative.

Acting as a Custodian

If banks do not maintain adequate data protection or security of the consumer's private keys, they may be subject to unfairness claims.

Therefore, if banks offer financial products or services, they must also act as a custodian of funds.

Misrepresenting FDIC insurance

FDIC-insured banks cannot misstate the eligibility of customer virtual assets ("CVA") for insurance.

Banks must:

- Be careful when describing the nature of CVAs
- Manage comms with 3rd party service providers

---

25. Consumer Fin. Prot. Bureau, CIRCULAR 2022-02, *Deceptive representations involving the FDIC's name or logo or deposit insurance* (May 17, 2022), https://www.consumerfinance.gov/compliance/circulars/circular-2022-02-deception-representations-involving-the-fdics-name-or-logo-or-deposit-insurance/.

TILA and Regulation Z

TILA's origin was enabling "the informed use of credit."[26] But its scope changed over the years to add substantive consumer protections. Thus, this section provides a couple of potential compliance considerations for disclosure-based and substantive requirements for offering certain types of credit.

First, TILA, through Regulation Z, generally regulates the offer or extension of consumer credit that meets specified criteria. Credit is not defined as being limited to fiat currency, much less U.S. dollars. Therefore, extensions of credit involving virtual assets may require compliance with TILA and Regulation Z. This section addresses compliance considerations for two scenarios: (1) a bank offers closed-end credit denominated in a virtual asset rather than fiat currency, and (2) a bank seeks to use virtual assets held on a consumer's behalf to repay the consumer's indebtedness on a credit card. TILA and Regulation Z may apply to many other scenarios involving extending credit that involves virtual assets or otherwise relies on blockchain technology. But these two examples show how considering disclosure and substantive requirements is necessary if a bank seeks to use virtual assets in transactions that would otherwise be subject to TILA and Regulation Z.

Closed-End Credit Denominated in Virtual Assets

As noted above, credit is not expressly limited to fiat currency. And for closed-end transactions, creditors must make certain disclosures to consumers before consummation of the transaction. While the CFPB provides model forms for creditors to use to meet these disclosure obligations, their use is not required; absent permissible changes, proper use of the model forms means creditors will be deemed to comply with Regulation Z concerning the disclosures.[27] However, the model forms *assume* a U.S. dollar-based extension of credit, e.g., the table uses "$" symbols to introduce certain disclosures, and the regulation requires that the "finance charge" be disclosed "as a dollar amount."[28] Therefore, if a bank wants to denominate a closed-end loan in virtual assets, the bank may need to alter the model form disclosures to ensure that they (i) accurately describe the closed-end credit transaction and (ii) comply with their regulatory disclosure obligations. Therefore, changing the model form to ensure accurate descriptions may mean that banks will *lose* the safe harbor afforded by the model forms.

For example, if a bank extended closed-end credit to a consumer via a virtual asset and such extension of credit was subject to TILA and Regulation Z, the bank would need to comply with TILA's closed-end disclosure obligations before doing so. These include, but are not limited to:

- Disclosing the "finance charge"—using that term—as a "dollar amount" and using language similar to "the dollar amount the credit will cost you";[29]

26. 15 U.S.C. § 1601(a); see also S. Rep. No. 392, at 1 (1967). ("The basic purpose of the truth in lending bill is to provide a full disclosure of credit charges to the American consumer.")
27. Regulation Z Official Commentary, Appendices G and H—Comment 1.
28. Regulation Z Official Commentary, 1026.18(d)-1.
29. 12 C.F.R. § 1026.18(d).

- The annual percentage rate, calculated as required under Regulation Z;[30] and
- The payment schedule.

To best comply with these and other disclosure obligations, the bank would likely need to consider at least the following:

- What type of virtual asset is the bank extending credit in? For example, extending credit via a stablecoin versus another virtual asset with wildly fluctuating value may complicate the bank's disclosure obligations. If the virtual asset used fluctuates in value, the method of determining the appropriate dollar value to assign to the loan is not specified.
- How will the bank require repayment? Again, the type of virtual asset used may impact its disclosure obligations, e.g., is the bank seeking repayment in the virtual asset itself or its dollar equivalent? If so, how is the bank calculating what amount must be repaid?

Put another way, extending credit using virtual assets that fluctuate in price will likely multiply compliance complexities versus using virtual assets that are pegged to the U.S. dollar and *meant* to maintain a stable value.

Credit Cards Secured by Virtual Assets

As more consumers acquire virtual assets, and as more banks hold virtual assets for consumers, both banks and consumers may wonder whether (i) the consumer can use his or her virtual assets as security for a credit card, or (ii) whether the bank can offset the consumer's indebtedness under a credit card plan using virtual assets that the bank holds on the consumer's behalf.

For substantive consumer protections, TILA and Regulation Z address these issues as follows: prohibiting offsets using funds deposited by the cardholder, or requiring that the consumer provide the bank with a valid security interest in such funds.[31] As discussed above, the CFPB believes that funds include virtual assets. Therefore, if a consumer holds virtual assets with a bank and is indebted to the bank under a credit card plan, the bank will need to assess whether the consumer intended the virtual asset to be held on deposit. If so, the bank may be prohibited from debiting the virtual asset to repay any indebtedness *unless* the bank acquires a valid consensual security interest in the virtual asset as described under Regulation Z and as authorized by state law.[32]

ECOA

If a bank extends credit using virtual assets subject to TILA, such extensions of credit will likely be subject to ECOA and Regulation B, which has a broader definition of credit and is

30. 12 C.F.R. § 1026.18(e), Appendix J to Part 1026—Annual Percentage Rate Computations for Closed-End Credit Transactions.
31. 15 U.S.C. § 1666(h); 12 C.F.R. § 1026(d).
32. 12 C.F.R. § 1026(d)(2).

not limited to consumer credit.[33] Therefore, banks will need to ensure that such products comply with every aspect of the credit transaction, including information requirements; terms of credit; revocation, alteration, or termination of credit; and collection procedures.[34]

While the ECOA prohibits discriminatory credit behavior, it also contains procedural provisions designed to both protect and educate consumers.[35] For the procedural requirements, this section focuses on adverse action notice requirements, and specifically the requirement that the creditor provide a "statement of specific reasons for the action taken."[36] Regulation B contains sample forms with a list of possible reasons for denial. These sample forms were created in substantially their existing form—including the list of possible reasons—in 1985.[37]

If banks seek to denominate extensions of credit in virtual assets, it is possible that banks may also look at an applicant's prior blockchain-based activity to help determine whether to extend credit. Taking this approach likely means that using the existing sample reasons will not permit banks to meet their ECOA and Regulation B obligation to provide the applicant with a statement of specific reasons. The CFPB recently addressed this issue in another emerging technology setting—the use of artificial intelligence in credit decisioning models.[38]

There, the CFPB stated that creditors cannot rely on the checklist of sample reasons to meet their ECOA obligations, nor may creditors use "overly broad or vague reasons" if doing so obscures "the specific and accurate reasons relied upon."[39] The same analysis would likely apply to any bank using an applicant's blockchain history (*e.g.,* interactions with specific decentralized applications or dApps, assets held on-chain, etc.) as a basis for determining whether to extend credit.

Creditors cannot evade their regulatory obligations because the factors considered may surprise consumers or the reasons are not intuitively related to the consumer's financial capacity. While use of blockchain analytics to assess consumer capacity is in its infancy, as more consumers transact using various blockchain protocols, such data may inform a consumer's capacity to repay credit extended. If banks seek to use such data—and assuming its use does not come from a consumer reporting agency, which will have different obligations under FCRA—banks will need to carefully assess *how* they disclose any reasons for an adverse action.

FCRA and Regulation V

FCRA[40] and its implementing regulation, Regulation V[41] exist, in part, to protect the rights of consumers to ensure accurate representation of their credit history. Blockchain analytics

33. 15 U.S.C. § 1691a(d); 12 C.F.R. § 1002.2(j); Official Commentary, 1002.2(j)-1.
34. 15 U.S.C. § 1691(a); 12 C.F.R. § 1002.2(m).
35. S. Rep. No. 94-589 (1976).
36. 12 C.F.R. § 1002.9(a)(2)(i).
37. 50 Fed. Reg. 48,018, 48,024 (Nov. 20, 1985).
38. Consumer Fin. Prot. Bureau, CIRCULAR 2023-03, *Adverse action notification requirements and the proper use of the CFPB's sample forms provided in Regulation B* (Sep. 19, 2023), https://www.consumerfinance.gov/compliance/circulars/circular-2023-03-adverse-action-notification-requirements-and-the-proper-use-of-the-cfpbs-sample-forms-provided-in-regulation-b/.
39. *Id.*
40. 15 U.S.C. §§ 1681-1681x.
41. 12 C.F.R. §§ 1022.1-1022.142.

companies compile blockchain transaction information into reports (Blockchain Reports), some of which may be used to create reports for various purposes for industry participants. To date, banks do not create Blockchain Reports, but if they use such reports or numerical scores produced from such reports for a "permissible purpose," e.g., to underwrite consumer loans, the companies providing Blockchain Reports could become "consumer reporting agencies" (CRAs).[42] If that occurs, banks may have to treat a blockchain analytics company as a CRA.

Banks acting as users of information obtained from CRAs must identify themselves to the CRA and certify the information requested will be used as specified in FCRA.[43] As part of its vendor due diligence process, a bank should ask whether service providers producing such blockchain-based transaction reports have the proper licenses or registrations required to operate as CRAs or furnishers. In addition, banks using Blockchain Reports to determine creditworthiness must disclose the use of such reports in adverse action notices. As discussed above, the specificity required in these notices may be a challenge for banks.

If a bank decides to produce blockchain-based consumer reports used to determine creditworthiness and such reports do not rely *solely* on the bank's own "transactions and experiences" with the consumer,[44] it may be deemed a CRA. A bank may also be deemed a furnisher if it submitted "information relating to consumers"[45] to a CRA for inclusion in a consumer report and be subject to additional obligations including the obligation to establish and implement reasonable written policies and procedures regarding the accuracy and integrity of the information that it furnishes to the CRA. This raises further questions about what it means to submit information relating to consumers and whether it would cover sharing on-chain data or just a consumer's blockchain network address.

Conclusion

Existing Federal consumer financial laws were not designed with the concept of blockchain technology in mind. Still, that fact does not excuse non-compliance. The above analysis is solely meant to provide a flavor of the *types* of compliance considerations banks will need to perform before providing virtual asset products to customers.

Further, assuming consumer adoption of virtual assets continues to increase, the CFPB and the prudential regulators will likely—or at least should—provide more targeted guidance on compliance. That said, such guidance may arrive first via enforcement action. The CFPB may also issue new rulemakings, whether under its Dodd-Frank Act authority or as part of an enumerated consumer financial law.[46] For example, the CFPB could use its authority to impose disclosure requirements on virtual asset activity, such as, for example, hidden or unexpected costs that the CFPB has received complaints about, as detailed in its Virtual Assets Complaints Analysis.

---

42. 12 C.F.R. § 1022.41; 1022.130.
43. 15 U.S.C. § 1681b(f).
44. *Id.* at § 1681a(d)(2)(A)(i).
45. 12 C.F.R. § 1022.41.
46. See, e.g., 12 U.S.C. §§ 5512, 5531(b), and 5532.

Taken together, consumer use of virtual assets will likely continue to increase. As it does, banks may offer products and services involving virtual assets. But in doing so, banks will need to scrutinize existing Federal consumer financial laws to best assess how to meet their compliance obligations while offering novel financial products and services.

Chapter 4
Custody, Redemption, and Ownership

Mark Attar and Stephen T. Gannon

Amara's Law: "We tend to overestimate the effect of a technology in the short run and underestimate the effect in the long run."

Introduction

The custody of digital assets is crucial for the safe and secure institutional use of digital assets, as well as for broader retail adoption. In this chapter, we will discuss several of the aspects of digital asset custody. First, we will define what it is and why it is important. Second, we will discuss the practical issues in connection with digital asset custody solutions as they currently exist, including their risks. Third, we will discuss the current legal framework as it applies to the customer of digital assets. As a preview, that legal framework is still very much in the process of development.

At the outset, one estimate worth noting is that approximately 20 percent of all bitcoins issued have been lost. Many of those familiar with the digital asset space are familiar with the story of James, the Welsh IT worker who kept 7500 bitcoin in a wallet on his hard drive, which at today's prices would be valued at above $300 million. Unfortunately, in 2013 James threw away his hard drive and has since been on a campaign (so far unsuccessfully) to get access to the local garbage dump to find the hard drive. The lesson, of course, is that the nature of digital records is tenuous and a failure to exercise due care can come with a severe downside.

Ownership of digital assets depends on the possession of public and private keys. Keys are extremely large, randomly generated numbers that prove ownership of a digital asset. As the phrase goes "not your keys, not your coins." Thus, broad adoption of digital assets requires the ability of investors not only to store their assets securely, but to be able to recover them if the keys are lost. The challenge is that the immutable transparency of digital assets comes without the possibility of administrative overrides. Thus, solutions to this risk must become broadly available and be accompanied by a substantial level of security and customer confidence.

Background

For context, it is helpful to begin with how custody is understood within traditional finance. There, custody services involve the holding and servicing of assets on behalf of others. To facilitate the provision of those services, custodians operate securities accounts and cash accounts for their clients. Securities accounts are used to record and safekeep investments and securities trades made by clients, while cash accounts reflect clients' cash holdings (which may be in multiple currencies) and which are placed on deposit with the bank which has a relationship with the custodian.[1] Core custody services typically involve safekeeping and record-keeping services; asset servicing; transaction, processing, and settlement; and, in some cases, banking services. It thus requires the simultaneous operation of two separate but related types of client accounts: one that holds securities and another that holds cash.[2] These assets are beneficially owned by the clients who retain their property rights and the assets and these investments are not reflected on a custodian's balance sheet. However, cash credited to a client's cash account is typically reflected on the balance sheet of a custodian as a deposit liability, just as with any normal bank deposit, because it represents a contractual claim to the payment of the cash balance (plus any accrued interest) from the bank.[3]

Historically, banking organizations have been the primary providers of custodial and fiduciary services and also may safeguard crypto assets when holding collateral or margin in secured financing and other client transactions. The role of custody banks in providing safekeeping services for their clients and acting as a trusted intermediary is well understood by the market as essential and safely supporting client assets in an increasingly complex global financial system.[4] The Office of the Comptroller of the Currency (OCC) describes this role at length in an Interpretive Letter declaring that national banks are authorized to engage in digital asset custody activities, noting that "safekeeping services are among the most fundamental and basic services provided by banks... . OCC guidance has recognized that banks may hold a wide variety of assets as custodians, including assets that are unique and hard to value."[5]

---

1. "The Custody Services of Banks," The Clearing House White Paper (Jul. 2016).
2. *Id.*
3. *Id.*
4. *See* Letter of BNY Mellon, Northern Trust, and State Street to the Basel Committee on Banking Supervision, Bank for International Settlements (Sept. 20, 2022) (hereinafter, "Basel Letter").
5. OCC Interpretive Letter 1170, *Authority of National Banks to Provide Crypto-Currency Custody Services for Clients* (Jul. 22, 2020).

Three core risk management principles support these safekeeping practices. First, safekeeping operations must be functionally separated from trading and other similar activities. Second, client assets must be segregated at all times from the bank's proprietary assets and from the assets of other clients. Third, proper control over client assets must be maintained at all times, including in the case of crypto assets, by control of the private keys in order to eliminate any single point of failure in the record of ownership.

Digital asset custody is a broad term that includes various methods of storing and protecting digital assets on behalf of their owners.[6] They are similar in a number of ways to those described above for traditional financial assets. A customer can decide to provide that custody for himself, or custody providers can take responsibility for securely storing those assets, including the ability to buy and sell them and keep appropriate records of (i) their ownership, (ii) corporate actions with respect to such assets (such as payment of dividends), (iii) valuation of the assets, and (iv) transfer of the assets. Other traditional considerations are how the assets are segregated (individual or omnibus), whether sub-custodians will be used, and any contractual limitations on liability.

Self-custody involves an investor holding its digital assets in its own wallet, which actually is a piece of software sitting on a computer. This wallet will hold both public keys and private keys. Public keys can be shared publicly, and are used to generate a deposit address for the owner's receipt of crypto. Private keys are larger sets of numbers which must remain absolutely private because they can be used to transfer digital assets to another person. Obviously, the primary risk involving self custody is that the individual customer is relying on himself to ensure the private keys are not lost and can be accessed when needed. This includes protecting the wallet against hacking and other risks, which can be more challenging for an individual customer than an institutional customer.

Third-party custody has become the preference of owners who would rather involve experienced intermediaries to safeguard their keys and bear some of the burden if the keys are lost. Moreover, certain institutional investors are obliged to use accredited (or qualified) custodians to safeguard their assets. The digital asset custody industry includes direct custodians and hybrid service providers. Among the direct custodians are crypto exchanges, such as Coinbase, financial institutions, including banks, and other established financial services concerns. Hybrid service providers offer individuals and businesses digital custody solutions through software and other technological means. In some cases, financial institutions will contract with a sub-custodian to provide such services. However, that may limit the type and number of clients, which investors may not be able to accept based on the sub-custodian's risk profile and the options it supports. Product-based custodial solutions are developing as well. For example, qualifying investors are now able to deposit digital assets with a custodian in exchange for depositary receipts, which are held as traditional securities in book-entry form at a registered securities clearing organization.[7]

---

6. *Digital Asset Custody 101: Guide to Self Custody, Wallet Options and More*, Fireblocks, https://www.fireblocks.com/digital-asset-custody/.

7. *See, e.g.*, Receipts Depositary Corporation, https://receiptsdepo.io/ (last visited Mar. 23, 2024).

There are different types of methods for the storage of digital assets. The most common are:

1. **Hot wallets**, which are connected to the Internet, meaning that the private keys needed for transactions are always online. This creates the advantage of speed and ease of trading digital assets. It has the disadvantage of being always connected to the internet, and therefore more vulnerable to security breaches.
2. **Cold wallets**, in which private keys are stored off-line on a device not connected to the Internet. This maximizes security but at the expense of access speed. Human involvement is required for the use of the private keys for each transaction so it can be recorded on the blockchain.
3. **Warm wallets,** which combine some of the features of cold and hot wallets. The keys are held online, but human involvement is needed to create the transaction and record it on the chain.

There are other methods of security, which can be applied to all forms of wallets, either singly or in combination, such as multisignature (Multisig) and multi-party computation (MPC) techniques. Multisig is a system which requires the signature of multiple individuals for transactions to be approved. No single person has total control over the funds so that if any single system is compromised, the owner's assets are still protected from theft. MPC splits a private key into different key shares that can be distributed across multiple devices so a hacker cannot obtain the entire key by breaching a single device.

With those points as background, we can now turn to what the practical framework of what a digital asset custodian would look like. For institutional investors, such as asset managers and advisers, custody services, generally, are the superior choice given the challenge of regulatory interpretations, risk management, technical capabilities, and evolving best practices. Contracting with a third party to oversee asset movements, valuation, settlement times, and security is typically the more prudent choice, provided it is accompanied by transparency around the financials, IT, risk management, and information security practices at the chosen custodian.

Practical Considerations

The following points should be taken into account in connection with choosing, monitoring, and engaging with a third-party, digital asset custodian:

- What are the structures or mechanisms the custodian uses to safeguard ownership rights (including cyber security, and other information security controls) and prevent the use of client assets by the custodian for its own account?
- What protections does the custodian offer to prevent the account from becoming part of the bankruptcy estate of the custodian, if it becomes insolvent?
- Does the custodian have a track record of successful operation? Does it have adequate financial resources, including insurance? Do third parties (such as auditors) review the custodian's operations?
- Does the custodian unilaterally control the assets and, if so, are there contractual protections in place for the investor?

- Does the custodian have the appropriate authorization or licenses required by the relevant regulatory authorities to enable an institutional investor to self custody, its own digital assets?
- Does the custodian have appropriate disaster recovery plans and capabilities?
- What digital assets does the custodian's platform support?
- What is the ease of access for a client to transfer or retrieve its assets?
- What system does the custodian use to report data such as net asset values, balances, transfers, and orders?
- What are the custodian's risk management, risk controls, and compliance/monitoring frameworks (especially regarding KYC/AML and record-keeping)?
- What is the process for key generation and management?
- What governance processes exist to ensure that management and the board of the custodian understand their duties and responsibilities?
- Is the custodian dependent on any third parties and, if so, does the custodian have in place an active risk assessment and monitoring program regarding such third parties?
- Does the custodian generate SOC reports [SOC 1 = financial controls; SOC 2 = operational and privacy controls] and/or have ISO certifications?[8]

The quality of the custody provider will ensure that investors are able to obtain the requisite simplicity, efficiency, and security that they need. Of course, custodial services are evolving and are working on improvements to processes that will balance security and speed, as well as efficiency and operational flexibility. Much as custody in traditional finance developed from rudimentary concepts to sophisticated central security depositories, the evolution of digital asset custody is likely to proceed on the same arc. And, as that evolution takes place, the legal framework, discussed immediately below, is highly likely to evolve with it.

Current Legal Framework for Digital Asset Custodians

Currently, there is no single source of law defining custody in the digital asset context. As explicitly recognized in the recent proposed legislation, there are shortcomings of existing law as it pertains to the custody of financial assets in general as "laws surrounding custody of financial assets is largely customary, uncodified, and poorly understood,"[9] and there is a lack of uniformity across jurisdictions regarding custody, which has not been addressed by regulators in the digital asset space. To gain further understanding of custody specific to the digital asset context where none currently exists, the analysis set forth below references multiple frameworks, including current federal and state regulatory regimes, contract law, and common law principles.

8. Industry Guide on Digital Asset Custody, AIMA.
9. *Lummis-Gillibrand Financial Responsible Financial Innovation Act*, S. 4356, 117th Congress (2021–2022).

I. U.S. Federal Law

a. Banking Regulation

i. Generally—There are no specific laws that govern policies and procedures regarding the custody of assets by banks. Most applicable rules impose obligations tied to the particular type of assets at issue.[10] Moreover, certain types of custody may invoke other legal ramifications, such as rules regarding fiduciaries (while custody is not typically deemed a fiduciary activity, other services may invoke fiduciary duties) and AML requirements under 31 C.F.R. § 103.

ii. The OCC charters, regulates, and supervises national banks, publishes guidance related to the consideration of banking custodial services. The OCC's Comptroller's Handbook on Custody Services (Handbook) addresses the fundamentals of securities custody and related services, as well as prudent risk management practices as applicable to the OCC's supervision of national banks and federal savings associations. The Handbook defines custody as "[t]he safekeeping, settlement, and servicing of securities for customers."[11] As noted in its Overview, the Handbook specifically states that "a custody relationship is contractual," and that services provided by a custodian are "typically the settlement, safekeeping, and reporting of customers' marketable securities and cash."[12] Throughout the Handbook, the OCC repeatedly notes that custodial relationships are contractual, and that custody is generally not considered a fiduciary capacity under 12 C.F.R. § 9 (fiduciary activities of national banks); however, the Handbook does note that a custodian could perform functions that are fiduciary in nature (such as exercising discretion in managing a securities lending cash collateral pool) and could be considered to be a fiduciary in certain jurisdictions.[13]

In July 2020, the OCC issued Interpretive Letter 1170, permitting regulated banks and financial institutions to custody cryptocurrencies provided certain conditions were satisfied. The letter notes the OCC's understanding of the growing demand for safe places to hold unique cryptographic keys associated with cryptocurrencies on behalf of customers and to provide related custody services. While referring to its prior guidance in the Handbook, the OCC noted that providing custody services for cryptocurrency falls within the longstanding authority to engage in safekeeping and custody activities and that such services could be provided in either a non-fiduciary or a fiduciary capacity.

Since July 2020, the OCC has provided additional guidance addressing whether it is permissible for national banks and Federal Savings associations to engage in certain cryptocurrency, distributed ledger, and stablecoin activities. For example, on November 18, 2021, the OCC issued Interpretive Letter 1179, clarifying the authority of banks to engage in certain

---

10. *See, e.g.,* 12 C.F.R. § 12 (regarding recordkeeping requirements for securities transactions handled by banks); ERISA Rules (regarding custody of retirement plan assets); and the Shareholder Communications Act (regarding the processing of proxies).

11. *Id.*, p. 73.

12. *Id.*, p. 1.

13. *See Id.*, pp. 10–11.

cryptocurrency activities. More recently, the OCC, together with the Board of Governors of the Federal Reserve System and the Federal Deposit Insurance Corporation, issued a joint interagency statement on crypto-asset risks to banking organizations.

b. Securities Regulation

i. SAB 121[14]—SEC Staff Accounting Bulletin (SAB) 121 sets forth standards and guidance for accounting for crypto assets for which an entity is required to safeguard and discusses fcertain SEC staffs' views regarding the accounting for entities to safeguard crypto assets held for their platform users. AICPA guidance regarding SAB 121 states that the determination of whether an entity is responsible for safeguarding crypto assets depends on the totality of the facts and circumstances, including consideration of the involvement of the entity and other third parties. Among the factors to be considered are the nature and level of the entity's involvement, the contractual terms of arrangements with the third party whose assets are being safeguarded, the degree to which the entity can transact in the crypto assets without the involvement of other parties, and who controls the flow of transactions.[15]

ii. SEC and FINRA Joint Staff Statement on Broker-Dealer Custody of Digital Asset Securities[16]—This joint statement notes that the fact that a broker-dealer (or its third-party custodian) maintains the private key may not be sufficient evidence by itself that the broker-dealer has exclusive control of the digital asset security. Moreover, the fact that a custodian holds the private key may not be sufficient to allow it to reverse or cancel mistaken or unauthorized transactions. In the statement, staff provides examples of noncustodial activities involving digital assets.

iii. SEC Statement and Request for Comment: Custody of Digital Asset Securities by Special Purpose Broker-Dealers[17]—In this statement, the SEC suggests that custody means that a broker-dealer has access to the digital asset securities and the capability to transfer them on the associated distributed ledger technology. For a broker-dealer to maintain custody, the digital asset security must be in the exclusive physical possession or control of the broker-dealer. A digital asset that is not in the exclusive possession or control of the broker-dealer would not be held in a manner that complies with

---

14. *See* Staff Accounting Bulletin No. 121, SEC (Apr. 11, 2022), https://www.sec.gov/oca/staff-accounting-bulletin-121.

15. With respect to certain market participants, such as broker-dealers, the SEC staff has developed a set of factors (not yet been published) designed to assist firms in assessing if SAB 121 applies. For example, if a broker-dealer's customers are able to transact in crypto-assets through a third-party crypto-asset platform that has established a relationship with the broker-dealer, SAB 121 may apply unless the factors are satisfied. In general, the factors relate to which entity possesses or controls cryptographic key information, which entity is acting as agent for the customer, and whether an agency relationship exists between the third-party crypto-asset platform and the broker-dealer. The broker-dealer also may be required to obtain an outside counsel opinion regarding the broker-dealer's contractual obligations under the arrangement and how the customer would be treated under bankruptcy law if the broker-dealer fails.

16. *See* Joint Staff Statement on Broker-Dealer Custody of Digital Asset Securities, SEC (Jul. 8, 2019) (on file with SEC) available at: https://www.sec.gov/news/public-statement/joint-staff-statement-broker-dealer-custody-digital-asset-securities.

17. *See* 17 CFR Part 240, https://www.sec.gov/files/rules/policy/2020/34-90788.pdf.

applicable regulatory requirements (i.e., Rule 15c3-3 under the Securities Exchange Act of 1934). The statement goes on to address potential policies, procedures, and controls that are necessary for a broker-dealer to safekeep digital assets.

iv. SEC Proposal on Safeguarding Advisory Client Assets[18]—On February 15, 2023, the SEC proposed to amend its investment adviser custody rule (Rule 206(4)-2 under the Investment Advisers Act of 1940, to be redesignated as Rule 233-1), addressing how registered investment advisers (RIAs) safeguard client assets. Rule 206(4)-2 specifies when an RIA is deemed to have custody of client funds or securities and requires an RIA that has such custody to maintain those assets at a qualified custodian (i.e., certain banks, broker-dealers, futures commission merchants, and foreign financial institutions). The proposal would expand the scope of assets that an RIA with custody of client assets would have to maintain at a qualified custodian to include, in addition to funds and securities, "other positions" held in the client's account, which would include "investments such as all crypto assets, even in the instances where such assets are neither funds nor securities." The proposal also specifies that a qualified custodian does not "maintain" a client asset for purposes of the rule if it does not have "possession or control" of that asset, which is defined as "holding assets such that the qualified custodian is required to participate in any change in beneficial ownership of those assets." The proposal raises a number of questions, including whether qualified custodians will be able to hold crypto assets in compliance with the proposal and whether certain custody providers, such as state-chartered trust companies that provide crypto custody services, are able to meet the conditions for being a qualified custodian under the proposal.

II. State Law

a. Efforts to Codify Digital Asset Custody Standards—Digital asset custody standards vary by state as illustrated by our discussion of several examples below. Similar to the federal regime, states generally have not sought to define custody in the digital asset context.

   i. For example, New York has acted to regulate virtual currency businesses within the state of New York. Any entity engaged in virtual currency business activity must obtain a BitLicense from the New York Department of Financial Services (NYDFS).

   ii. On January 23, 2023, NYDFS issued guidance to virtual currency entities (VCEs) on custody and disclosure practices to protect customers in the event of an insolvency or similar proceeding. The NYDFS guidance is intended to provide greater clarity regarding the standards and practices to ensure that VCE custodians are providing a high level of customer protection under the BitLicense and limited purpose trust company frameworks, with specific focus on segregation of and separate accounting for customer virtual currency, the VCE custodian's limited interest in and use of customer virtual currency, sub-custody arrangements, and customer disclosure.

   iii. Additional state law examples—e.g., Louisiana, Idaho.

---

18. *See* 17 CFR Parts 275, 279, https://www.sec.gov/files/rules/proposed/2023/ia-6384.pdf.

b. Bailment—As a general concept, a bailment is the process of placing personal property or goods in the temporary custody or control of another. A bailment is only created when the bailor relinquishes "exclusive possession, control, and dominion" of the property to the bailee. If a bailment does exist, then the bailee is generally liable for damages resulting from negligence in connection with the bailment—i.e., the failure to take the same level of care that persons of common prudence in their own situation and business usually use in the custody and keeping of similar property belonging to themselves.[19]

c. Fiduciary Concepts—The relationship between a custodian and its client is established and governed by contractual terms "which sets out the scope of the services to be provided, key terms and conditions relevant to the services, the standard of care that the custody bank will exercise in carrying out its duties and the governing law of the contract."[20] Thus, custodians usually are not considered fiduciaries in the traditional sense, though commercial terms may vary. Nonetheless, fiduciaries such as investment advisers and asset managers often use custodians and therefore will be inclined to choose only those who meet very high standards of trust and confidence. Fiduciary principles covering investment advice have developed within several related legal areas. Historically, fiduciary concepts are rooted in the common law of trust and agency. More recently, federal statutes, such as the Investment Advisers Act of 1940 and the Employee Retirement Income Security Act of 1974. (ERISA) have supplemented the common law and grown and in importance. The Investment Company Act of 1940 (regulating mutual funds and other investment companies) is an additional trigger for fiduciary duties owed by advisers to registered funds. And to the extent digital assets are considered commodities, case law under the Commodities Futures Trading Commission (CFTC) and the common law impose a range of duties, including fiduciary duties in some cases.

Fiduciary duties in general are often composed of two separate duties, one of loyalty and one of care (which includes the duties of competence and diligence). These differ from other standards of conduct, such as the duty of suitability. States can impose a fiduciary duty as part of their unethical business practice rules, or through other rules or case law.[21] Under state law, in some cases, ad hoc or fact-based fiduciary relationships may arise. While principles of contract law would typically exclude that kind of relationship between customer and custodian, the elements of trust and agency in the relationship between the parties should be carefully considered, and the contract and related agreements closely reviewed with respect to the potential creation of such a duty. Unfortunately, the fiduciary duties of loyalty and care are both indeterminant and imprecise. Accordingly, facts should be reviewed carefully in order to minimize the risk that a custodial relationship could evolve into a fiduciary one.

---

19. *See generally*, R.H. Holmholz, *Bailment Theories and the Liability of Bailees*, 42 Kansas Law Rev. 97 (1992).
20. Basel Letter at p. 3
21. A. Laby, *Fiduciary Principles In Investment Advice*, at pp. 12–13, *Oxford Handbook of Fiduciary Law* (Oxford University Press, 2019).

III. Ongoing Developments

Several recent developments demonstrate the intertwining of regulation as it may impact banking and the performance of custodial duties for digital assets. First, in connection with the release of SAB 121, members of Congress [Rep. Partick McHenry (R-NC) and Sen. Cynthia Lummis (R-WY)] sent a letter to federal banking regulators questioning the "massive capital charge" that requiring banks and other financial institutions to place digital assets on their balance sheets would trigger, thus preventing "prudentially regulated entities from engaging in digital assets" when "on the contrary, we should be encouraging prudentially regulated financial institutions to provide digital asset services precisely because they are subject to the highest standards of capital, liquidity, recovery and resolution, custody, cyber-security, and risk management."[22] Notably, the SEC's recent approval of Bitcoin ETFs has generated similar actions from bank industry groups who on February 14, 2024, submitted a letter to the SEC proposing amendments to SAB 121 which would allow banks to participate as custodians for Bitcoin EFFs.[23] Among other things, the letter underscores "that on balance sheet treatment will preclude highly regulated banking organizations from providing a custodial solution for digital assets at scale ... . [and] digital asset custodial services are currently being offered by various non-banking organizations, thereby keeping activity outside of the prudential perimeter and avoiding necessary oversight by regulators." These common interests appear to demonstrate a small but perhaps significant convergence in the interests of digital asset entities and traditional banking. The banks' frustration is understandable, particularly when viewed in the context of crypto custody services being provided by Deutsche Bank (partnering with Taurus) in the EU, Standard Chartered (partnering with Zodia) in Hong Kong, and DBS Bank in Singapore. Thus, the SEC's reaction to the banking industry's request will be very much worth monitoring.

Second, on June 6, 2023, Interagency Guidance on third-party risk management was published by the Federal Reserve Board, the FDIC, and the OCC.[24] It is broad in scope and describes principles applicable to the diligence and selection of a bank's third-party relationships, the ongoing monitoring of those relationships and considerations for the termination of relationships. To the extent that banks seek to use sub-custodians or partners (as above with Deutsche Bank/Taurus and Standard Chartered/Zodia) linked to the provision of digital asset custodial services, they will have to take into account the prescripts of this guidance.

Third, general attention should be paid to recent developments in the bankruptcies of crypto-related entities. In such an event, the custodian holding a client's crypto assets at the time of bankruptcy should support the client's ownership rights over such assets held in custody. For example, Article 8-503(a) of the Uniform Commercial Code (UCC) provides that

---

22. Letter from Sen. Cynthia M. Lummis (R-WY) and Rep. Patrick McHenry (R-NC) to Hon. Michael Barr, Vice Chair Supervision, Fed. Rsvr. Sys., Michael Hsu, Acting Comptroller, OCC, Hon. Marty Gruenberg, Chairman Board, Fed. Deposit Ins. Corp., and Hon. Todd Harper, Chairman of the Board, Nat'l Credit Union Admin., (Mar. 2, 2023) (on file with Sen. Cynthia Lummis).

23. Letter from the Bank Policy Institute, American Bankers Association, Financial Services Forum, and Securities Industry and Financial Markets Association to Hon. Gary Gensler, Chair SEC (Feb. 14, 2024), https://bpi.com/wp-content/uploads/2024/02/Joint-Trades-SAB-121-Letter-to-SEC-2.14.24-vF.pdf.

24. *Interagency Guidance on Third-Party Relationships*, 88 Fed. Reg. 111 (Jun. 9, 2023), https://www.govinfo.gov/content/pkg/FR-2023-06-09/pdf/2023-12340.pdf.

financial assets held by a securities intermediary, such as a custodian, for a customer are not property of the securities intermediary and are not subject to claims of creditors of the securities intermediary. Article 8-102(9) of the UCC specifies that a "financial asset" includes any property that is held by a securities intermediary, such as a custodian, for another person in a "securities account," if the parties have expressly agreed that the property is to be treated as a financial asset under Article 8. And under §541(a) of the U.S. Bankruptcy Code, crypto assets held at a custodian would not be considered property of the estate because the custodian would not have any title (legal or equitable) to any of the crypto assets unless otherwise provided for in the custodial contract, which would be highly unusual.

Conclusion

As noted at the beginning, digital asset custody is at an inflection point with respect to the acceleration of institutional exposure to crypto and all that means in terms of liquidity and the advancement of mainstream acceptance. Its future will impact the ability of crypto advisers to provide a high-quality customer experience that is safe, secure, and convenient. Thus, understanding the regulatory and technological cross-currents in this space will be critical to providing digital asset clients with the advice they need.

Chapter 5
Know-Your-Customer/BSA

David Stier, Jason Covert, and Emily Honsa Hicks

> We have money laundering rules that cover banks and credit unions and stockbrokers and gold dealers and even Western Union, but the current rules don't cover big parts of the crypto industry. And crypto likes it that way ... The rules should be simple: same kind of transaction, same kind of risk, means the same kind of rules.
>
> —Sen. Elizabeth Warren on the introduction of the February 2023 Digital Asset Anti-Money Laundering Act (Feb. 14, 2023).

Developed in the 1970s through the Bank Secrecy Act (BSA),[1] the goal of the Anti-Money Laundering (AML) regulatory regime is lofty and honorable: ensuring that financial intermediaries develop reasonably designed, risk-based controls to help prevent the U.S. financial system from being used to facilitate money laundering, terrorist financing, evading economic sanctions, and other illicit activity. A half a century later, the AML regime in the United States still represents the constant balance and tension between safeguarding our financial system from bad actors and preserving privacy cherished by democratic nations.

Yet despite the clarion cries of politicians on one hand and the ardent objections of privacy advocates on the other, many cryptocurrency and cryptocurrency adjacent intermediaries are not only *subject* to AML rules, but they are complying with those rules. What's more, they are complying often primarily by leveraging blockchains—the very technology that made cryptocurrency possible in the first place. In fact, these publicly available, auditable,

1. 31 USC 5311 *et seq*.

and immutable ledgers of financial transaction activity could be one of the most important crime-fighting and AML tools since the birth of the BSA in the 1970s. Companies such as TRM, Chainalysis, Elliptic, and others collectively employ hundreds of individuals from software engineers to former law enforcement officials and public policy experts to create and sell the most cutting-edge and effective blockchain analytics and AML tools available to the private sector *and* law enforcement.

Primer on BSA/AML in the United States

Congress has tasked various agencies to achieve their BSA/AML goals; those agencies promulgate regulations covering (or purporting to cover) traditional finance (Tradfi), fintechs, and digital asset companies; conducting examinations; and bringing enforcement actions. Depending on their business model and product offerings, and unless a specific and often narrowly tailored exemption applies, fintech providers may fall under the jurisdiction of the BSA and/or the USA PATRIOT Act—administered by the U.S. Treasury's Financial Crimes Enforcement Network (FinCEN). Whether as traditional financial institutions, securities broker-dealers, futures commodities merchants or introducing brokers, payment processors, and/or Money Services Businesses (MSBs), each type of "financial institution" regulated by the BSA shares similar regulatory and compliance-focused Know Your Customer (KYC) obligations designed to prevent the U.S. financial system from being used to facilitate money laundering or terrorist financing and are required by the BSA and its implementing regulations to collect, maintain and share with law enforcement certain customer and transaction records.[2]

Specifically, under BSA regulations, an AML program for nearly all financial institutions, including MSBs, must:

- develop risk-based policies, procedures, and controls reasonably designed to prevent money laundering and terrorist financing, including:
  - (a) performing due diligence and collecting KYC information about customers;
  - (b) creating and maintaining records called for under the BSA;
  - (c) filing Suspicious Activity Reports (SARS), when necessary, and complying with the Funds Travel Rule, including providing information about the sender and recipient of funds involving transactions of $3,000 or more; and
  - (d) responding to law enforcement requests.

2. Typically, fintech and digital asset companies must determine whether they fall within the definition of being a money transmitter under state and federal rules. The definition of money transmission under federal law is broad and includes the "acceptance of currency, funds, or other value that substitutes for currency from one person and the transmission of currency, funds or other value that substitutes for currency to another location by person or by any means." Unless a specific (and often very narrow) exemption applies to the specific product or business line (such as digital asset mining companies and equipment, peer-to-peer trading platforms serving un-hosted wallets, and anonymizing software providers), such companies must register with FinCEN, obtain a license in the state(s) in which they conduct business (*i.e.*, solicit or serve customers), and implement an AML program.
Additionally, the Virtual Asset Service Provider (VASP) guidelines promulgated by the international money laundering standard setting body, the Financial Action Task Force (the FATF) while similar in many key respects to the U.S. federal requirements, differ in connection with the dollar threshold and types of sender and recipient (customer) information required to be reported under the Funds Travel Rule, as well as the treatment and exemptions available for truly decentralized actors.

- designate an AML Compliance Officer to enforce AML policies, procedures, and controls.
- develop employee training programs for appropriate personnel.
- have an independent audit function to monitor and test the AML program.
- obtain approval from the institution's Board of Directors.[3]

Moreover, traditional financial institutions such as brick and mortar banks must also:

- Develop a written Customer Identification Program (CIP) appropriate for the size and type of business for verifying the identity of each customer to the extent reasonable and practical.[4] The financial institution must, at a minimum, obtain and retain basic customer information including the customer's name, date of birth, address and identification number and compare the information against lists of known or suspected terrorists.[5]
- Comply with the FinCEN Customer Due Diligence (CDD) Rule which requires financial institutions to adopt and implement risk-based CDD policies, procedures, and processes based on the institution's specific and unique products and services, customers, and geographic locations (among other factors) for all customers, but especially those who present a higher risk for money laundering and terrorist financing.[6]

CDD procedures must include obtaining and analyzing sufficient information to understand the nature and purpose of relationships to develop a customer risk profile; conducting ongoing monitoring to identify and report suspicious transactions and, on a risk basis, to maintain and update customer information (including information regarding the beneficial owners (BOs) of legal entity customers). They should be commensurate with the institution's BSA/AML profile, with an increased focus on higher-risk customers, contain a clear statement of responsibilities, and provide standards for conducting and documenting due diligence analysis, including guidance for resolving issues when insufficient or inaccurate information is obtained.

Along with monitoring and SARS reporting, institutions, particularly in the cryptocurrency space, are increasingly developing KYT capabilities, that is, real-time monitoring and tracking transactions in fiat and on blockchains. Financial institutions may rely on non-documentary methods to perform CIP, but there is regulatory uncertainty as to whether blockchain-based information-gathering methods (described below) would be appropriate.[7] On top of this uncertainty, although financial institutions can rely on other financial institutions which have federal functional regulators (such as the FDIC, Federal Reserve, and/or the Office of the Comptroller of the Currency (OCC)) to verify customer information,[8] this option is rarely available to crypto-native companies, which, if registered, are registered as money services businesses.

---

3. See 31 CFR 1022.210(a).
4. See 31 CFR 1020.220.
5. See *id.*
6. See 31 CFR 1020.210(b)(5).
7. See 31 CFR 1020.220(a)(2)(ii)(B).
8. See 31 CFR 1020.220(a)(6).

KYC & KYT Challenges and Opportunities Unique to Blockchain-Connected Entities

Blockchain-connected entities face several unique BSA-related challenges and opportunities:

- The fast-developing global digital asset regulations and increasing sophistication of illicit conduct, including hacks and attacks by nation-state actors, potentially impacting the effectiveness of compliance programs and the ability to file SARS timely.
- Different blockchains, including ones with different transaction validation methods (such as Bitcoin vs. Ethereum) that do not seamlessly operate with one another (also known as interoperability), leaving significant volumes of customer data outside the dataset from which KYC controls traditionally draw.
- Integrating the vast volume of blockchain data with more traditional KYC data across systems and compliance personnel sufficiently experienced in each.

Despite these significant challenges, the tools and advances driven by blockchain technology represent unique opportunities for combatting money laundering and terrorist financing. As Coinbase, a global, centralized digital asset exchange, summarized in a comment letter in response to a U.S. Treasury proposed rulemaking:

The ease of tracing transactions on the blockchain offers significant benefits to law enforcement, allowing them to detect and disrupt illicit activity by mapping specific transactions to illicit actors. They can then trace the transfer of ill-gotten funds through different digital wallet addresses and seek to connect those addresses to specific individuals... As an official at the Commodity Futures Trading Commission recently noted, it 'is easier for law enforcement to trace illicit activity using Bitcoin than it is to trace cross-border illegal activity using traditional banking transactions, and far easier than cash transactions.[9]

Tradfi typically relies on proprietary, private, and opaque ledgers, as well as the honesty of customers to gather KYC. Under this model, consumers provide personal information multiple times, to multiple financial institutions (anywhere they wish to open an account) which may result in inconsistency or information blind spots. By contrast, the recently developed blockchain KYT offers advances in the space, as real-time data can be used to construct preventative *risk-based controls* as required by the BSA. This KYT can be done efficiently, and cost-effectively, and can be specifically tailored with real-time data on the blockchain. KYT is immediate (or close to immediate), allowing Virtual Asset Service Providers (VASPS) to track assets in real time as soon as a transaction happens; it can be independently validated (i.e., it is derived from a source other than the customer) and it does not rely on analog confirmations.[10]

Relatedly, blockchain technology may enable private and public sector collaboration in the development of novel tools for the advancement of KYC and KYT. For instance, in 2022 the FDIC and FinCEN held a private sector TechSprint to develop a "scalable, cost-efficient, risk-based solution to measure the effectiveness of digital identity proofing to

9. Coinbase Institute, *Crypto Innovation is Essential to Curtailing Illicit Finance*, Coinbase, https://www.coinbase.com/public-policy/advocacy/documents/crypto-innovation-is-essential-to-curtailing-illicit-finance.
10. See *id.*

ensure that individuals who remotely (i.e., not in person) present themselves for financial activities are who they claim to be."[11] Using blockchain and encryption technology such as zero-knowledge proofs (ZKPs),[12] homomorphic encryption,[13] or both, and with FinCEN's encouragement, companies may seek to develop privacy-preserving identity verification and management, often called decentralized ID (DID). DID would allow a customer to share traditional KYC information (birthdate, social security number, address) together with the date that their identity was verified.[14]

Going forward, this already-vetted information could be memorialized on the blockchain with an attestation or an immutable "soulbound" token.[15] Further, it could be shared with other financial institutions as an indication that the customer has complied with a certain level of KYC, without revealing (and thus compromising) the customer's personal identifying information. This technology could *significantly* reduce compliance costs and onboarding times, thus allowing financial institutions to focus on identifying money laundering and terrorist financing threats more quickly and effectively. However, as described above, it is unclear whether, under the existing FinCEN regulatory regime, financial institutions could comply with their CIP obligations by accepting customer information in the form of soulbound tokens. Absent a shift in the regulatory environment, it is also extremely unlikely that Tradfi could rely on MSBs or other crypto-native companies to have collected and verified the customer information stored inside.[16]

Recent Regulatory Guidance and Enforcement Trends

Recent BSA/AML regulatory guidance and enforcement trends demonstrate the current quandary faced by fintechs and crypto-native companies; comments and proposals provided by fintechs and crypto-native companies during the rulemaking process do not appear to receive the same weight from prudential regulators, perpetuating the overlay of Tradfi rules

---

11. *See* Press Release, Financial Crimes Enforcement Network, FDIC FinCEN digital identity tech sprint—key takeaways and solution summaries (Sept. 9, 2022), (available at https://www.fincen.gov/news/news-releases/fdic-fincen-digital-identity-tech-sprint-key-takeaways-and-solution-summaries).

12. ZKPs are "techniques to verify claims without revealing the information itself. In this process, a "prover" shares proof of their claim with a "verifier," who then verifies the accuracy of the proof without learning any additional information." Aad, Imad (2023), Mulder, Valentin; Mermoud, Alain; Lenders, Vincent; Tellenbach, Bernhard (eds.), *'Zero-Knowledge Proof', Trends in Data Protection and Encryption Technologies*, Cham: Springer Nature Switzerland, pp. 25–30.

13. Homomorphic encryption allows computation on encrypted data, meaning that "data can remain confidential while it is processed, enabling useful tasks to be accomplished with data residing in untrusted environments." Frederik Armknecht, Colin Boyd, Kristian Gjøsteen, Angela Jäschke, Christian Reuter, Martin Strand, *A Guide to Fully Homomorphic Encryption*. Cryptology ePrint Archive (2015).

14. See *generally* Coinbase Institute, *Crypto Innovation is Essential to Curtailing Illicit Finance* (Jan. 19, 2023), https://www.coinbase.com/public-policy/advocacy/documents/crypto-innovation-is-essential-to-curtailing-illicit-finance)

15. Soulbound tokens "refer to digital identity tokens that represent the characteristics or reputation of a person or entity." They are "publicly verifiable and non-transferable non-fungible token (NFT) that represent an individual's credentials, affiliations, and commitments." At least one centralized cryptocurrency exchange has issued its own soulbound token to serve as a digital verification solution for customers that have completed KYC requirements. Jagit Singh, *What Are Soulbound Tokens (SBTs) and How Do They Work?* Cointelegraph (Nov. 19, 2022), https://cointelegraph.com/news/what-are-soulbound-tokens-sbts-and-how-do-they-work.

16. See *generally* Coinbase Institute, *Crypto Innovation is Essential to Curtailing Illicit Finance* (January 19, 2023), https://www.coinbase.com/public-policy/advocacy/documents/crypto-innovation-is-essential-to-curtailing-illicit-finance.

to a Defi world. Moreover, many of those same regulators are aggressively seeking to flex their enforcement authority over Defi through the use of Tradfi regulations. Here are just a few examples of this dilemma.

Beneficial Ownership Rule

Pursuant to the 2021 Corporate Transparency Act, FinCEN issued proposed rules and sought input from stakeholders on a set of game-changing regulations in September 2022. These included the recently promulgated Ultimate Beneficial Ownership rule (BO Rule), effective January 1, 2024.[17] The new BO Rule requires a large swath of domestic and foreign companies to disclose to FinCEN several new categories of information, including the actual beneficial owners of many foreign and domestic corporate entities. FinCEN is also spearheading the creation of the Beneficial Ownership Secure System (BOSS), a BO database that will contain massive volumes of information for the use of law enforcement—with limited judicial oversight in many instances. Traditional BSA-regulated financial institutions will also have limited-access to the BOSS and will be required to make use of it in performing KYC.[18]

Questions remain, and the BO Rule raises significant challenges for both Tradfi, fintechs, Centralized Exchanges and especially the decentralized finance (Defi) community:

- *Control.* The scope of the current CDD rule and, in particular, its definition of who controls a company, is currently narrower than the definition of control for purposes of the BO Rule.[19]
- *Personhood.* Assuming it has registered as an entity with a state's secretary of state, how does an entity that is formed as a Decentralized Autonomous Organization (DAO) where the founders have, in fact, relinquished control over and operation of the DAO to computer code (smart contracts) comply with the BO reporting requirements?
- *Interoperability.* How will current blockchain analytics and intelligence companies interact with the BOSS, *i.e.*, will law enforcement seek to feed traditional (non-blockchain intelligence) about beneficial owners into the growing databases of blockchain analytics companies and/or will FinCEN seek to import data from the blockchain to

17. *See Beneficial Ownership Information Reporting Rule Fact Sheet*, FinCEN (Sept. 29, 2022), http://www.fincen.gov/beneficial-ownership-information-reporting-rule-fact-sheet.

18. *See Beneficial Ownership Information Reporting: Frequently Asked Questions*, FinCEN, https://www.fincen.gov/boi-faqs. ("Financial institutions will also have access to beneficial ownership information in certain circumstances, with the consent of the reporting company.")

19. Under the current CDD rule, in addition to collecting information on individuals with 25 percent ownership, banks must collect information on any individual with significant responsibility to control, manage, or direct a legal entity. However, the CTA's definition of beneficial owner does not limit the reporting of individuals in substantial control to one person. Instead, a reporting company must list any and all individuals who satisfy the definition of control, including (i) having authority over the appointment or removal of any senior officer or a majority of the board of directors (or similar body), or (ii) directing, determining, or having substantial influence over important decisions made by the reporting company. FinCEN explained that the CTA's definition of substantial control "designed to close loopholes that allow corporate structuring that obscures owners or decision-makers" and, adopting the CDD rule definition of control would benefit primarily reporting companies that were overly complex (perhaps by design). Importantly, as part of the CTA, FinCEN will be revising the CDD rule, which may eliminate the current discrepancies between the rule and the CTA.

help inform the BOSS. This raises potentially significant privacy and cyber-security considerations for blockchain users.

- *Burden on Financial Institutions, Fintechs, and Others.* Financial institutions with crypto-related customers will need to check the BOSS and may also need to make use of blockchain analytics even though the two systems may not be aligned or interoperable—for example, an individual who has substantial control over a shell company may transact on the blockchain even though current blockchain tools may not have mapped that individual's traditional KYC information to her presence (or wallets) on the blockchain. This may create a far more resource intensive exercise for financial institutions and their compliance staff.

June 2023 Intra-Agency Regulatory Guidance for Financial Institutions on Third-Party Relationships

On June 6, 2023, The Board of Governors of the Federal Reserve System (Board), the FDIC, and the OCC, (collectively, the banking agencies) issued interagency guidance on managing risks associated with third party-relationships.[20] While the guidance adopts a principles-based approach and does not specifically address fintech partnerships, the introduction makes clear that a banking organization's decision to partner with third parties, including fintechs, "does not diminish or remove [the bank's] responsibilities to ensure that activities are performed ... in compliance with applicable laws and regulations," including "those addressing financial crimes." This emphasis on compliance with laws and regulations addressing financial crimes was a clear signal to banking organizations that their regulators will expect to see increased third-party risk management in the areas of BSA/AML compliance, especially with respect to fintech and crypto-native partnerships.

In the guidance, the banking agencies intentionally declined to address specific third-party relationships, such as those with fintechs or crypto-native companies, citing the over-arching principles-based approach to the third-party risk guidance. Nevertheless, the agencies did note that "it is important for a banking organization to understand how the arrangement with a third party, including a fintech company, is structured so that the banking organization may assess the types and levels of risks posed and determine how to manage those third-party relationships accordingly."[21] This decision to avoid bright line rules provides the banking agencies with greater flexibility to address emerging areas such as cryptocurrency and fintech development, but leaves these same industries and their potential banking partners struggling to understand how they should approach one another from a safety and soundness perspective.

Additional Guidance from the NCUA, FINRA, and SEC

Additional guidance from financial services regulators and self-regulatory organizations further illustrates concerns about BSA/AML implications of cryptocurrency—and the blockchain—becoming mainstream. In May 2022, the National Credit Union Administration

---

20. Interagency Guidance on Third-Party Relationships: Risk Management, 88 Fed. Reg. 37920 (Jun. 9, 2023).
21. *Id.* at 37923.

(NCUA) issued a bulletin to its members "Federally Insured Credit Union Use of Distributed Ledger Technologies [(DLT)]." The bulletin and related letter to the industry acknowledged that credit unions had—to that point—predominantly sat on the sidelines of engaging with DLT out of fear of regulatory blow-back. The NCUA encouraged credit unions, where appropriate, to make risk-based decisions to benefit their members and communities,[22] however, it also highlighted BSA-related legal and compliance risks such as:

- When deploying the DLT, will the credit union comply with applicable laws and regulations, such as BSA requirements, including customer due diligence, KYC, and anti-money laundering requirements?
- Are each of the nodes on the DLT network BSA compliant?
- If the application involves the use of smart contracts, is testing of the underlying architecture in place and documented?
- Has the credit union confirmed with whom and to what extent oversight, governance, and maintenance of the smart contract application reside and exist?

Similarly, on January 10, 2023, FINRA published its 2023 Report on FINRA's Examination and Risk Monitoring Program, highlighted increased integration of fintech and crypto-related activities into the business models of traditional financial institutions. The report emphasized the need for those institutions' AML programs to evolve alongside these new products and services.[23] And on July 31, 2023, the SEC's Division of Examinations issued a Risk Alert related to observations from AML compliance examinations of broker-dealers.[24] The SEC's risk alert was followed one month later by a Securities and Exchange Commission (SEC) enforcement action against Archipelago Trading Services, Inc. for its failure to have or implement a reasonably designed AML program. The SEC's recent emphasis on AML enforcement coincides with its increased focus on regulating cryptocurrency and digital assets through enforcement actions.

Recent Regulatory Focus on BSA/AML Compliance

The 2020 COVID-19 pandemic ushered in an era where a sizable number of traditional brick-and-mortar banks began partnering with fintechs to expand their footprints and increase customer engagement and the volume of borrowers they could assist, particularly in the frenzied roll-out of the federal Paycheck Protection Program. Furthermore, traditional banks have also started to expand their business lines to include cryptocurrency platforms and services. Financial regulators have taken notice and are scrutinizing whether risk management and compliance aspects of these partnerships and business lines fail to establish effective BSA/AML programs. In 2022, the OCC brought two notable enforcement actions

---

22. *See* Letter from Nat'l. Credit Union Admin. To Federally Insured Credit Unions on use of distributed ledger technologies (May 2022) (available at https://ncua.gov/regulation-supervision/letters-credit-unions-other-guidance/federally-insured-credit-union-use-distributed-ledger-technologies).

23. *See* FINRA, *2023 Report on FINRA's Examination and Risk Monitoring Program* (Jan. 2023), https://www.finra.org/sites/default/files/2023-01/2023-report-finras-examination-risk-monitoring-program.pdf.

24. *See* SEC Risk Alert on Observations from Anti-Money Laundering Compliance Examinations of Broker-Dealers (Jul. 31, 2023) (available at https://www.sec.gov/files/risk-alert-aml-compliance-examinations-bd-073123.pdf).

in this space. First, in April 2022 the OCC entered into a consent agreement with Anchorage Digital Bank, the first federally chartered crypto lender, for its failure to establish effective BSA/AML controls. Next, in late August 2022, the OCC entered into a consent agreement with Blue Ridge Bank, NA, a subsidiary of a publicly traded bank holding company, for BSA/AML failures in connection with its third-party contractual relationship with fintechs. Each consent agreement required the bank and its Board to make significant improvements to its BSA/AML program, including strengthening compliance, risk management, and audit processes; retaining qualified personnel; and reporting frequently to the OCC.

And the scrutiny from financial regulators will likely only intensify in nature. On September 28, 2023, the OCC issued its Fiscal Year 2024 Bank Supervision Operating Plan, which provides notice to financial institutions of the agency's supervision priorities and objectives for the following year. Within the list of agency priorities is the examination of financial institution's risk management processes related to distributed ledger technology products and services, including "cryptoasset custody, tokenization of real-world assets and liabilities, payments, and other uses to support business operations."[25]

Similarly, the enforcement environment in the last year has seen increased activity from the U.S. Department of Justice (DOJ), the U.S. Treasury Department's Office of Foreign Asset Control (OFAC) and FinCEN, the Commodity Futures Trading Commission (CFTC) and the SEC, each of which have filed key enforcement actions or indictments against cryptocurrency (and fintech) players whose actions and/or business models have allegedly facilitated money laundering, sanctions evasion, or terrorist financing.

In lieu of Congress passing comprehensive cryptocurrency and blockchain legislation or the agencies passing regulations, the industry has faced the challenge of regulating by enforcement (or regulating by indictment in the case of DOJ). The following are just a few examples of this approach to enforcement and the difficulty the Defi industry faces in discerning what activities it may lawfully conduct:

- In August and November 2022, OFAC designated Tornado Cash, a cryptocurrency mixer, a Specially Designated National (SDN). In August 2023, the DOJ indicted two Tornado Cash founders for charges of conspiracy to commit money laundering, sanctions evasion and operating as an unlicensed money transmission business, alleging they knowingly assisted bad actors including North Korea hackers, the Lazarus Group, in moving stolen funds. These charges were especially significant because the founders had formed a DAO, relinquished the administrative keys--and thus decision-making—to the DAO, the platform operated through smart contracts (software code), and the transmission of illicit funds was performed by independent third-party relayers.

Other key enforcement actions in the AML and Sanctions Evasion space involved:

- In January 2023, FinCEN and DOJ deployed powerful enforcement tools against Bitzlato, a China-based cryptocurrency exchange that allegedly facilitated sanctions

25. *See* Press Release, OCC, Fiscal Year 2024 Bank Supervision Operating Plan (2023) (available at https://www.occ.treas.gov/news-issuances/news-releases/2023/nr-occ-2023-109a.pdf).

evasion by Russian cyber-criminals. FinCEN used a new tool to designate Bitzlato as a "primary money laundering concern," essentially cutting it off from the global financial system and DOJ charged Bitzlato's founder with, among other things, operating an unlicensed money transmission business wholly or in substantial part in the United States—a "general intent" or "strict liability" crime—in violation of 18 USC § 1960.

- In September 2023, the CFTC charged and simultaneously settled cases against three Defi protocols for offering digital asset derivatives trading but failing to register with the CFTC and failing to establish BSA compliance programs, including a CIP to facilitate KYC diligence on customers.[26]

Finally, in October 2023, FinCEN proposed to regulate (by regulation). Citing significant money laundering and terrorist financing risks to the U.S. financial system as well as national security concerns related to cryptocurrency mixers and mixing services, FinCEN deployed its seldom-used "Special Measures" powers pursuant to Section 311 of the USA PATRIOT Act, in a notice of proposed rulemaking. If promulgated as proposed, the rule would designate transactions with cryptocurrency mixers or mixing services as a "Primary Money Laundering Concern" and require BSA-regulated Tradfi and MSBs to monitor and report to FinCEN transactions with a mixer or mixing service within 30 days of each transaction.

Regulatory Signaling for OCC Banks Entering Crypto

Whether or not one gives credence to the regulating by enforcement trend, a number of enforcement actions have provided insight into how regulatory frameworks for Tradfi engagement with fintechs and the blockchain may evolve.

Beginning in 2020, Blue Ridge Bank, National Association (Blue Ridge) had approximately $959 million in assets and $722 million in deposits when it began aggressively growing its partnerships with various fintechs. The fintechs with which Blue Ridge partnered included companies providing personal loans for debt consolidation, income-based financing for students in higher education, card remittance, and forex transactions, among many other consumer-based financial services. By June 30, 2022, Blue Ridge had grown to $2.7 billion in assets, with approximately $395 million in deposits related to fintech relationships, up from approximately $189 million just six months earlier. The bank also had approximately $25 million in loans held for sale or investment related to fintech relationships, and more than $55 million in assets under management related to fintech relationships. While the bank experienced explosive growth in fintech partnerships, it appears the bank failed to make commensurate investments in compliance, internal controls, and third-party risk management related to those same relationships. On August 29, 2022, the bank's primary regulator, the OCC, finalized an enforcement action against Blue Ridge by way of a Formal

26. *See* Press Release, CFCT, CFTC issues orders against operators of three DeFi protocols for offering illegal digital asset derivatives trading (Sept. 7, 2023) (on file with CFTC). In one case, although the protocol took steps to block US-based Internet Protocol (IP) addresses, the CFTC concluded that such steps "were not sufficient to actually block US users from accessing the … [p]rotocol." *In the Matter of Opyn, Inc.*, Order Instituting Proceedings Pursuant to Section 6(c) and (d) of the Commodity Exchange Act, Making Findings, and Imposing Remedial Sanctions, CFTC Docket No. 23-40, Sept. 7, 2023.

Agreement after the regulator identified unsafe or unsound practices relating to third-party risk management of fintech partnerships, BSA/AML risk management, and suspicious activity reporting, among other deficiencies.[27]

For those financial institutions that intend to partner with fintechs, the provisions contained in the Blue Ridge Formal Agreement can serve as a best-practices road map. Generally speaking, the financial institution should do the following when considering partnering with fintechs:

- ensure that its BSA/AML program is commensurate to the risk associated with the fintech partnerships;
- evaluate its BSA/AML program as a whole prior to onboarding new fintech partnerships, including the BSA risk assessment process, BSA audit program, BSA compliance personnel and staffing, customer due diligence and enhanced due diligence requirements, and suspicious activity monitoring and reporting;
- adopt and implement a written fintech risk management program that is reviewed and approved by the bank's board, ensuring the program's complexity is commensurate with the risk and complexity of the bank's fintech partnerships.

The fintech risk management program is a crucial component in this process and should provide, at a minimum, for the following[28]:

- **Written Policies, Procedures, and Processes.** The policies, procedures, and processes governing the bank's fintech partnerships should be written and approved by the board and should address how a bank identifies and assesses risks from fintech products, services, and activities. The policies, procedures, and processes should also detail how a bank assesses, selects, and oversees third-party fintech partners, including criteria for board review and approval. Finally, they should also include the bank's strategic plan for providing necessary resources, infrastructure, technology controls, and organizational capabilities to manage the third-party fintech partnerships.
- **BSA Risk Assessments.** The bank's program should include the completion of BSA risk assessments for each fintech partner based on the unique products, services, and activities of the fintech, including the fintech's process for mitigating BSA risks. These BSA risk assessments should be comprehensive and address all products, services, customers, entities, geographies, and activities provided by or through the fintech partner.
- **Compliance Oversight**. The fintech risk management program should include a compliance oversight program that evaluates the products, services, and activities of the fintech, contains internal controls for compliance monitoring, and provides a clear process for addressing activities by the fintech that fail to comply with the bank's policies and procedures or violate applicable laws and regulations. The compliance

27. See OCC, Enforcement Action No. 2022-043 (Aug. 2022), https://www.occ.gov/static/enforcement-actions/ea2022-043.pdf.

28. See generally In re Blue Ridge Bank, National Association, OCC EA 2022-043 (Aug. 29, 2022), available at https://www.occ.gov/static/enforcement-actions/ea2022-043.pdf.

program should also contain explicit provisions allowing the bank appropriate access to conduct ongoing monitoring of the fintech's activities and performance, as well as contingency plans for the effective termination of the fintech partnership, if necessary. Additionally, the program should provide for the maintenance of documentation, including through a management information system, and reporting that permits proper board and management oversight and accountability related to fintech partnerships.

- **Audit Plan and GAAP Assessment.** The risk management program should contain an audit plan, to be completed by a qualified independent auditor, that includes reviews to assess internal controls, information technology, compliance, and operational risk associated with fintech partnerships. The program should also provide for a written assessment from a qualified, independent CPA to ensure the manner in which the fintech and the bank account for transactions initiated through the fintech partnership conforms with GAAP and that the financial reporting related to the fintech's activities through the bank is in line with contractual terms between the bank and fintech.
- **Staffing.** Finally, the program should outline how the bank will evaluate and implement adequate staffing of bank employees, with requisite experience in third-party management and technology to help manage and oversee the risks associated with fintech partnerships.

Current Advantages of Already-BSA-Regulated-Entities

The way forward through this legal maze for fintechs and crypto-native companies will likely be through established pathways. While many proponents of blockchain technology and cryptocurrencies balk at Tradfi 'elders' now seeking seats at the table (and the inherent compromises that their participation will require) they are joining the party, nonetheless. Established firms such as Blackrock, Franklin Templeton, BNY Mellon, Deutsche Bank, and Citi have all recently asserted their presence in the brave new world of blockchain and cryptocurrency despite institutional resistance. This is fortunate, because although direct investment and decentralized control are core values of the blockchain movement, it is an unavoidable reality that existing operational risks and restrictions may deter or prevent many individuals from considering these assets. As described above, traditional institutions likewise can—and if the FinCEN proposed rule is passed, would be required to—enhance existing BSA/AML compliance programs to address emerging risks related to digital assets that still fall within known and managed categories, such as high-risk businesses like VASPs offering 'mixing' services.

Exchange Traded Funds

A great example of the possibilities available through the combination of Tradfi and Defi can be seen in the proliferation of exchange-traded funds (ETFs)—investments combining the breadth of mutual funds but traded via shares, like individual stocks, on stock exchanges at real-time market prices. ETFs generally allow a lower minimum investment and allow greater flexibility to enter and exit through market trading than mutual funds. While a number of such funds exist that track cryptocurrencies, some notable funds include the Schwab Crypto Thematic ETF and Fidelity Crypto Industry and Digital Payments ETF.

Also, currently available are Crypto Futures ETFs, which track cryptocurrency futures contracts for an expected price of Bitcoin at a later date (not Bitcoin ownership). Spot Crypto ETFs, on the other hand, would represent actual custody of cryptocurrency held by an ETF manager. Spot Crypto ETFs are generally not equivalent to a direct investment but instead will reflect the performance of the price of Bitcoin, allowing investors to use traditional brokerage accounts and traditional securities markets/exchanges without acquiring, holding, or trading Bitcoin directly themselves via a digital asset exchange. Shares in the fund would be backed by custodian-held Bitcoin assets, so investors would not be required to establish digital wallets or hold account keys.

While futures-type ETFs and cryptocurrency trusts are available to investors now, for years, the SEC has declined to approve spot crypto ETFs out of concerns that such ETFs would be excessively vulnerable to manipulation. However, on August 29, 2023, the U.S. Court of Appeals for the District of Columbia ruled that the SEC was arbitrary and capricious in rejecting an application to list an ETF that tracks the price of Bitcoin. As a result, spot crypto ETFs appear imminent. Notably, the pending Grayscale Investments LLC application that was the center of the SEC case has been joined in the queue by similar applications from industry veterans Franklin Templeton[29] and BlackRock.[30]

Custody Services

Another example of established players entering the fairly nascent marketplace is in the space of cryptocurrency custody services. Despite the novelty of digital assets, the OCC has concluded that providing cryptocurrency custody services "is a modern form of traditional bank activities related to custody services" and that there is a present need for banks to offer to "safeguard" consumers' "most valuable assets, which today for tens of millions of Americans includes cryptocurrency."[31] Along with their approval of this activity, the OCC cautioned banks that other regulators, like the SEC, may impose additional restrictions, and noted that "understanding the risks of cryptocurrency, the due diligence process should include a review for compliance with anti-money laundering rules. Banks should also have effective information security infrastructure and controls in place to mitigate hacking, theft, and fraud."[32] Despite these cautionary notes, this unambiguous invitation was enough for a number of traditional banks to get serious about the world of cryptocurrency custody. Two notable examples are Bank of New York Mellon (BNY Mellon) and Deutsche Bank.

As early as 2018, BNY Mellon was considering the regulatory hurdles involved in crypto custody services, acknowledging that "any regulated financial institution operating in this space would be expected to apply rigorous controls to ensure the appropriateness of the counterparties and assets they are interfacing with, comparable to AML/KYC procedures

29. Franklin Templeton Application, SEC, available at https://www.sec.gov/Archives/edgar/data/1992870/000113743923001074/ftdhts1092023.htm.

30. Danny Nelson, *Franklin Templeton Joins Bitcoin EFT Race*, CoinDesk. (Oct. 12, 2023), http://www.coindesk.com/business/2023/09/12/franklin-templeton-joins-bitcoin-etf-race/.

31. Press Release, OCC, Federally Chartered Banks and Thrifts May Provide Custody Services For Crypto Assets, (Jul. 22, 2020) (on file with OCC).

32. Interpretive Letter #1170, OCC (Jul. 22, 2020), https://www.occ.gov/topics/charters-and-licensing/interpretations-and-actions/2020/int1170.pdf.

in existence for other asset types."[33] BNY Mellon had an overt eye on crypto custody services and the associated challenges—and rewards—by 2019, noting that a "lack of safe, qualified custody is ... a significant barrier preventing institutional investors from joining the crypto market in greater numbers. This seems poised to change as their interest is growing and solutions are being developed by major, trustworthy players."[34] Then in 2021, the bank announced its Digital Assets task force, along with its intention to finally enter the market,[35] and in October 2022, BNY Mellon became the first large bank to launch its own crypto custody platform offering. In doing so, it touted an established legal and regulatory framework, an existing reputation as the world's largest custodian, and a potential user interface consolidating traditional and digital assets.[36]

BNY Mellon may have been the first, but the oldest bank in the United States was soon joined by the largest German bank, Deutsch Bank, which announced its intention to offer crypto custody via a partnership arrangement with a Swiss company in September 2023[37] after having quietly asserted interest in February 2021.[38]

However, despite the assurances provided by the entry of such established players and some marginal regulatory assent,[39] new regulatory hurdles have emerged. At the time of publication, the SEC has proposed a rule[40] that adds additional requirements for custodians generally and fails to ameliorate the issues posed by SEC Staff Accounting Bulletin No. 121, which requires a global custody bank holding clients' cryptocurrency to reflect such as both asset and liability. Other aspects of the proposed rule have led industry groups to warn that it will compromise qualified custodian's ability to provide digital asset custody services to their clients.[41]

Tokens/Tokenized Service Offerings

A final example of Tradfi broadening the capabilities of relatively nascent crypto activity is Citi Bank's Tokenized Service Offerings. Citi recently concluded a proof of concept with several banks and the New York Federal Reserve to link central bank digital currencies

---

33. Kara Kennedy, *Crypto Custody*, BNY Mellon (Oct. 2018), https://www.bnymellon.com/us/en/insights/all-insights/crypto-custody.html.

34. *Cryptocurrencies, Custody and Third-party Access*, BNY Mellon (May 2019), http://www.bnymellon.com/us/en/insights/all-insights/cryptocurrencies-custody-and-third-party-access.html.

35. Penny Crossman, *Digital Assets Are Here to Stay: BNY Mellon Embraces Crypto*, American Banker (Feb. 23, 2021), http://www.americanbanker.com/news/digital-assets-are-here-to-stay-bny-mellon-embraces-crypto.

36. *Digital Asset Custody*, BNY Mellon, http://www.bnymellon.com/us/en/solutions/digital-assets.html#digital-asset-custody.

37. Elizabeth Howcroft, *Deutsche Bank To Hold Crypto for Institutional Clients*, Reuters (Sept. 14, 2023), http://www.reuters.com/business/finance/deutsche-bank-hold-crypto-institutional-clients-2023-09-14/.

38. Ian Allison, *Deutsche Bank Quietly Plans to Offer Crypto Custody, Prime Brokerage*, Coindesk (Feb. 12, 2021), http://www.coindesk.com/business/2021/02/13/deutsche-bank-quietly-plans-to-offer-crypto-custody-prime-brokerage/.

39. Armknecht et al., *supra* note 13.

40. Proposed Rule: Safeguarding Advisory Client Assets. 88 FR 14672, March 9, 2023. The comment period was reopened until October 30, 2023. See Safeguarding Advisory Client Assets; Reopening of Comment Period, 88 FR 59818 (Aug. 30, 2023), http://www.federalregister.gov/documents/2023/08/30/2023-18667/safeguarding-advisory-client-assets-reopening-of-comment-period.

41. See, for example, Securities Industry and Financial Markets Association's Comment on Proposed New Rule re: Safeguarding Advisory Client Assets (May 8, 2023), http://www.sifma.org/wp-content/uploads/2023/05/Safeguarding-Advisory-Client-Assets.pdf.

and tokenized digital assets including bank deposit tokens through a Regulated Liability Network.[42] The United States-based bank is now piloting token services for institutional clients. The service is intended to integrate tokenized deposits and smart contracts to Citi's cash management and trade finance services, with a stated aim to create a digital solution serving the "same purpose as bank guarantees and letters of credit in the trade finance ecosystem."[43] In launching the services, Citi conducted a pilot of the service in collaboration with Maersk, a shipping company, and a canal authority that was successful in demonstrating that instant payments via smart contracts could be provided via programmable transfer of tokenized deposits. This type of innovation by market-leading financial institutions offers a glimmer of the promise of blockchain and smart contract technology, long touted by its proponents but often conceptually impenetrable to those less familiar with the underlying concepts—unquestionable advances with intrinsic risks managed by experienced, regulated institutions subject to significant obligations with respect to BSA/AML compliance.

As traditional financial institutions move in the direction of offering tokens, even more complexity will arise with respect to determining applicable BSA/AML requirements, particularly with regards to customer and transaction identification, and banks may need to supplement their standard methods with additional information unique to the cryptocurrency space. However, it is assuredly a competitive advantage that these banks have the market share and preexisting compliance programs to enhance rather than build from the ground up.

Depending on one's vantage point, when it comes to money laundering, the blockchain is either part of the problem (in that it has the potential to facilitate money laundering) or part of the solution (in that it has the potential to make money laundering more challenging). Larry Fink, CEO of the world's largest asset manager, BlackRock, reportedly said both: "Bitcoin is an index of money laundering" (*in 2017*) and "Bitcoin could revolutionize finance" (*in 2023*).[44] As Tradfi seeks to bridge the gap by making digital assets more available to investors, it remains to be seen whether Tradfi DLT-supported products will be adopted by crypto-advocates and enthusiasts. But what is clear from the current regulatory enforcement environment is that scrutiny of BSA/AML compliance related to fintechs and crypto-native companies will only increase going forward. The industry players that can recognize this reality and facilitate partnerships that survive regulatory scrutiny stand to benefit the most in this ever-evolving area.

---

42. Participants included BNY Mellon, Citi, HSBC, Mastercard, The New York Innovation Center at the Federal Reserve Bank of New York (NYIC), PNC Bank, Swift, TD Bank, Truist, US Bank and Wells Fargo. See Regulated Liability Network at http://regulatedliabilitynetwork.org/.

43. Press Release, Citi Group, Citi develops new digital asset capabilities for institutional clients (Sept. 18, 2023) (on file with Citi Group).

44. Helene Braun, *BlackRock CEO's Turnabout on Bitcoin Elicits Cheers, Skepticism of Crypto Cred*, Coindesk (Jul. 7, 2023), https://www.coindesk.com/business/2023/07/07/blackrock-ceo-larry-finks-turnabout-on-bitcoin-elicits-cheers-skepticism-from-crypto-insiders/.

Chapter 6
Office of Foreign Assets Control and Sanctions

Mike Carter and Bobby Lowe

Primer on the Rules and Regulations

The Office of Foreign Assets Control (OFAC) is an office of the U.S. Treasury that administers and enforces economic and trade sanctions based on U.S. foreign policy and national security goals against targeted individuals and entities such as foreign countries, regimes, terrorists, international narcotics traffickers, and those engaged in certain activities such as the proliferation of weapons of mass destruction or transnational organized crime.[1] All U.S. persons, including financial institutions, must comply with OFAC regulations. Although a sanctions compliance program is not legally required, OFAC encourages institutions to take a risk-based approach to designing and implementing an OFAC compliance program.

In general, the regulations that OFAC administers require financial institutions to do the following:

- Block accounts and other property of specified countries, entities, and individuals; and
- Prohibit and reject unlicensed trade and financial transactions with specified countries, entities, and individuals.

OFAC was established to oversee, implement, and enforce U.S. sanctions programs and to ensure that U.S. entities block assets destined for people and enterprises that are subject to

1. Authority: 8 U.S.C. 1189; 18 U.S.C. 2332d, 2339B; 19 U.S.C. 3901–3913; 21 U.S.C. 1901–1908; 22 U.S.C. 287c, 2370(a), 6009, 6032, 7205, 8501–8551; 31 U.S.C. 321(b); 50 U.S.C. 1701–1706, 4301–4341; Pub. L. 101–410, 104 Stat. 890, as amended (28 U.S.C. 2461 note).

U.S. sanctions. U.S. Sanctions generally fall into two categories: (1) sanctions that prevent U.S. entities from doing business with or moving assets in and out of, particular countries; and (2) sanctions that prevent U.S. entities from doing business with or moving assets to and from, specific people. OFAC publishes a list of countries or regions and specific jurisdictions subject to sanctions programs and also a list of individuals and companies owned or controlled by, or acting for or on behalf of, targeted countries. It also lists individuals, groups, and entities, such as terrorists and narcotics traffickers designated under programs that are not country specific. Collectively, these individuals and companies are called Specially Designated Nationals or SDNs and their assets must be blocked. U.S. citizens, permanent resident aliens, U.S. companies, and foreign subsidiaries owned or controlled by U.S. companies are generally prohibited from dealing with them.[2]

Prohibited transactions are trade or financial transactions and other dealings in which U.S. persons may not engage unless licensed by OFAC or expressly exempted by statute. In some cases, an underlying transaction may be prohibited, but there is no blockable interest in the transaction (*i.e.,* the transaction should not be accepted, but there is no OFAC requirement to block the assets). In these cases, the transaction is simply required to be rejected, (*i.e.,* not processed) and reported in accordance with the OFAC Reporting System (ORS).

Financial institutions are prohibited from completing any transaction involving the receipt of funds from, transmittal of funds to, or conducting business with customers located in, any country against which the United States government has economic sanctions in place prohibiting such transactions.

Types of OFAC Sanctions

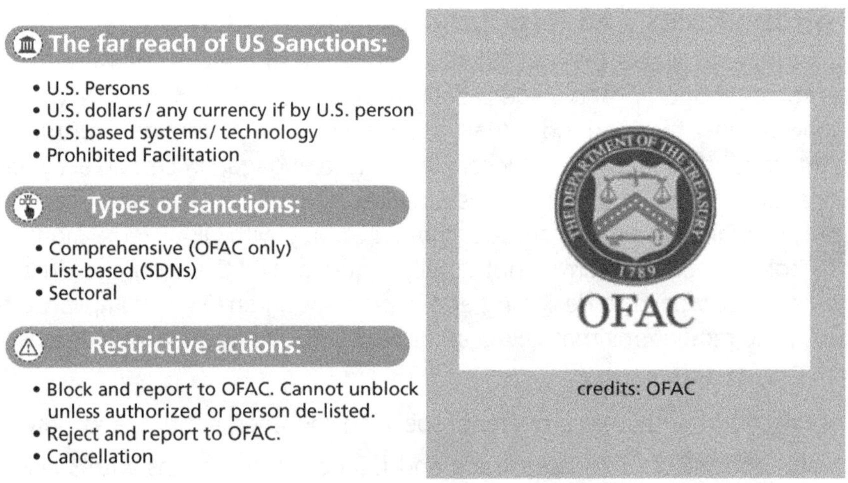

Current List of OFAC comprehensively sanctioned nations or regions

2. The "U.S. person" designation applies to citizens or green card holders, wherever located (i.e., even outside the United States), as does the prohibition on transactions with citizens of comprehensively sanctioned jurisdictions, making OFAC compliance challenging for blockchain transactions. Assisting another person to violate sanctions, or for facilitating sanctions violations, is also punishable.

- Cuba
- Iran
- North Korea
- Russia
- Syria
- The following regions of Ukraine: Crimea, Donetsk, and Luhansk

OFAC Rules and Regulations Apply to Digital Assets and Service Providers

OFAC has also published both a compliance guide as well as guidance specific to digital assets, noting, "Persons including technology companies, administrators, exchangers, and users of digital currencies; and other payment processors should develop a tailored, risk-based compliance program, which generally should include sanctions list screening and other appropriate measures."[3]

Banks with global footprints or digital asset customers need to be cognizant of other international sanctions programs that may apply to them including, but not limited to, the European Union, United Kingdom's HM Treasury, and United Nations. In principle, various global sanctions programs often require similar and overlapping restrictions and compliance controls for obligated institutions, however, there can be complicated compliance considerations, especially in the case of virtual assets where cryptocurrency may transit several jurisdictions with varying sanctions restrictions within minutes.

With respect to sanctions, the obligations of digital asset service providers generally mirror those of financial institutions, and, in many jurisdictions, they are regulated and supervised as a variation of a financial institution. Banks and other financial institutions should be keenly aware that providing services to digital asset service providers exposes them to secondary sanctions risks that should be mitigated through robust due diligence and continuous monitoring as prescribed in OFAC's *A Framework for OFAC Compliance Commitments*.[4]

Meeting Core Sanctions Obligations

OFAC has published *A Framework for OFAC Compliance Commitments* and other industry-specific guidance documents[5] regarding the agency's expectations for an effective sanctions compliance program. The framework embraces a technology-neutral, risk-based approach and relies on five primary pillars:

---

3. OFAC, "Questions on Virtual Currency," *FAQs*, U.S. Dep't Treas. https://ofac.treasury.gov/faqs/topic/1626.

4. Press Release, U.S. Dep't Treas., OFAC issues a framework for compliance commitments (May 2, 2019) (on file with U.S. Dep't. Treas.).

5. OFAC, "OFAC Information for Industry Groups," *Additional OFAC Resources*, U.S. Dep't. Treas., https://ofac.treasury.gov/additional-ofac-resources/ofac-information-for-industry-groups.

Elements of an effective sanction's compliance program

Framework for OFAC compliance commitments: five essential components

1. Management commitment	Senior management must ensure compliance personnel are delegated sufficient authority, autonomy, and resources; review and directly approve the compliance program and should foster a "culture of compliance."
2. Risk Assessment	No "one size fits all" approach to sanctions compliance. Risk based controls require a regular, holistic assessment of all possible OFAC risk touchpoints. Stressed importance of due diligence efforts at various points in on boarding customers and entering corporate transactions.
3. Internal Controls	Requires risk-based written policies and procedures to "identify, interdict, escalate, report (as appropriate), and keep records of" potential risk. Establish clear expectations. and be strictly enforced. Compliance personnel should be empowered to integrate these controls into the daily operations of all relevant business units.
4. Testing & Audit	Organizations should employ an independent and thorough auditing process to regularly identify any strengths and gaps in controls, as well as emerging threats.
5. Training	Mandatory training for all relevant personnel on a regular (at least annual) basis, with more specialized training for higher risk employees. The scope of training should be commensurate with the company's risk profile and regularly updated as needed.

More specifically, OFAC and various other regulatory agencies expect financial institutions and digital asset service providers to:

- Develop a tailored risk assessment addressing the organization's specific products, services, geographic, customer, and operational sanctions risks.
- Create and implement written policies and procedures for complying with sanctions regulations and guidance. These policies and procedures should be tailored to the company's business activities and should cover all aspects of sanctions compliance, including customer due diligence, transaction screening, and reporting.
- Implement a risk-based watchlist screening program to identify and assess the risk of each customer. The program should include procedures for identifying and verifying the identity of customers and beneficial owners, as well as screening customers against applicable sanctions lists.
- Implement a risk-based transaction screening program to detect and prevent transactions that violate OFAC sanctions. The screening program should include procedures for screening all transactions, including wire transfers, ACH transactions, and other payment methods. Transaction screening may incorporate a combination of automated, rules-based, manual, and intelligence-based methods to prevent and detect potential sanctions violations.
- Prevent transactions that violate sanctions imposed by the U.S. government or other relevant authorities.
- Prevent transactions with persons or entities on the SDN list or any other relevant watchlists.
- Undergo routine end-to-end, pre-, and post-implementation testing of the sanctions compliance program, including watchlist screening and transaction monitoring controls.

- Maintain accurate and up-to-date information in its watchlist filtering program, including regularly updating watchlists and verifying the accuracy of customer and transaction data.
- Implement procedures for escalating and reporting OFAC program-violating activity to the appropriate authorities. These procedures should include steps for freezing assets, conducting investigations, and filing reports appropriate to the facts and circumstances surrounding a particular customer, account, or transaction.
- Maintain a record-keeping system to ensure that all sanctions compliance activity is accurately documented and can be easily retrieved in the event of an audit or investigation.
- Provide training and awareness programs to all employees to ensure that they understand their sanctions compliance obligations and are able to effectively implement the entity's sanctions compliance program.
- Conduct independent audits and testing of the company's sanctions compliance program to assess its effectiveness and identify any weaknesses or gaps that need to be addressed.
- Receive appropriate support for the sanctions compliance program by senior management. This includes promoting a culture of compliance, and
- As a risk mitigating measure, maintain a Voluntary Self-Disclosure[6] program in case a control measure fails, and a sanctions event occurs.

The Costs of Sanctions Compliance Failures

From 2020 through 2023, OFAC has issued sixty-eight enforcement actions totaling over 1.6 billion dollars in fines.[7] At least seven of those enforcement actions directly involved a digital asset service provider failing to appropriately implement some portion of, or in whole, an effective sanctions compliance program related to their facilitation of blockchain transactions.

In 2021 OFAC published a *Sanctions Compliance Guidance for the Virtual Currency Industry* (the OFAC VC Guidance or VC Guidance),[8] making clear that it "may impose civil penalties for sanctions violations generally based on a strict liability legal standard. This means that, in many cases, a U.S. person may be held civilly liable[9] for sanctions violations even without having knowledge or reason to know it was engaging in such a violation."[10]

---

6. Appendix A to Part 501—Economic Sanctions Enforcement Guidelines: "Voluntary self-disclosure means self-initiated notification to OFAC of an apparent violation by a Subject Person that has committed, or otherwise participated in, an apparent violation of a statute, Executive order, or regulation administered or enforced by OFAC, prior to or at the same time that OFAC, or any other federal, state, or local government agency or official, discovers the apparent violation or another substantially similar apparent violation."
7. Sourced from OFAC as of December 11, 2023, *see* OFAC, Civil Penalties and Enforcement Information, U.S. Dep't Treas. https://ofac.treasury.gov/civil-penalties-and-enforcement-information (last accessed Dec. 11, 2023).
8. OFAC, *Sanctions Compliance Guidance for the Virtual Currency Industry*, U.S. Dep't Treas. (Oct. 2021), https://ofac.treasury.gov/media/913571/download?inline.
9. *Id.*
10. *Id.*

Although the strict liability standard no doubt strikes fear into companies seeking to comply, the OFAC VC Guidance also clarifies that "OFAC takes into consideration the totality of facts and circumstances surrounding an apparent violation to determine the appropriate enforcement response. For example, OFAC may consider as mitigating factors a virtual currency company's implementation of a risk-based OFAC compliance program and remedial measures taken in response to an apparent violation." This underscores the importance of developing, implementing, and improving a risk-based compliance program suitable to the risks presented by the business, geography, customers, and related factors.

Furthermore, *Appendix A to Part 501—Economic Sanctions Enforcement Guidelines*[11] outlines the schedule of monetary penalties (as of 2023):

- $1,000 with respect to a transaction valued at less than $1,000;
- $10,000 with respect to a transaction valued at $1,000 or more but less than $10,000;
- $25,000 with respect to a transaction valued at $10,000 or more but less than $25,000;
- $50,000 with respect to a transaction valued at $25,000 or more but less than $50,000;
- $100,000 with respect to a transaction valued at $50,000 or more but less than $100,000;
- $200,000 with respect to a transaction valued at $100,000 or more but less than $200,000;

Of note, the nature of blockchain transactions executing as micro-transactions may subject a financial institution to compounding instances of a sanctions violation as potentially perceived by OFAC.

Addressing Blockchain-Centric Sanctions Risks

The VC Guidance highlights the "increasingly critical role" that "the virtual currency industry, including technology companies, exchangers, administrators, miners, wallet providers, and users" plays in "preventing sanctioned persons from exploiting virtual currencies to evade sanctions and undermine U.S. foreign policy and national security interests." The OFAC VC Guidance then outlines numerous, practical sanctions compliance techniques and approaches for both digital asset service providers and financial institutions with customers or business lines involving digital assets, many of which have been highlighted in recent OFAC enforcement actions and are used by experienced digital asset compliance practitioners, including:

- Implementing a robust digital identity program that effectively assesses the validity of customer documentation and combats synthetic ID fraud used by criminals and those seeking to evade sanctions controls.

11. Appendix A to Part 501, Title 31.

- Where possible, leveraging blockchain tools to maintain, verify, and transmit customer names, dates of birth, addresses, and identification numbers along with applicable transaction details, especially for higher-risk cross-border transactions;
- Conducting on-chain monitoring of blockchain transactions to identify sanctioned crypto addresses, mixers, and illicit actors through direct and indirect transaction routes. This includes reviews of customers with repeated indirect blockchain exposure to high-risk addresses or clusters;
- Implementing, where technically feasible,[12] inbound and outbound transaction blocking to crypto addresses designated by OFAC or as high-risk for sanctions exposure by third-party blockchain intelligence tools;
- Routinely assessing and conducting enhanced due diligence on customers who engage in frequent use of digital assets with privacy-enhancing features;
- Flagging counterparty digital asset exchanges that are inappropriately licensed or are "nested" with and reliant upon the compliance controls of a different exchange. Often, nested exchanges will have few sanctions compliance controls in place, creating indirect sanctions exposure that could quickly result in direct exposure given the rapid nature of digital asset movements;
- Conducting geolocation screening, including Internet Protocol (IP) and virtual private network (VPN) monitoring. Geolocation tools can help determine the physical location of an individual, entity, or IP address based on various data points, such as GPS coordinates, IP addresses, or mobile device data;
- Performing address verification, especially for customers who use VPNs or reside in regions adjacent to countries or regions subject to comprehensive OFAC sanctions;
- Implementing a robust digital asset assessment process that documents the compliance risks related to how a specific product operates, its technical features, the developers, how the product is generally used, and what types of customers use it;
- Conducting appropriate due diligence when entering into a business or financial relationship with a digital asset service provider. As a general rule, the provider should possess commensurate levels of compliance controls and risk appetite. The provider should also be transparent with regard to how it operates its sanctions compliance program and the results of its routine independent program testing.

12. A current limitation in screening Blockchain transactions relates to the ability to query, in real-time, a customer's withdrawal address against third-party Blockchain data and automatically block outbound transactions with certain addresses classified as being higher risk at the time the customer's transaction is initiated. Third-party Blockchain queries and subsequent blocking are subject to the availability of information at a point in time, as well as any downtime of systems attribution or data feedback via API. In many cases, the attribution of a Blockchain address as "risky" does not occur until weeks, months, or even years after the original transaction.

OFAC Crypto-Related Alerts: A Comparison

OFAC	Crypto Related	Total
Enforcement Actions	8	108
Sanction List Updates	14	206
Regulations and Guidance	1	112

The Promises of Blockchain in Complying with Sanctions Regulations

For compliance teams, blockchain as an underlying technology offers an unparalleled opportunity to address traditional sanctions evasion risks through stronger data controls, counterparty verification, identity governance, and supplemental tracing of transactions through a given blockchain ecosystem. Blockchain technology is capable of directly addressing the following sanctions evasion typologies common to the banking system:

- Efforts to omit or falsify information in transaction messages, sometimes referred to as wire stripping;
- Use of shell companies to obscure ultimate beneficiaries;
- Routing payments through third countries or multiple institutions to obscure origin, destination, or counterparties; and
- Customers requesting payments to or from a newly sanctioned jurisdiction.

Distributed Ledger Technology is inherently designed to address those traditional typologies because the data is immutable, is permissive to a transparent audit trail for each transaction, and is capable of incorporating complete and reliable originator, intermediary, correspondent, and beneficiary data.

In fact, the Society for Worldwide Interbank Financial Telecommunication (SWIFT), an interbank messaging network used by over 11,000 global banks facilitating tens of millions of transactions per day, has begun to explore distributed ledger technology to "deliver the business functionalities and data richness required to support automated real-time liquidity monitoring and reconciliation."[13] Traditional SWIFT messages rely on the quality of data inputs and information relays through originating and multiple intermediary financial institutions. This transaction information could be (and historically has been) manipulated or otherwise obscured to prevent the appropriate screening of transactions for potential sanctions by the initiating and ending financial institution. For example, in June 2014, BNP Paribas, S.A. the global financial institution headquartered in Paris pled guilty to "large-scale,

13. *Swift Completes Landmark DLT Proof of Concept*, Swift (Mar. 8, 2018), https://www.swift.com/news-events/news/swift-completes-landmark-dlt-proof-concept.

systemic violations of U.S. economic sanctions" for stripping references to Cuba from wire and SWIFT messages.[14]

As cross-border payments trend toward blockchain technology and digital assets, other opportunities for enhanced sanctions compliance present themselves to financial institutions, including crypto-native entities and their banking partners.

A key component to meeting sanctions obligations in the digital assets space is the implementation of blockchain transaction monitoring. Generally, blockchain transaction monitoring differs from traditional transaction monitoring in that it relies on intelligence-based rules instead of (or in addition to) patterns, thresholds, or other mathematical algorithms. Intelligence-based monitoring enables direct and indirect attribution of a specific blockchain transaction to a risky or potentially suspicious source or intermediary, including sanctioned persons, entities, or jurisdictions. This is particularly helpful in assessing transaction risk and customer or counterparty risk before engaging in a transaction or customer relationship that may violate OFAC or other sanctions program obligations.

Further, digital asset service providers and financial institutions can leverage blockchain data by relying on their customers' digital identities to verify and screen transaction counterparties and conduct persistent KYC throughout the customer lifecycle. Blockchain technology may also be used for Customer Identification Programs (CIP) which has the potential to replace traditional poor data quality, fuzzy name list matching, and associated manual work for data immutability and screening speed.

Because of its transparency and traceability, the blockchain is capable of providing a level of clarity to financial services providers that may be embraced as part of a comprehensive compliance approach including sanctions, anti-money laundering (AML), anti-fraud, data protection, and other areas by leveraging its transparency and traceability. Though no solution mitigates all risk, pairing a blockchain-focused approach with enterprise-level sanctions controls may significantly decrease the likelihood and severity of a sanctions violation and the ensuing penalties.

The Risks of Blockchain in Complying with Sanctions Regulations

Blockchain products also present unique challenges to digital asset service providers and traditional financial institutions. First, users of digital assets are more likely to be anonymous in under-regulated jurisdictions, enhancing secondary exposure to persons in sanctioned geographies or who are listed as SDNs. The speed and borderless nature of blockchain transactions also increase the chances that standard sanctions screening methods deployed to oversee blockchain transactions may be rendered less effective or subverted entirely.

From a technical standpoint and as various agencies within the U.S. government, including the CFTC and U.S. Treasury have recognized, privacy-enhancing features and mixers or

14. See Press Release, Office of Public Affairs, HSBC Holdings Plc. And HSBC Bank USA N.A. admit to anti-money laundering and sanctions violations, forfeit $1.256 billion in deferred prosecution agreement (Dec. 11, 2012) (on file with U.S. Dept. of Just.); Press Release, Office of Public Affairs, BNP Paribas agrees to plead guilty and pay $8.9 billion for illegally processing financial transactions for countries subject to U.S. economic sanctions (Jun. 30, 2014) (on file with U.S. Dept. Just.); United States of America v. BNP Paribas S.A., 14 Cr.460 (LGS) (S.D.N.Y. Apr. 30, 2015).

mixing services present elevated AML and sanctions compliance risks because they may be used to obfuscate transaction flows and attributional information and frustrate sanctions compliance program controls. Although such tools are not inherently illicit, digital asset service providers and traditional financial institutions should be mindful of and review the frequency and value of transactions involving high-risk tools in connection with their risk-based approach and documented risk appetite. Additionally, as described in Chapter 7, *supra*, in October 2023, the U.S. Treasury proposed designating transactions with mixers or mixing services under its USA PATRIOT Act Special Measures authority. The comment period for the proposed rule ended in January 2024 and, if promulgated as proposed, it will require reporting to the Treasury's Financial Crimes Enforcement Network (FinCEN) many such transactions.

Chapter 7
Risk Management and Governance

Michael Glotz

Establishing a Robust Risk Framework for Digital Asset Business

The burgeoning digital landscape has ushered in unprecedented opportunities and risks for businesses venturing into the realm of digital assets. This chapter provides an in-depth guide on instituting a robust risk framework for digital asset businesses. Delving into critical components such as board governance, executive governance, crypto asset management processes, enterprise risk management, independent assessments, strategic management, advanced analytics, blockchain integration, and information and cybersecurity, this comprehensive framework aims to fortify legal practitioners against the evolving complexities of the digital asset landscape. This chapter will explore each of the nine Pillars of Holistic Digital Asset Risk Framework, including Model Risk Management.

The Nine Pillars of the Holistic Digital Asset Risk Framework

The Holistic Digital Asset Risk Framework below (Figure 1) highlights the Nine Pillars of a robust risk framework as a guide to help you develop a specific framework for your organization to manage ongoing digital asset risk.

Figure 1 Holistic Digital Asset Risk Framework

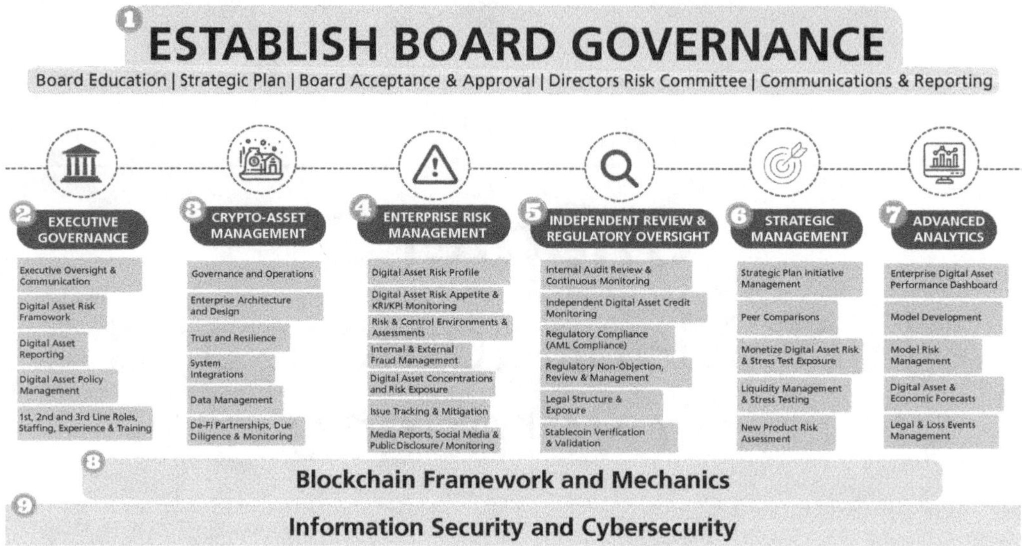

Pillar One: Establishing Effective Board Governance

Establishing effective board governance for digital assets ensures that the Board of Directors has the right information, context, and defined responsibility to ensure that they provide an effective oversight role for investors. It is the Board's responsibility to ensure that management institutes an effective risk framework given the size and complexity of the digital assets' infrastructure in place in the organization, as well as ensuring it meets the Board's risk appetite.

Key Components: Establishing Effective Board Governance

a. Board Education: As the vanguard of strategic decision-making, board members must undergo comprehensive training tailored to equip all members with a nuanced understanding of digital assets, blockchain technology, and emerging risks.

b. Risk Oversight: Ensuring effective risk oversight at the board level is paramount, as is developing and approving a strategic plan, appointing a designated board member or committee in overseeing digital asset risks, integrating risk discussions into regular board meetings, and maintaining a proactive stance toward risk mitigation.

c. Ongoing Communication and Reporting: Transparency is critical in the digital asset landscape, as is implementing a robust reporting system that provides regular updates on digital asset performance, risk exposure, compliance, and fosters informed decision-making.

d. Risk Appetite and Policy Limits: Managing exposure to specific digital assets in accordance with a board-established Risk Appetite Statement that includes concentration and limits for digital assets. In addition, the Board shall set and review other policy limits to mitigate risks associated with particular assets, adapting to the ever-changing market conditions.

e. Board Risk Committee: It is best practice to appoint a specialized committee within the board for oversight of digital asset risks. The importance of diversity in expertise within this committee and its role in ensuring comprehensive risk governance is the foundation of a strong risk management framework.

Pillar Two: Establishing Comprehensive Executive Governance

Establishing effective executive governance for digital assets to ensure that the leadership team has the right information, context, and defined responsibility to ensure that they appropriately manage risk associated with digital assets. It is the responsibility of the Chief Executive Officer (CEO) and Executive Management to ensure that an effective risk framework is appropriately designed, funded, implemented, and continuously managed.

Key Components: Establishing Comprehensive Executive Governance

a. Digital Asset Policy Development: Crafting a comprehensive digital asset policy is foundational to effective management governance. This section highlights the importance of a policy that aligns with legal and regulatory requirements, highlights key risk limits and the need for regular updates to adapt to the dynamic digital landscape.
b. Digital Asset Risk Framework: A tailored risk framework specific to digital assets employed in the organization is crucial for day-to-day operations. The development and integration of such a framework into the organization's decision-making processes is fundamental to the success of the organization.
c. Identifying and Staffing First, Second, and Third Line of Defense functions: Clearly defining the roles and responsibilities of different lines of defense ensures a robust risk management structure. The importance of collaboration and communication between these lines determines is critical. Each line of defense needs to be properly staffed and funded. Leadership of each line of defense should be on the executive leadership team reporting to the CEO.
d. Executive Risk Committee: An executive committee (separate from the Board Risk Committee) dedicated to overseeing and managing digital asset risks at an organizational level is essential. This committee will provide regular communication channels between the committee and the organization's leadership team and board's risk committee, ensuring alignment and effective reporting.

Pillar Three: Digital Asset Operations Management (First Line of Defense)

Establishing effective digital asset operations management will ensure that each functional area implements documented processes, procedures, information, context, and defined responsibilities to ensure that they appropriately manage risk in each assigned function area.

Key Components: Digital Asset Operations Management

a. Governance and Operations: Governance forms the bedrock for efficient operations. One must ensure that an effective governance program, organization, and staffing are in place to ensure that digital asset operations and operational processes align with organizational goals. This includes appropriate training and ongoing development of all associates.
b. Architecture and Design: The architecture and design of digital asset management systems need to be robust and secure. The importance of designing systems with scalability and potential threats in mind, and the regular assessment and updating of the architecture is a fundamental part of the organization's infrastructure.
c. Trust and Resilience: Trust and resilience are imperative in the volatile digital asset landscape. We require the establishment of trust mechanisms and resilience measures, along with the development of contingency plans for potential disruptions for the organization to operate effectively ongoing.
d. Systems Integrations: Seamless integration of digital asset systems with existing organizational systems is crucial. Regular assessments to identify and address integration risks should be documented and reported as part of each functional unit's process documentation.
e. Data Management: Secure and compliant data management is a cornerstone of crypto asset management. The implementation of robust data management systems, including regular audits and monitoring processes is fundamental to a well-run organization.
f. DeFi Partnerships, Due Diligence, and Monitoring: Organizations engaged in decentralized finance (DeFi) partnerships must employ strategies to stay informed about developments in the DeFi space and managing associated risks. This includes strong vendor management procedures and vendor monitoring protocol.

Pillar Four: Enterprise Risk Management (Second Line of Defense)

Enterprise Risk Management (ERM) is an integrated and continuous process for managing enterprise-wide risk—including strategic, financial, operational, compliance, and reputational risk—to minimize unexpected performance variance and maximize intrinsic firm value. This process empowers the board and management to make more informed risk/reward decisions by addressing fundamental requirements with respect to governance and policy (including risk appetite), risk analysis, risk management, and monitoring and reporting. Instituting a strong ERM Program is essential to managing digital assets in a high-risk environment, and the appointment of a Chief Risk Officer, reporting to the CEO, is a best practice to ensure the ERM Program is properly designed, funded, staffed, and effectively instituted in the organization.

Key Components: Enterprise Risk Management

a. Build Risk Appetite Statement for Digital Assets: Clearly defining and communicating the organization's risk appetite for digital assets is foundational, as is the alignment of risk appetite with the overall organizational risk strategy by way of industry awareness and interviews across the organization. This Digital Asset Risk Statement should be consistent with, and a part of, the overall organization's Risk Appetite Statement.

b. Monitor Risk Appetite Key Performance and Risk Indicators: Establishing key performance indicators (KPIs) and Key Risk Indicators (KRIs) for monitoring adherence to digital asset risk appetite is essential, as is regular review and updating of KPIs and KRIs based on changing market conditions.
c. Perform Internal and External Fraud Assessments: Proactive assessment of internal and external fraud risks is crucial as are regular assessments and the implementation of preventive measures and controls to mitigate fraud risks.
d. Establishment and Monitoring of Digital Asset Concentration Limits: Setting and regularly reviewing concentration limits for digital assets is imperative to manage portfolio risk. The diversification of digital asset portfolios to reduce concentration risk is a key risk management technique that needs to be investigated in each organization.
e. Oversee Issue Tracking and Remediation: Effective issue tracking and resolution for digital asset operations and the implementation of robust systems for tracking and resolving issues, ensuring timely communication and resolution, is another fundamental process in ERM.
f. Institute a Strong AML/BSA Program for Digital Assets: Developing and maintaining a comprehensive Anti-Money Laundering (AML) and Bank Secrecy Act (BSA) program that is regularly updated to align with evolving regulatory requirements is essential.
g. Training and Development: The second line of defense needs adequate training and ongoing development in the digital assets area to be truly effective.

Pillar Five: Independent Assessments (Third Line of Defense)

As digital assets become increasingly integrated into financial ecosystems, the need for robust risk internal audit and independent assessment practices is more critical than ever. The advent of digital assets, including cryptocurrency and tokenized assets, has ushered in a new area of financial innovation. To ensure integrity of the financial systems, internal audit and independent assessments play a pivotal role in this context, providing assurance, oversight, and validation of digital asset management processes.

Internal Audit. The importance of internal audit and independent assessment in digital asset management cannot be overstated. These functions serve as critical components of a comprehensive risk management framework, providing transparency, mitigating risks, ensuring compliance, and enhancing the overall resilience of organizations operating in the digital asset space. By investing in robust internal audit processes and seeking independent assessments, financial institutions and entities involved in digital asset management can build trust, strengthen their risk management practices, and navigate the complexities of this transformative financial landscape with confidence.

Independent Auditors. Engaging independent auditors for regular audits of digital asset operations is a cornerstone of risk management, along with transparent communication of audit findings to the board and relevant committees and with the implementation of corrective actions based on audit recommendations.

Key Components: Independent Assessments

a. Transparency and Accountability: Digital asset management involves complex processes from custody to security to trading and valuation. Internal audit functions service as a critical internal control mechanism, ensuring that these processes are transparent, accountable, and aligned with organizational objectives. Conducting regular audits, internal auditors can identify and rectify potential issues, thereby enhancing the overall reliability of digital asset management.
b. Skills, Ability, and Knowledge Required: The Third Line of Defense needs the appropriate skills, ability, and knowledge to be effective. Outside resources are generally required as having all the appropriate staff in-house may be difficult to acquire and maintain. In addition, an effective training and development program is required for all company associates.
c. Compliance, Legal, and Regulatory Alignment: The regulatory environment for digital assets is still evolving, and adherence to compliance standards is crucial for both legal and reputational reasons. Internal auditors play a key role in ensuring the digital asset management practices comply with relevant regulations and industry standards. Their independent assessment provides organizations with the confidence that they are operating within the bounds of the law.
d. External Assurance: Independent assessment by external auditors brings an additional layer of objectivity and credibility. External Auditors provide an unbiased perspective on the effectiveness of controls, the accuracy of financial reporting, and the overall governance framework of the digital assets' engagement. The external validation enhances stakeholders' trust in the organization's digital asset practices.
e. Cybersecurity and Resilience: The decentralized and digital nature of assets requires heightened focus on cybersecurity. Internal Audit teams are instrumental in evaluating the cybersecurity measures implemented for digital asset storage and transactions. By conducting thorough assessments of cybersecurity protocols, auditors contribute to the overall resilience of digital asset management systems.

Pillar Six: Strategic Management

Given the ever-changing environment for digital assets, having a well-designed strategic management program is fundamental for ensuring that initiative is properly managed and changes with technological innovation. The board should review and approve all updated strategic plans and be appraised of the status of strategic initiatives on a quarterly basis.

Key Components: Strategic Management

a. Strategic Plan Reference to Digital Assets: Integrating digital asset strategies and considerations and alignment of digital asset strategies with broader business objectives will ensure well organized operations. Strategic plans should be updated on an annual basis and strategic imperative status should be tracked at least quarterly.

b. Capital Stress Testing for Digital Assets: Stress testing to assess the impact of adverse market conditions on digital asset portfolios is essential. The development of contingency plans based on stress test results should be reviewed and updated at least annually.

c. Liquidity Stress Testing for Digital Assets: Regular stress testing to assess liquidity risks associated with digital assets is imperative. The establishment of liquidity reserves (on-balance sheet and off-balance sheet) to address potential liquidity challenges is critical.

d. Building a New Product Risk Assessment: A comprehensive risk assessment framework for evaluating new digital asset products is crucial and conducting a thorough risk analysis before implementing new products is a must. You may want to ensure that the Board approves all new digital asset products.

Pillar Seven: Advanced Analytics

In the rapidly evolving landscape of finance, the rise of digital assets has brought about opportunities and challenges. Advanced analytics should be employed to monitor, model, and report on risks associated with digital assets. Plans to utilize advanced analytics should be shared with the management team and board to better manage risk in a timely manner.

Key Components: Advanced Analytics

a. Model Development and Risk Management: Effective model risk management is critical to ensure the reliability and accuracy of financial models. Institutions must embrace innovative approaches, leverage advanced technologies, and remain agile in response to evolving market conditions and regulatory requirements. More on this topic is covered in depth in the following pages.

b. Utilizing AI to Monitor Key Risk and Performance Indicators: Implementing advanced analytics tools to monitor key performance indicators (KPIs) and key risk indicators (KPIs) related to digital assets is essential. The use of data-driven insights to inform decision-making and strategy is a leading practice, and the technology is here today.

c. Monitoring and Reporting of Loss Events: Implementing a system for tracking, analyzing, and reporting loss events related to digital assets is crucial. Loss of event data to enhance risk management strategies is another leading practice.

Pillar Eight: Establishing a BlockChain Framework and Mechanics

Developing a clear framework for integrating blockchain technology into digital asset operations is paramount. The importance of staying informed about advancements in blockchain technology and collaborating with industry experts to leverage blockchain for enhanced security and efficiency is critical. While critical, in-depth exploration of the components of this technical topic is outside of the scope of this publication.

Key Components: Blockchain Framework and Mechanism

a. Defining use cases.
b. Selection criteria for the Blockchain Platform.
c. Consensus mechanism decision.
d. Implementation of smart contracts.
e. Thorough testing, deployment, and maintenance.

Pillar Nine: Information Technology and Cybersecurity

Robust information and cybersecurity measures are non-negotiable in the digital age, but the development and implementation of comprehensive security measures to safeguard digital assets against evolving cyber threats is a vast topic that cannot be covered within the framework of this chapter but is a practice on its own. One key risk management concept is insurance—ensuring that your organization has adequate cybersecurity insurance is critical to long-term survival.

Model Risk Management for Digital Assets

Model risk management, a subset of Pillar Seven of the Digital Risk Management Framework, is important enough to warrant further coverage here. In the rapidly evolving landscape of finance, the rise of digital assets has brought about unprecedented opportunities and challenges. As financial institutions and investors increasingly incorporate digital assets into their portfolios, the need for robust model risk management has become paramount. Model risk refers to the potential for adverse consequences resulting from errors in financial models or their misapplication. In the context of digital assets, which are often characterized by high volatility and complex market dynamics, effective model risk management is crucial to ensure the reliability and accuracy of financial models. The failure of models, such as those governing the Terra/LUNA, has led to catastrophic results.

Model Risk Management: Challenges

a. Volatility and Market Dynamics: Digital assets such as cryptocurrencies, are notorious for their price volatility. The dynamic and sometimes unpredictable nature of these markets poses challenges for traditional modeling approaches. Models that fail to account for rapid price changes and sudden market shifts can lead to inaccurate risk assessments and financial losses.
b. Decentralization and Lack of Central Authority: Blockchain's decentralized nature challenges traditional models that rely on centralized authorities for data validation. Model developers must account for the absence of a central clearinghouse and design models that are resilient to distributed consensus mechanisms.
c. Smart Contracts and Automated Processes: Smart contracts, self-executing agreements with the terms of the contract directly written into code, introduce a new layer of complexity. Model risk management must address the potential for vulnerabilities in smart contracts and automated processes, ensuring they align with regulatory requirements and organizational risk tolerance.

d. Data Privacy and Security Concerns: While blockchain provides enhanced security through cryptographic techniques, it also poses unique challenges in terms of data privacy. Ensuring that sensitive information is adequately protected while maintaining the benefits of transparency requires careful consideration in model development.

e. Interoperability and Standards: The lack of standardized protocols and interoperability between different blockchain networks presents challenges for model risk management. Financial institutions must navigate the complexities of integrating various blockchain systems and ensure that their models can adapt to diverse technological environments.

Key Components: Model Risk Management

a. Model Risk Management Policy: This policy should cover topics such as model governance, model risk rating, independent reviews of model on a cycled basis depending on model risk level, model documentation standards, and model reporting.

b. Model Risk Ratings: All models should be rated based on the level of risk it imposes on the organization and cover such attributes as information security risk, volatility, level of liquidity risk, level of capital risk, impact to customers, etc.

c. Independent Model Validation: All models should be independently validated in a standard cycle depending on risk rating. High-risk models should be independently validated every 12 to 18 months or when the model has been substantially changed. Moderate risk models should be independently validated every 12 to 30 months or when the model is substantially changed. Low-risk models should be independently validated every 24 to 60 months depending on key factors.

d. Model Documentation Standards: Documentation standards need to exist to ensure that all models are properly documented.

e. Model Stress Testing: All models should be stress tested to understand the range of outputs in the model and whether they are reasonable. In addition, the range of financial impacts to the organization should be understood and communicated to the executive team and Board.

Model Risk Management: Opportunities and Best Practices

a. Transparency and Immutable Audit Trails: Blockchain's transparent and immutable nature provides an opportunity to enhance auditability. Models leveraging blockchain technology can benefit from transparent audit trails, allowing for real-time monitoring and validation of transactions, ultimately reducing the risk of errors or fraudulent activities.

b. Smart Contract Auditing: Specialized auditing processes for smart contracts can mitigate risks associated with their execution. Regular audits, code reviews, and security assessments help identify vulnerabilities in smart contracts, ensuring that they operate as intended and align with regulatory requirements.

c. Collaboration and Industry Standards: Collaborative efforts within the industry to establish standards for blockchain technology can facilitate model risk management.

Institutions should actively engage in industry consortia and standardization bodies to contribute to the development of best practices and frameworks.

d. Continuous Monitoring and Adaptation: Given the dynamic nature of blockchain technology, continuous monitoring and adaptation of models are essential. Institutions should have mechanisms in place to update models in response to changes in blockchain protocols, security standards, and regulatory requirements.

Figure 2 highlights the key starting point for establishing your Holistic Digital Asset Risk Framework.

Figure 2 How to Get Started with Crypto-Asset Products

Conclusion

As digital asset infrastructure becomes increasingly integral to the global economy, the need for a comprehensive risk framework cannot be overstated. This chapter serves as a roadmap to navigate the complexities of the digital landscape, ensuring that legal practitioners are well-equipped to address the multifaceted challenges of digital asset businesses. By integrating these strategies, banks, fintechs, insurance companies, and asset management companies can build resilience, enhance governance, and position themselves for success in the dynamic and ever-evolving digital frontier.

Chapter 8
Privacy and Cybersecurity in Blockchain

Mike Borgia and Patrick Austin

Privacy and Cybersecurity Considerations in Blockchain Technology

Blockchain predicates on principles of consensus, decentralization, and cryptography to generate trust in a transaction. The National Institute of Standards and Technology (NIST) defines blockchains as "tamper evident and tamper resistant digital ledgers implemented in a distributed fashion (*i.e.*, without a central repository) and usually without a central authority (*i.e.*, a bank, company, or government)."[1] Nevertheless, as utilization of blockchain technology has proliferated the financial sector, blockchain privacy and security issues have come to light and warrant examination.

This chapter outlines privacy principles codified in international and U.S. data privacy laws, and growing tensions with utilization of blockchain technology in financial transactions. One example of such tension: a fundamental pillar of blockchain technology–consensus.[2] Consensus is achieved by providing participants with access to a distributed ledger to permit review of the entire history of transactions executed on that blockchain. Each participant can verify the accuracy of information stored. However, if stored transaction information is available to anyone with access to the blockchain, regulatory and compliance

1. Dylan Yaga et al., *Blockchain Technology Overview*, NIST, U.S. Dept. Comm'r (Oct. 2018), https://nvlpubs.nist.gov/nistpubs/ir/2018/NIST.IR.8202.pdf.
2. Amitai Porat et al., *Blockchain Consensus: An Analysis of Proof-of-Work and Its Applications*, Secure Compu. Sys. – Stan. Univ. (2017), https://www.scs.stanford.edu/17au-cs244b/labs/projects/porat_pratap_shah_adkar.pdf.

issues arise if that transaction information contains personal information, as defined under international or U.S. data privacy laws.[3]

This chapter is divided into two sections. Section I focuses on privacy and data processing issues. Section II focuses on cybersecurity. Both sections discuss related legal risks and identify action steps to mitigate cyber threats when using blockchain technology.

Public and Private Blockchains: Different Privacy and Security Concerns

Before delving into privacy and cybersecurity issues associated with blockchain technology, we must highlight an important distinction within blockchain technology: public blockchains versus private blockchains. Public blockchain networks generally enable anyone to join and permit participants to remain anonymous. A public blockchain typically utilizes internet-connected computers to validate transactions to achieve consensus among participants. One of the most well-known, and popular examples of a public blockchain is bitcoin. Bitcoin achieves consensus via bitcoin mining.[4] Computers that access the bitcoin network are often referred to as miners. Those computers attempt to solve a complex cryptographic problem to create proof of work, thereby validating a particular transaction.[5] Aside from public keys, there are minimal identity and access controls associated with a public blockchain network.

There also are private blockchain networks. These networks utilize identity controls to confirm membership. They also set access privileges. Together, these organizations create a members-only blockchain network. A private blockchain managed through a permissioned network achieves consensus via selective endorsement, whereby known users verify a particular transaction. Only members afforded specific access and permissions have the ability to maintain the transaction ledger. As a result, a private blockchain network generally requires greater identity and access controls.

The use of private and permissioned blockchain networks has privacy and security-related advantages due to greater control over what data is entered, who is authorized to enter the data, and how it may be entered. Even so, given the proliferation of bitcoin and other public, permissionless blockchain networks, privacy and security professionals need to be prepared to analyze legal, compliance, and regulatory issues that arise within both public and private blockchain frameworks.

I. Privacy Considerations in the Utilization of Blockchain Technology

Data privacy has become a major policy and regulatory concern in the digital age, and privacy laws in both the European Union (EU) and United States (US) include provisions affecting providers and users of blockchain technology. While the EU has more privacy protective

3. CMS, *The Tension Between GDPR and the Rise of Blockchain Technologies* (Jan. 2019), https://cms.law/en/media/international/files/publications/publications/the-tension-between-gdpr-and-the-rise-of-blockchain-technologies.

4. Fraida Fund, *Bitcoin: Reaching Consensus in Distributed Systems*, NYU Polytechnical School of Engineering (Mar. 7, 2016), https://witestlab.poly.edu/blog/get-rich-on-fake-bitcoins/.

5. Porat et al., *supra* note 2.

legal framework than the US, a proliferation of privacy laws in the US—particularly at the state level—complicates the data privacy landscape for blockchain technologies.

Data privacy is, in effect, the ability to determine who is able to view personal data, how that data can be utilized, and how long others can access said data.[6] The EU, through its General Data Protection Regulation (GDPR),[7] maintains a rigorous standard for personal data protection applicable to both the EU and European Economic Area (EEA). The GDPR is intended to protect personal data, which is defined as any information relating to an identified or identifiable natural person.[8] The term natural person is defined as one who can be identified, directly or indirectly, in particular by reference to an identifier such as a name, an identification number, location data, an online identifier, or to one or more factors specific to the physical, physiological, genetic, mental, economic, cultural or social identity of that natural person.[9] The GDPR applies to the processing of personal data of individuals in the EU when an entity offers goods or services to EU individuals and when entities engage in online behavioral monitoring of EU individuals.[10] Controllers and processors of personal data are required to take specific actions to document their data processing programs and comply with the GDPR's principles and regulatory obligations.[11]

Conversely, data privacy laws in the US consist of a patchwork, owing largely to the US's federal system. Broadly speaking, federal privacy laws are sectoral—i.e., they apply specifically to certain economic sectors, such as financial services, health care and others, or to specific types of data, such as personal data of children. Most generally applicable privacy laws found at the state level.

The most prominent data privacy law for financial services is the Gramm-Leach Bliley Act and its various implementing regulations (GLBA).[12] GLBA, among other things, restricts how and to whom covered "financial institutions"[13] may disclose customer's personal financial data, referred to as "nonpublic personal information,"[14] and require financial institutions to provide customers the right to opt out of certain disclosures.[15] The GLBA contains a provision requiring the Federal Trade Commission (FTC) to implement regulations designed to carry out the GLBA's financial privacy provisions. The FTC is also tasked with enforcing its

6. CMS, *supra* note 3.
7. Regulation (EU) 2016/679 entered into force on May 25, 2018.
8. Council Regulation 2016/679, art. 4, 2016 O.J. (L119) (EU).
9. *Id.*
10. Council Regulation 2016/679, art. 3, 2016 O.J. (L119) (EU).
11. Council Regulation 2016/679, art. 24–43, 2016 O.J. (L119) (EU).
12. 15 U.S.C. § 6801-6809, §§ 6821-6827.
13. This term is broadly defined in the GLBA regulations and may include, but is not limited to: banks, savings associations, credit unions, non-bank mortgage lenders, mortgage brokers, businesses that extend credit or service loans, insurance underwriters and agents, businesses that provide check cashing or wire transfer services, etc., 12 C.F.R. Part 1016 (Regulation P).
14. This term is defined as any "personally identifiable financial information" that a financial institution collects about an individual in connection with providing a financial product or service unless that information is otherwise "publicly available," FTC, *How to Comply with the Privacy of Consumer Financial Information Rule of Gramm-Leach-Bliley Act* (Jul. 2022), https://www.ftc.gov/business-guidance/resources/how-comply-privacy-consumer-financial-information-rule-gramm-leach-bliley-act.
15. See, e.g., 12 C.F.R. Part 1016 (Regulation P).

Privacy of Consumer Financial Information Rule (Privacy Rule). The Privacy Rule applies to businesses that are "significantly engaged"[16] in "financial activities."[17]

Regarding the FTC, it is worth noting that this federal agency can, and does, take law enforcement action against financial institutions and other businesses for alleged violations of consumer privacy laws and/or alleged failures to maintain the security of sensitive consumer information. In many instances, the FTC charges businesses with alleged violations of Section 5 of the FTC Act. Section 5 prohibits unfair and deceptive acts and practices in or affecting commerce.[18]

In addition to the GLBA and FTC, the Right to Financial Privacy Act of 1978 (RFPA) imposes limitations and legal obligations on financial institutions prior to disclosing customer's financial records to federal authorities.[19] Similar to the GLBA, the RFPA requires notice be provided to a customer when a request is made by federal authorities seeking the customer's financial records. Customers must also be afforded the opportunity to object to any disclosure of their records by a financial institution to federal authorities.[20]

At the US state level, the California Consumer Privacy Act of 2018, as amended by the California Privacy Rights Act of 2020 (CCPA),[21] is generally considered to be the most comprehensive data privacy law in the US. The CCPA has many similarities to GPDR. For example, the CCPA is designed to protect "personal information" (the CCPA corollary to the GDPR's personal data). The CCPA defines "personal information" to include "any information that directly or indirectly identifies, describes, or can reasonably link to a particular California resident consumer or household.[22] Another similarity between the GDPR and CCPA is the scope of consumer protections and compliance obligations. For example, businesses in California subject to the CCPA must provide notice, access, and disclosure, including details regarding third-party disclosures or sales, of an individual's personal information.[23] The CCPA also provides individuals with the "right to be forgotten,"[24] subject to certain limitations, which is comparable to GDPR's right to erasure.[25]

Other states—including Colorado, Connecticut, Florida, Indiana, Texas, Utah, and Virginia—passed data privacy laws sharing similarities to the CCPA, but with unique, state-specific thresholds and regulatory requirements. For the purposes of this chapter, we will focus our analysis on the CCPA, given the law's comprehensiveness and its role as a legislative template for consideration and modification by other states.

---

16. Businesses must take into account all the facts and circumstances of its financial activities to determine if it is "significantly engaged" in financial activities, FTC, *supra* note 14.
17. Examples of relevant financial activities that may place a business within the ambit of the Privacy Rule include lending, exchanging, transferring, or safeguarding money or securities, brokering loans, servicing loans, debt collecting, providing financial, investment, or economic advisory services, etc.
18. FTC, "Protecting Consumer Privacy and Security," *Privacy and Security Enforcement*, https://www.ftc.gov/news-events/topics/protecting-consumer-privacy-security/privacy-security-enforcement.
19. FDIC, "Chapter VIII. Privacy—Right to Financial Privacy Act," *FDIC Consumer Compliance Examination Manual* (Jun. 2006).
20. *Id.*
21. Cal. Civ. Code §§ 1798.100 - 1798.199.100.
22. Cal Civ. Code § 1798.140(o).
23. Cal. Civ. Code §§ 1798.100, 1798.110, 1798.115, and 1798.130.
24. Also referred to as the "right to deletion," Cal. Civ. Code § 1798.105.
25. Council Regulation 2016/679, art. 17, 2016 O.J. (L119) (EU).

State-Based Privacy Regimes[26]

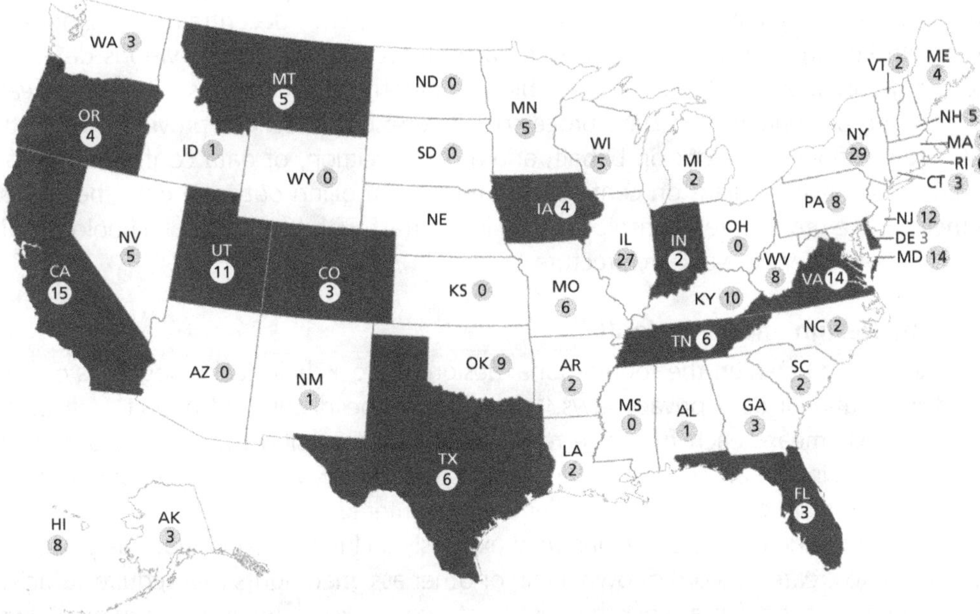

The above figure shows the states in color that have passed 'modern' privacy laws like GDPR and CCPA as well as a count per state of privacy related bills introduced in their latest sessions.

PRACTICE TIP

Prior to subjecting your organization to the regulatory requirements of the CCPA, determine if your organization is exempt from the CCPA's jurisdictional orbit. For example, the CCPA exempts certain businesses and types of information regulated by other laws.

For example, information collected by financial institutions and financial services businesses subject to the GLBA or the California Financial Information Privacy Act (CalFIPA) is exempt from the auspices of the CCPA.

@BANKING.ON.BLOCKCHAIN

26. https://leginfo.legislature.ca.gov/faces/codes_displayText.xhtml?division=3.&part=4.&lawCode=CIV&title=1.81.5.

Shared Framework of Data Privacy Laws

A notable similarity shared by the data privacy laws in the US and EU is an adherence to a data protection framework that is inherently in conflict with decentralized technologies such as blockchain. This widely adopted data protection framework envisions data controllers (e.g., organizations) with the capability to determine the purposes for, and means of, processing personal data.[27] Data processors, referred to as service providers under the CCPA, are envisioned to work on behalf, and at the direction, of data controllers. A data protection framework reliant on centralized entities controlling both the data they collect and their service provider relationships stands in contrast with blockchain technology's distributed peer-to-peer network architecture.

Tension by Design and by Default

There is a tension between the foundational design of blockchain technologies as existing US and international data privacy laws.[28] Specifically, the distributed aspect of a blockchain essentially means each full node responsible for processing transactions and building the blockchain has access to the blockchain transaction data.[29] This means, in many instances, there is no centralized controller of data entered into the blockchain, including personal data. In addition, blockchains may expressly include personal data as payload if they attempt to create a record of ownership or other assigned rights that require sufficient identifying information.[30] If a blockchain is structured in such a manner, it could very well make the blockchain subject to a data privacy law such as the GDPR, CCPA, GLBA, or the litany of state-based privacy laws in the US.

Bitcoin is said to be pseudonymous, meaning it has been de-identified by "replacing direct identifiers with a pseudonym, such as a randomly generated value."[31] However, it is unclear that bitcoin and other blockchains can meet the strict definitions of pseudonymous data under privacy laws. Once attributed to an individual through various means, a lifetime of pseudonymous transactions can become public knowledge and linkable to that individual. Applications have been developed to monitor the communications between nodes on a blockchain, which can then link transactions and specific internet protocol addresses. In addition, cryptocurrency wallet software can be subjected to a forensic analysis, even without the passphrases or keys that are typically necessary to access and use a crypto wallet.

Data Subject Rights in the Context of Blockchain

The tensions between blockchain technology and various data privacy laws becomes even more apparent in light of the statutory and regulatory rights afforded to data subjects seeking to modify or delete any personal information of the data subject maintained or shared by a data controller.

---

27. Through the collection, use, and management of personal data provided to data controllers by data subjects.
28. CMS, *supra* note 3.
29. *Id.*
30. Panel for the Future of Science and Technology, *Blockchain and the General Data Protection Regulation*, Eur. Parl. (July 2019), https://www.europarl.europa.eu/RegData/etudes/STUD/2019/634445/EPRS_STU(2019)634445_EN.pdf.
31. "Pseudonymization," *Glossary – Computer Security Resource Center*, NIST, https://csrc.nist.gov/glossary/term/pseudonymization.

Both the CCPA and GDPR afford data subjects various rights when it comes to the collection, processing, storage, and sharing of their personal data. For example, data subjects—under both the CCPA and GDPR, possess the right to request that a data controller (typically an organization) correct and/or delete any personal data maintained by the controller pertaining to the data subject.

These rights create significant compliance challenges for blockchain-based technologies due to the core architecture of the technology. As mentioned, by design, blockchains are not easily modifiable. This is because, once recorded, the data in any given block typically cannot be altered retroactively without alteration of all subsequent blocks. Even if, arguendo, deletion of a private key or the encryption of payload data were contemplated, it creates compliance difficulties with a data subject's right to correction. Blockchains featuring recordkeeping tools, such as smart contracts, could potentially address updates and data modifications by recording additional transactions. However, these later transactions would not technically delete data previously stored on the blockchain.

Data Minimization and Storage Limitation Principle in the Context of Blockchain

In addition to the right to correct and/or delete personal data, other thorny regulatory requirements for blockchain contained in the GDPR and CCPA are adherence to the principles of data minimization and storage limitation. In regard to the data minimization principle, it obligates data controllers—while collecting, using, sharing, and retaining the personal information of data subjects—to be "reasonably necessary and proportionate" to achieve the purposes for which the personal information was collected.[32] Blockchain technologies, by design, will encounter difficulties achieving compliance with such a principle because most blockchains feature a plurality of nodes, each of which stores the entire blockchain. The automatic replication of blocks containing personal information across all nodes could be considered a further sharing of personal information that likely is not necessary to achieve the purpose for which the personal information was collected (e.g., in the context of a particular financial transaction, degree verification, and so forth). Basically, the sharing of the private information is necessary at least once for verification purposes, but the continued replication of such personal information across all nodes is not.

The storage limitation principle effectively prohibits organizations from retaining personal information for longer than is reasonably necessary to accomplish the disclosed purpose for which the personal information was collected.[33] Once again, this creates inherent conflict with traditional blockchain technologies since they are designed to be permanent and immutable ledgers. By design, they retain every block of information added to the chain.

A straightforward method for blockchain users to navigate data privacy laws and regulations predicated on the collection, use, storage, and sharing of personal data is to implement protocols to avoid inputting personal data on a blockchain. However, such a method is rife with pitfalls and practical challenges due to the broad definitions for "personal data"

32. Council Regulation 2016/679, art. 5(1), 2016 O.J. (L119) (EU); Cal. Civ. Code § 1798.100(a)(1)-(3).
33. *See* Council Regulation 2016/679, art. 5(1), 2016 O.J. (L119) (EU); Cal. Civ. Code § 1798.100(a)(3).

and "personal information" across various regimes. Attempting to avoid the use of personal data in blockchain transactions also poses significant hurdles for blockchains using public-private key encryption to manage transactions among individuals.

The inherent tensions described in this section raise the open question as to whether standard on-chain storage blockchain models can ever fully achieve compliance with the GDPR, CCPA, and other data privacy regimes.

Data Privacy Framework Options for Blockchain

Despite the tensions and compliance challenges associated with applying data privacy laws, there remain options for consideration aimed at trying to harmonize blockchain technology with the regulatory requirements set forth in the GDPR, CCPA, and other data privacy regimes.

For example, the French data protection authority *Commission Nationale de l'informatique et des Libertés* (CNIL) issued guidance applying the data privacy framework of the GDPR to blockchain transactions. The CNIL guidance states that blockchain participants with full writing rights to enter transactions on a blockchain, and to send the data for validation to miners, are considered data controllers for the purposes of assessing a blockchain transaction under the GDPR.[34] The CNIL guidance also deems blockchain accessors who can retain full copies of a blockchain, but have read-only rights, to be data controllers.[35] In addition, the CNIL guidance considers blockchain miners capable of validating transactions and creating new blocks to be data controllers in the context of the GDPR.

The rationale provided by the CNIL for treating these blockchain participants as data controllers is the fact that they determine the purposes and means for processing personal data entered on a blockchain. Hence, they meet the GDPR's definition of data controller.[36] In contrast, the CNIL guidance advises that accessors and miners to a blockchain that do not make such determinations are not considered controllers. In addition, the CNIL guidance notes that blockchain participants entering personal data on a block for strictly personal purposes would not be considered controllers due to the GDPR's "household exception."[37] Nevertheless, if a third party acts on a participant's behalf, the CNIL advises they may be considered processors and would need to enter into data processing agreements to comply with the GDPR.[38]

"Off-Chain" Model for Addressing Privacy in Blockchain

Along with attempting to conform current data privacy frameworks to blockchain participants, another pathway for addressing the tension between data privacy regulations and blockchain is to consider the utilization of an "off-chain" model for blockchain transactions. For context, a traditional "on-chain" blockchain model strings together each block and adds them to a

---

34. CNIL, Blockchain and the GDPR: Solutions for a Responsible Use of the Blockchain in the Context of Personal Data (Oct. 29, 2018), https://www.cnil.fr/en/blockchain-and-gdpr-solutions-responsible-use-blockchain-context-personal-data.
35. *Id.*
36. Council Regulation 2016/679, art. 4(7), 2016 O.J. (L119) (EU).
37. Council Regulation 2016/679, art. 2(2)(c), 2016 O.J. (L119) (EU).
38. CNIL *supra* note 34.

chain.[39] An off-chain model, in contrast, system stores information off-chain in a third-party storage node while still retaining a digital ledger in the form of a blockchain.[40] The location of the stored data, along with its hash, would be retained on the blockchain. The hash would act as a fingerprint (i.e., a unique identifier) of the data and evidence that the data is stored on the third-party storage node.[41] This would afford the option to delete or modify personal information stored within the third-party node without directly impacting the blockchain. As a result, modifying personal information within the storage node would not require modification of the entire blockchain.[42] Furthermore, with the off-chain model, personal information contained within the storage node is not automatically replicated across every node. Rather, the personal information is confined to the node designated for storage.[43]

If both the utilization of blockchain technology and the adoption of data privacy regulations continue to proliferate, an off-chain model of blockchain holds promise as a proverbial "middle ground" for organizations engaging in blockchain transactions that must also comply with applicable data privacy laws and regulations.

II. Cybersecurity Considerations in the Utilization of Blockchain Technology

The US Cybersecurity and Infrastructure Security Agency (CISA) defines cybersecurity as "the art of protecting networks, devices, and data from unauthorized access or criminal use and the practice of ensuring confidentiality, integrity, and availability of information."[44] In effect, cybersecurity encompasses the mechanisms used to insure the confidentiality, integrity, and availability of information, including information utilized in the course of blockchain transactions.[45]

Assessing the Cybersecurity Landscape

Before delving into the interplay between cybersecurity and blockchain technology, it is necessary to survey the current cybersecurity landscape, including relevant regulatory authorities, agencies, and laws.

In Section I of this chapter, we discussed the GDPR in the EU and its role in regulating data privacy. On the cybersecurity end of the spectrum, the European Union Agency for Cybersecurity (ENISA)[46] is tasked with supporting EU member states, businesses, and institutions related to cybersecurity. Specifically, ENISA is responsible for establishing a cybersecurity certification framework for products and services, increasing operational cooperation

39. Yaga et al., *supra* note 1.
40. Christian Liu et al., *A Tool for Moving Blockchain Computations Off-Chain*, BSCI '21: Proceedings of the 3rd ACM Int'l. Symposium on Blockchain and Secure Infrastructure (May 29, 2021), https://dl.acm.org/doi/10.1145/3457337.3457848.
41. *Id.*
42. *Id.*
43. *Id.*
44. *What Is Cybersecurity?*, Cybersecurity & Infrastructure Security Agency, https://www.cisa.gov/news-events/news/what-cybersecurity.
45. CMS, *supra* note 3.
46. *See* ENISA: European Union Agency for Cybersecurity, https://www.enisa.europa.eu/.

to help EU Member States with handling cybersecurity incidents, promoting security best practices, and supporting the coordination of the EU in the event of a major cross-border cyber incident. There is also the Security of Network and Information Systems Directive (NIS2 Directive),[47] which was proposed by the European Commission and implemented by all EU countries as part of a larger EU Cybersecurity strategy.[48] The NIS2 Directive requires "essential entities"[49] and "important entities"[50] to take technical, operational, and organizational measures to manage risks to their network and information systems and to minimize the impact of potential incidents on users of the entity's service.[51] The NIS2 Directive also requires covered entities to implement baseline security measures to address specific risks and implement policies on risk analysis and information security, incident handling, business continuity, supply chain security, information systems development practices including vulnerability disclosure, cryptography, encryption, and multifactor authentication.

Another notable EU regulation is the Digital Operational Resilience Act (DORA), which creates a binding, comprehensive information and communication technology (ICT) risk management framework for the EU financial sector. DORA[52] establishes technical standards that financial entities and their critical third-party technology service providers must implement in their ICT systems by January 17, 2025. For example, covered entities are required to, among other things, conduct continuous risk assessments of their ICT systems, document and classify cyberthreats, establish business continuity and disaster recovery plans addressing different cyber risk scenarios, establish systems to monitor, manage, log, classify, and report ICT-related incidents, and document dependencies between assets, systems, processes, and providers.[53]

In the US, laws and regulations addressing cybersecurity share a similar patchwork model previously discussed for domestic data privacy laws. There is an array of laws, regulations, and policies at both the federal and state levels, many of which are enforceable on a sector-specific or industry-specific basis.[54]

---

47. Directive 2022/2555, of the European Parliament and Council of 14 Dec. 2022 on measures for a high common level of cybersecurity across the Union, amending Regulation (EU) No 910/2014 and Directive (EU) 2018/1972, and repealing Directive (EU) 2016/1148 (NIS 2 Directive), 2022 O.J. (L 333) (80) (EU).

48. Briefing on EU Legislation in Progress: The NIS2 Directive (Feb. 2023), https://www.europarl.europa.eu/RegData/etudes/BRIE/2021/689333/EPRS_BRI(2021)689333_EN.pdf.

49. Includes, but is not limited to, entities in the following sectors: banking and financial market, digital infrastructure, energy, health, public administration, space, transport, and water.

50. Includes, but is not limited to, entities in the following sectors: digital providers such as social networks and search engines, postal and courier services, manufacturing, research, and waste management.

51. Directive 2022/2555, *supra* note 47.

52. Applies to all financial institutions in the EU, including traditional financial entities such as banks, investment firms, and credit institutions, along with non-traditional entities, such as crypto asset service providers and crowdfunding platforms. DORA also applies to third-party service providers that supply financial firms with information and communication technology systems and services (e.g., cloud service providers and data centers) and businesses providing critical third-party information services, such as crediting rating services and data analytics providers.

53. *Digital Operation Resilience Act ('DORA')*, AIMA, https://www.aima.org/regulation/keytopics/digital-operational-resilience-act.html.

54. An example of a sector-specific cybersecurity regulation is the breach notification rules contained in the Health Insurance Portability and Accountability Act (HIPAA), which applies to health care providers, health plans, health care clearinghouses, and, in some instances, business associates of these businesses called covered entities.

At the federal level, there is Executive Order 14028 (Improving the Nation's Cybersecurity)[55] and the Strengthening American Cybersecurity Act of 2022 (including its companion Cyber Incident Reporting for Critical Infrastructure Act).[56] Of particular relevance to financial institutions is the Sarbanes–Oxley Act of 2002 (SOX)[57] which applies to all publicly traded companies in the US, wholly owned subsidiaries, accounting companies that perform audits on other businesses, and foreign companies conducting business in the US. In order to comply with SOX, covered companies are required to have policies and procedures in place focused on preventing, detecting, and disclosing material cybersecurity risks and incidents.[58] Covered companies also need to retain compliance records reflecting the utilization of data safeguards and procedures such as quality access management, preventative security measures, and redundant and secure backups.[59] SOX also requires covered companies to maintain security systems capable of detecting data breaches and there must be a communication plan in place for notifying leadership and investors of identified breaches.[60]

Another relevant federal law for financial institutions is the Bank Secrecy Act (BSA), also known as the Currency and Foreign Transactions Reporting Act. The BSA was enacted to help prevent financial institutions from laundering money, either willfully or through force via a cyberattack. The Office of the Comptroller of the Currency (OCC) oversees compliance with the BSA and conducts regular audits to verify the legitimacy of currency transactions. Financial institutions accepting money from customers—including national banks, agencies of foreign banks, federal saving associations, etc.—must comply with the BSA.

At the state level, data breach notification statutes have been enacted in all 50 states, the District of Columbia, Guam, Puerto Rico, and the Virgin Islands.[61] In addition, some states have implemented standalone cybersecurity laws, including Massachusetts and New York. For example, the Massachusetts Standards for the Protection of Personal Information of Residents of the Commonwealth (Massachusetts Cybersecurity Law), requires all individuals owning or licensing personal information regarding residents of Massachusetts to develop, implement, and maintain a comprehensive information security program.

Similar to Massachusetts Cybersecurity Law, the data security provisions of the New York SHIELD Act impose legal obligations on organizations owning or licensing private information of New York residents. Covered organizations are required to develop, implement, and maintain cybersecurity programs based on assessed risk, ongoing monitoring, incident response planning, and limited data retention and disposal.

Multiple state-level regulatory entities have also adopted sector-specific cybersecurity regulations. For example, the New York Department of Financial Services oversees compliance with, and enforces, a series of cybersecurity rules that impose security requirements on

---

55. *Executive Order on Improving the Nation's Cybersecurity*, Cybersecurity & Infrastructure Security Agency, https://www.cisa.gov/topics/cybersecurity-best-practices/executive-order-improving-nations-cybersecurity.
56. S. 3600, 117th Cong. (2022).
57. H.R. 3763, 107th Cong. (2002) (enacted).
58. Stephen Wagner and Lee Dittmar, *The Unexpected Benefits of Sarbanes-Oxley*, Harv. Bus. Rev. (Apr. 2006), https://hbr.org/2006/04/the-unexpected-benefits-of-sarbanes-oxley.
59. *Id.*
60. *Id.*
61. *2022 Security Breach Legislation*, NCSL (Sept. 2022), https://www.ncsl.org/technology-and-communication/2022-security-breach-legislation.

regulated entities.[62] Those security requirements include encryption, multi-factor authentication, breach notification, and so forth.[63]

PRACTICE TIP

Organizations, particularly financial institutions, need to thoroughly assess and evaluate which laws and regulations - whether international, federal, and/or state level - they are subject to and what compliance obligations are imposed under applicable law.

In many instances, financial institutions are subject to a series of complex rules and regulations that may involve overlapping reporting obligations and security requirements.

@BANKING.ON.BLOCKCHAIN

Cybersecurity Concepts Relevant to Blockchain Technology

The World Economic Forum identifies several cybersecurity concepts relevant to blockchain.[64] These concepts include confidentiality, integrity, and availability—which is oftentimes referred to as the CIA Triad[65] in the context of cybersecurity—along with security by design and by default. Below we discuss each cybersecurity concept and its relevance to the utilization of blockchain.

- Confidentiality: As a security concept, confidentiality means sensitive information will not be disclosed to unauthorized individuals, entities, or processes.[66] Different implementations of a blockchain offer varying degrees of confidentiality, but the general rule is that a blockchain might offer only a comparable level of confidentiality as a traditional database. In fact, public blockchains generally offer less assurance of confidentiality.[67]
- Integrity: As a security concept, integrity focuses on guarding against improper information modification or destruction, and includes ensuring information non-repudiation

62. N.Y. Codes R. & Regs. tit. 23, § 500.
63. *Id.*
64. WEF and Hitachi, *Inclusive Deployment of Blockchain for Supply Chains: Part 5* (Dec. 2019), https://www3.weforum.org/docs/WEF_Inclusive_Deployment_of_Blockchain_for_Supply_Chains_Part_5.pdf.
65. Jennifer Cawthra et al., *Data Integrity: Detecting and Responding to Ransomware and Other Destructive Events*, NIST Special Publication 1800-26A (Dec. 2020), https://www.nccoe.nist.gov/publication/1800-26/VolA/index.html.
66. Richard Kissel, ed., Glossary of Key Information Security Terms, NIST (Jul. 3, 2019), http://nvlpubs.nist.gov/nistpubs/ir/2013/NIST.IR.7298r2.pdf.
67. WEF and Hitachi, *supra* note 64.

and authenticity.[68] Blockchains typically possess built-in characteristics of immutability and traceability, which provide organizations with a means to ensure data integrity. Nevertheless, considering data is likely to be transmitted from an organization's source system to a blockchain, organizations must ensure the exchange channels are secure as this is no doubt a point of attack and entry for attackers.[69]

- Availability: As a security concept, availability is the assurance of "timely and reliable access to, and use of, information."[70] The decentralization and peer-to-peer characteristics of blockchain technology provide a stronger shield to combat disruption, as opposed to conventional distributed application architectures (e.g., client-server). Nevertheless, blockchains can be subject to denial-of-service (DoS) attacks.[71] As a result, adequate protection measures remain necessary for blockchain transactions, both at the network and application level.[72]
- Security by design and by default: This concept means security is embedded in the foundation of a system and activated by default.[73] Security by design and by default carries significant implications for blockchain, such as embedding update features or kill switches into smart contracts and taking steps to ensure security is considered at the beginning of the life cycle of a transaction.

Blockchain Concepts Relevant to Cybersecurity

The blockchain concepts of decentralization, consensus mechanisms, smart contracts, endpoints, and key management are all highly relevant to cybersecurity.[74] Each blockchain concept is discussed below.

- Decentralization: As a concept, decentralization is the transfer of authority away from a central source of power.[75] Security governance has traditionally been a centralized process, so decision-making can be executed quickly in critical situations. Decentralized governance is a paradigm shift that organizations transitioning to blockchain will need to navigate. The direct consequences of decentralization are decreased control over systems and oversight, as well as increased difficulty ensuring physical security and shutting down a system if need be. For example, ensuring the security of the DLT nodes may prove difficult when organizations may not even know which nodes are part of the distributed infrastructure. In addition to decreasing the control of an organization, decentralization increases the attack surface of ledgers—given that, in most blockchain types, all of the nodes hold the same version of the ledger.

---

68. Kissel, *supra* note 66.
69. Eric Piscini, David Dalton, and Lory Kehoe, *Blockchain and Cyber Security*, Deloitte (2017), https://www2.deloitte.com/tr/en/pages/technology-media-and-telecommunications/articles/blockchain-and-cyber.html.
70. Kissel, supra *note* 66, 68.
71. Understanding Denial-of-Service Attacks, CISA (Feb. 1, 2021), https://www.cisa.gov/news-events/news/understanding-denial-service-attacks.
72. *Id.*
73. WEF and Hitachi, *supra* note 64, 67.
74. *Id.*
75. *Id.*

- Consensus mechanisms: These mechanisms enable records to be added to the distributed ledger in a blockchain.[76] There are multiple consensus mechanisms that try to solve complex trade-offs, such as scalability, collusion resistance, computational cost, and real-timeliness. Vulnerabilities in such consensus mechanisms are significant as they could compromise the integrity of the blockchain which would thereby compromise trust in the system. Different consensus mechanisms lead to different requirements and levels of security. For example, some blockchains use multiple mechanisms to reach consensus. Security requirements must also consider these in conjunction with each other, a weaknesses may be amplified in this context.
- Smart contracts: These types of contracts consist of computerized protocols that automatically execute the terms of a contract upon a blockchain once predefined conditions are met.[77] A smart contract is a double-edged sword—the contents are visible to all members of the blockchain, meaning that hackers can freely search for vulnerabilities. Patching smart contracts is not as straightforward as patching a traditional piece of software, which is why secure coding and auditing are a must. However, the combined shortage of cybersecurity and blockchain talents makes securing smart contracts a real challenge.[78]
- Endpoints: In effect, endpoints consist of the hardware and software elements used to access a blockchain.[79] Due to the utilization of cryptographic algorithms in blockchain technology, blockchain users are generally required to create and manage cryptographic keys used to authenticate transactions and ensure a record is associated with a legitimate data input agent. When a cryptographic key is compromised, a malicious record can be faultily associated with a user. Alternatively, a stolen secret key could be used to manipulate data used to determine who is liable for penalties. Ultimately, the use of cryptographic keys is relatively commonplace by blockchain participant. As a result, the securitization of these keys is critically important across blockchains.

Examples of Blockchain Cyberattacks

While blockchain technologies endeavor to produce a tamper-proof ledger of transactions, blockchain networks are not impervious to cyberattacks and other malicious activities. Bad actors still retain the capacity to manipulate known vulnerabilities in blockchain infrastructure.

Examples of cyberattacks deployed against blockchain networks include phishing, routing, 51 percent attacks, Sybil, and endpoint vulnerabilities. Each type of attack is described below, in addition to steps organizations can take to shield themselves.[80]

---

76. *Id.*
77. Stuart D. Levi and Alex B. Lipton, *An Introduction to Smart Contracts and Their Potential and Inherent Limitations*, Harv. L. Sch. F. Corp. Gov. (May 26, 2018), https://corpgov.law.harvard.edu/2018/05/26/an-introduction-to-smart-contracts-and-their-potential-and-inherent-limitations/.
78. *Id.*
79. WEF and Hitachi, *supra* note 64.
80. *Id.*

Phishing Attacks

Phishing is an attack focused on attaining a user's credentials.[81] Bad actors send emails to wallet key owners designed to look as though they are from a legitimate source. The emails typically ask wallet key owners for their credentials using fake hyperlinks. If a phishing attack is successful, a bad actor would gain access to a user's credentials and thereby have access to sensitive information of the user and the blockchain network.

For example, cryptocurrency exchange firm Coinbase was the target of a successful phishing attack that led to a leak of employee personal data.[82] The phishing attack against Coinbase began when employees received SMS messages requesting they urgently log into their official email accounts to receive an important message. An employee inadvertently clicked on the malicious link and entered their email ID and password on a fraudulent login page. When the attackers obtained the user's credentials, they attempted to gain remote access to the Coinbase network. Twilio, a customer engagement platform, was subjected to the same type of phishing attack, and like Coinbase, employees inadvertently shared their login credentials to attackers leading to a data breach.[83]

PRACTICE TIP

To prevent phishing attacks:

- Improve browser security by installing a verified add-on to notify you about unsafe websites.
- Improve device security by installing malicious link detection software as well as dependable antivirus software.
- Be weary of communications asking for sensitive information, such as wallet secrets or financial information.
- Don't click on the link until you have thoroughly reviewed it. Instead of clicking on the links, enter the address into your browser.
- Avoid open Wi-Fi networks when using an electronic wallet or other important banking transactions.
- Make sure your system and software are up to date.

@BANKING.ON.BLOCKCHAIN

Routing Attacks

Routing attacks are cyberattacks directed at an internet service provider to reduce their operational capacity or prevent users from accessing a blockchain network. An attacker can divide a network into two (or more) distinct components using routing attacks. The attacker

---

81. *Phishing*, NIST, https://www.nist.gov/itl/smallbusinesscyber/guidance-topic/phishing.
82. Akshaya Asokan, *Crypto Exchange Coinbase Details SMS Phishing Attacks*, BankInfo Security (Feb. 21, 2023), https://www.bankinfosecurity.com/crypto-exchange-coinbase-details-sms-phishing-attacks-a-21274.
83. Mathew J. Schwartz, *Twilio Customer Data Breached via SMS Phishing of Employees*, BankInfo Security (Aug. 8, 2022), https://www.bankinfosecurity.com/twilio-customer-data-breached-via-sms-phishing-employees-a-19734.

blocks the communication between nodes in a certain chain and the ones that are outside of it. This way, the attacker creates parallel blockchains. When the attack ends, all blocks mined within the smaller chain are discarded. Any transactions and earnings of the attacked miners would be discarded as well.[84]

PRACTICE TIP

To prevent routing attacks:

- **Implement secure routing protocols (with certificates).**
- **Use data encryption.**
- **Change passwords regularly; use strong passwords.**
- **Educate yourself and your employees about the hazards associated with information security.**

@BANKING.ON.BLOCKCHAIN

Exploitation of Endpoint Vulnerabilities

The vulnerability of endpoints is another important security concern in blockchain security.[85] The blockchain network's endpoint is where users interact with the blockchain: on electronic devices such as computers and mobile phones. Hackers can observe user behavior and target devices to steal the user's key. This is one of the most visible blockchain security issues.

PRACTICE TIP

To prevent the exploitation of endpoint vulnerabilities:

- **Do not save blockchain keys on your computer or mobile phone as text files.**
- **Download and install antivirus software for your electronic devices.**
- **Review the system regularly, keeping track of the time, location, and device access.**

@BANKING.ON.BLOCKCHAIN

84. Howard Poston, *Attacking the Blockchain Network*, Infosec (Oct. 13, 2020), https://resources.infosecinstitute.com/topics/blockchain-security-overview/attacking-the-network/.

85. Jae Hyung Lee, *Systematic Approach to Analyzing Security and Vulnerabilities of Blockchain Systems* (MIT Sloan School of Management, Working Paper No. 2019-05, 2019), https://web.mit.edu/smadnick/www/wp/2019-05.pdf.

51 Percent Attacks

Blockchain mining requires a significant amount of computing power, especially for large-scale public blockchains. However, if a miner, or a group of miners, develops a sufficient amount of resources, there is the possibility they could attain more than 50 percent of a blockchain network's mining power. In this scenario, a miner, or group of miners, with more than 50 percent of the power would mean effectively possessing control over the entire blockchain ledger. With that control comes the ability to manipulate the ledger. As a result, a 51 percent attack occurs when a single individual, group of individuals, or an organization seizes control of an entire ledger.[86] Once 51 percent control is attained, a bad actor can modify the order of transactions and prevent them from being confirmed. In addition, they would have the authority to reverse previously completed transactions, resulting in double-spending. These attacks are more likely to occur in a blockchain's early stage and are a risk associated with public blockchains. For example, Ethereum Classic—an open-source, blockchain-based, decentralized computing platform and distributed cryptocurrency supporting smart contract functionality—has suffered multiple 51 percent attacks. One attack led to the reorganization of over 7,000 blocks, which is the equivalent of two days' worth of mining.[87]

PRACTICE TIP

To prevent a 51 percent attack:

- **Improve mining pool monitoring.**
- **Make certain that the hash rate is higher.**
- **Avoid using proof-of-work consensus procedures.**

@BANKING.ON.BLOCKCHAIN

Sybil Attacks

The name Sybil refers to the titular character in Flora Rheta Scheiber's novel[88] about an individual diagnosed with a multiple identity disorder. Similarly, a Sybil attack involves bad actors creating and using a number of false network nodes to flood the blockchain network and crash the system. Additionally, in a Sybil attack, bad actors can use the false network nodes to try and secure majority consensus in order to disrupt the blockchain. This is why bad actors typically deploy a 51 percent attack immediately following a Sybil attack.[89]

86. *Id.*

87. Zack Voell, *Ethereum Classic Hit by Third 51% Attack in a Month*, CoinDesk (Aug. 29, 2020), https://www.coindesk.com/markets/2020/08/29/ethereum-classic-hit-by-third-51-attack-in-a-month/.

88. Flora Rheta Schreiber, Sybil (2009).

89. Amanda Davenport, Sachin Shetty, and Xueping Liang, *Attack Surface Analysis of Permissioned Blockchain Platforms for Smart Cities*, Nat'l Sci. Found. (2018), https://par.nsf.gov/servlets/purl/10083311.

PRACTICE TIP

To prevent a Sybil attack:

- Use appropriate consensus algorithms.
- While these algorithms may not completely prevent these attacks, they make them impossible for the hacker to carry out.
- Monitor other nodes' behavior and check for the nodes that are only forwarding blocks from one user.

@BANKING.ON.BLOCKCHAIN

Taking steps to prevent cyberattacks and, equally important, being proactive in mitigating the extent of damage in the wake of an attack is critically important due to the potential liability associated with a data breach. A relevant example is the class action lawsuit filed against Atomic Wallet, a noncustodial cryptocurrency wallet that suffered a data breach impacting at least 5,500 crypto accounts on the platform and leading to $100 million in losses.[90] The class action suit alleges Atomic Wallet failed to provide any information to investors regarding the hack and failed to report the incident to law enforcement.[91]

Another example is a class action lawsuit filed against Coinbase, a prominent crypto exchange. The lawsuit, filed in the US District Court for the Northern District of Georgia, alleged the crypto exchange failed to establish and maintain adequate cybersecurity measures causing investors to lose access to their wallet and account, the assets and investments in those accounts, along with sensitive personally identifiable information stored in Coinbase accounts.[92]

Risk Considerations in the Context of Blockchain

As indicated above, organizations that use blockchain technology are exposed to risks similar to those associated with traditional business processes while introducing nuances for which businesses need to consider. In this section, we review the strategic, financial, information security, and business continuity risks generally associated with the utilization of blockchain technology.[93]

- **Strategic risk:** Adopting blockchain technology, or engaging in a blockchain transaction, can raise strategic concerns and questions for an organization, such as of defining the applicable value proposition, brand and reputation management, and

90. Helen Partz, *Atomic Wallet Faces Lawsuit over $100M Crypto Hack Losses: Report*, CoinDesk (Aug. 23, 2023), https://cointelegraph.com/news/crypto-atomic-wallet-faces-class-action-over-100m-crypto-hack-losses.
91. *Id.*
92. George Kattula v. COINBASE GLOBAL, INC., et al,, Civil Action 1:22-CV-3250-TWT (N.D. Ga. Jul. 6, 2023).
93. WEF and Hitachi, *supra* note 64.

handling change management.[94] Furthermore, given the peer-to-peer nature of blockchain technology, it is important for an organization to determine the right network to participate in, as their business strategy could be impacted by the different entities participating on the blockchain.

- **Financial risk:** The deployment of blockchain technology is typically to help facilitate transfers of value.[95] As a result, a variety of financial risks needs to be considered while designing blockchain applications, platforms, and infrastructure. Risks such as the potential for financial loss, transaction settlement finality, consortium funding-related risks, and intellectual property protection issues need to be analyzed and assessed. In addition, there are multiple accounting and reporting challenges that should be considered when depending on blockchain-based applications for financial transactions and for information used in financial reporting.
- **Information security risk:** Blockchain technology has the capacity to provide for greater transactional security, but it does not provide account and/or wallet security. The distributed database and the cryptographically sealed ledger prevent any corruption of data. However, the value stored in an account is still susceptible for an account takeover by a bad actor. In addition, as discussed, there are cybersecurity risks to the blockchain network if a malicious actor takes over 51 percent of the network nodes for a duration of time, especially in a closed permissions framework.
- **Business continuity risk:** Blockchain technologies are generally resilient due to the redundancy resulting from the distributed nature of the technology. However, the business processes built on blockchains may be vulnerable to technology and operational failures as well as cyberattacks. Organizations need to have a robust business continuity plan and governance framework to mitigate such risks.

Five-Step Plan for Managing Blockchain Cybersecurity Risks

The prior section identified key security risks organizations will likely confront in the utilization of blockchain technology. This section provides a blueprint[96] for how to manage and mitigate identified risks.

Step 1: Define the Security Objectives of Your Organization

Defining security objectives serves as a foundational element of an effective risk assessment. As a result, identifying and calibrating security objectives must be done first since the identified objectives will inform the remaining steps.

94. "Risk Factors," *Blockchain Toolkit*, WEF, https://widgets.weforum.org/blockchain-toolkit/risk-factors/index.html.
95. *Id.*
96. "Risk Management," *Blockchain Toolkit*, WEF, https://widgets.weforum.org/blockchain-toolkit/cybersecurity/index.html#blockchain-cybersecurity-risk-management.

PRACTICE TIP

Questions to ask that can help define relevant security objectives include the following:

- In light of the business model that will be supported by blockchain, what are the key security objectives to foster?
- Is confidentiality more or less important than availability?
- Should anonymity be guaranteed?

Which parts of the system must preserve data integrity other than a blockchain platform?

@BANKING.ON.BLOCKCHAIN

Step 2: Perform a Threat Assessment

Once security objectives are defined, the next step is to conduct a threat assessment. This assessment will aid an organization in understanding how the blockchain transaction or application could be vulnerable or susceptible to particular types of cyberattacks.[97] The threat assessment should consider and contemplate different scenarios ranging from human accidents to natural catastrophes and deliberate cyberattacks.

PRACTICE TIP

Differentiating among threats by categorizing them according to capabilities and intent is a good way to measure the potential for disruption. For example, a government agency may have capabilities, but no intent to attack a particular blockchain. In contrast, certain bad actors may be interested in harming the reputation of a particular organization but lack the ability to overcome certain security barriers.

@BANKING.ON.BLOCKCHAIN

Step 3: Perform a Vulnerability Assessment

Once a threat assessment is completed, the next step is to conduct a vulnerability assessment. This type of assessment aids a project team in better understanding and appreciating

97. *Id.*

aspects of the blockchain transaction or application solution that could be susceptible to attack and what weak spots could lead to adverse outcomes.[98]

PRACTICE TIP

Identifying such vulnerabilities can be challenging. Nevertheless, it is recommended organizations regularly perform penetration testing on all aspects of the blockchain solutions they deploy. In particular, attention needs to be paid to testing smart contracts. Defining a process early on to secure smart contract code is critical to reduce the vulnerabilities.

@BANKING.ON.BLOCKCHAIN

Step 4: Define Risk Probabilities

Once the vulnerability assessment is complete the next step is to define risk probabilities. Effectively defining risk probabilities allows for prioritization.[99] Risks emerge from the intersection of vulnerabilities and threats as defined in the previous steps. Prioritize risks by determining the likelihood of particular vulnerabilities intersecting with particular threats, and if that happens, determine the criticality of the impact. A highly impactful risk that is very unlikely to occur will be managed differently from a somewhat impactful risk that is likely to occur regularly.

Step 5: Decide What to Do with Each Risk

Once specific risks that may arise during the utilization of blockchain technology have been identified, the next step is to address each risk individually.[100] Below are specific strategies for managing particular risks:

- **Mitigate or reduce the risk.** Tackle the threat and/or the vulnerability directly to contain its impact. In the context of a blockchain transaction, containing impact is perhaps more challenging than with other technologies. This is why emphasis should be placed on reducing vulnerabilities and deterring threats. This strategy offers the best risk control but is generally costly. This strategy is generally recommended to address high and critical risks.

---

98. *Id.*
99. *Id.*
100. *Id.*

- **Accept the risk:** This strategy involves acknowledging the existence of the risk and appropriately budgeting for the risk, should it come to fruition. Though, such a strategy is best advised for low-to-medium risks.
- **Avoid the risk:** Consider re-working the approach in order to eliminate the specific security challenge entirely. In many instances, doing this will entail trade-offs and accepting the removal of certain functionalities or solution users.
- **Transfer the risk:** Consider involving a third party, such as an insurance company or an external service provider, to address the identified risk.

Takeaways

Privacy and cybersecurity remain significant concerns as more individuals and organizations utilize blockchain technology. While blockchain technology possesses promising features such as transparency and decentralization, it also has inherent challenges when it comes to protecting sensitive information, complying with current data privacy frameworks, and ensuring network security. However, with the development of privacy-enhancing technologies and robust cybersecurity measures, there remains the possibility that the issues and challenges discussed in this chapter can be remedied thereby making blockchain a secure and private platform for various applications.

Chapter 9
Rugpulls, Scams, and Fraud

Heidi Wilder

Introduction

The cryptocurrency industry is fast evolving. But as the technology evolves, so does the illicit activity. While many readers have heard of cryptocurrency being used for high profile illicit activity, such as terror finance, sanctions evasion, and dark markets, this activity remains relatively rare. Scams, however, are a more common and growing area of illicit activity in space.

This chapter provides an accessible overview for financial institutions with limited experience in the crypto realm, shedding light on traditional scams that have adapted to the crypto space, and newer threats unique to it.

The following diagram aims to help readers better understand the categories discussed below.

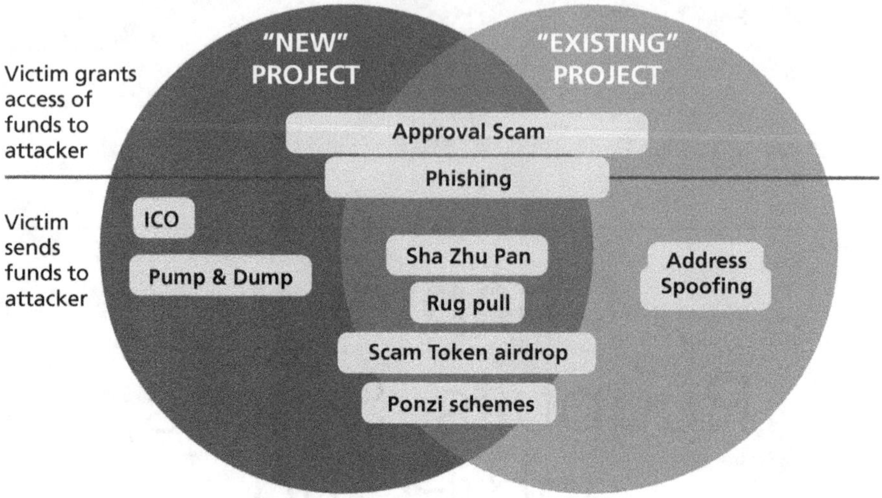

While some of the above terminology may appear novel, most of these categories are familiar scams that blockchain makes easier and irreversible.

Basic Phishing and Social Engineering

Definition and History

Phishing and social engineering are common scams that have found new life in the crypto world. These scams involve tricking individuals into divulging sensitive information through creating fraudulent webpages. (Phishing in this sense is not to be confused with spearphishing, which is a more targeted version of the tactic.)

How They Operate

Scammers create fake domains, projects, apps, or deploy malicious contracts, utilizing deceptive tactics to trick users into either revealing their private keys or passwords, or approving the use of their tokens.

Case Study: MEW and Fraudulent Bridges and Impersonating Friendlies

Private Key Phishing—MyEtherWallet

MyEtherWallet (MEW) used to be the primary Ethereum wallet of choice in 2018–2019. Its popularity was also a boon for scammers who created similar domains emulating MEW's actual URL. Because MEW required users to enter their private keys, scammers could easily swipe all user funds when victims fell for their scheme.

The scheme operates using the following the steps:

1. *Creation of Deceptive Site:* The attacker makes a fake website that looks like MyEtherWallet.
2. *Phishing Link Distribution:* The attacker sends messages to users or posts on social media with an urgent request, containing a link to the fake site.
3. *Social Engineering Tactics:* The messages trick users into clicking the link by creating a sense of urgency.

4. *User Clicks on the Phishing Link:* Users, thinking it's urgent, click the link and go to the fake site.
5. *Submission of Sensitive Information:* On the fake site, users are asked to enter private keys.
6. *Information Capture*: The attacker collects the entered private keys.
7. *Unauthorized Access and Fund Theft:* With stolen private keys, the attacker accesses the real Ethereum wallet of the victim, taking control of funds.

More recently, this same tactic has evolved to steal not only user funds but also non-fungible tokens (NFTs). Essentially, anything the user owns with that wallet.

Approval (Ice) Phishing—Lido Airdrop Scam

Lido is a popular decentralized app (dApp) that allows users to stake certain cryptocurrencies on validators and earn yield. In addition to its popularity, there have been multiple rumors and speculation around a potential additional token airdrop through which users of the dApp might receive valuable tokens in proportion to their usage of the dApp. This speculation also exists for other popular dApps such as Uniswap and Layer 2s (such as zSkync), many of which have experienced similar airdrop scams.

This scam follows a similar pattern to the MEW phishing example above, except for one key difference: rather than stealing private keys, the attacker goes after certain tokens the victim may hold. Because of the way some tokens are designed, victims may not even be aware of the theft taking place as there is no transaction on chain for them to check.

The scheme operates using the following the steps:

1. *Creation of Deceptive Site:* The attacker makes a fake website announcing a Lido token airdrop.
2. *Phishing Link Distribution:* The attacker sends messages to users or posts on social media with an urgent request, containing a link to the fake site.
3. *Social Engineering Tactics:* The message tricks users into clicking the link by creating a sense of urgency.
4. *User Clicks on the Phishing Link:* Users, thinking it's urgent, click the link and go to the fake site.
5. *Connect wallet:* On the fake site, users are asked to connect their wallets. This allows the scammers to see what tokens they have.
6. *Ask the victim to grant permission to tokens:* The scam website will then ask users to grant permission to certain tokens. Because granting permission does not appear as a transaction in the user's wallet interface, and thus does not show a change in the balance of the user's tokens, users may automatically approve the request. In addition, these permissions can even be obscured so the victim has no idea what they are giving permission for.
7. *Authorized Access and Fund Theft:* Once permission is provided by the user, the scammers access the victim's tokens to claw them out.

Address Spoofing

Though public wallet addresses are a random alphanumeric string, services exist that can sort through millions of random wallet address until they land on desirable combinations of letters and numbers. These are called vanity addresses. Generating your own vanity address, such as 0xc0ffee can be accomplished in a few minutes with the help of free and easy to use programs like Profanity.

Attackers leverage Profanity, not to make vanity addresses, but to mimic the first and last characters of a particular address a user has transacted with before in order to trick the user into sending funds to the spoofed address.

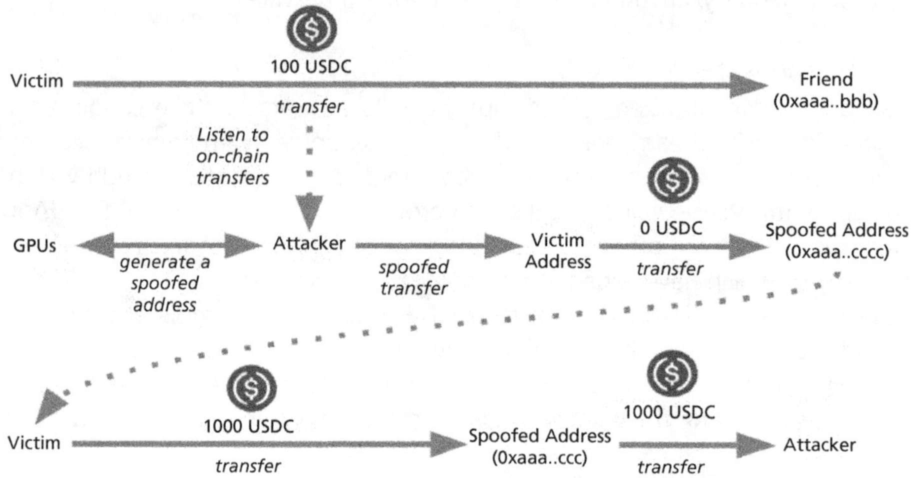

https://www.coinbase.com/blog/zero-transfer-phishing-part-1-attack-analysis

In an effort to simplify crypto addresses, wallets will often shorten a crypto address a user has sent to or received from to the first couple of characters and last couple of characters. As a result, however, this increases the probability of a user accidentally sending funds to a spoofed address.

The scheme operates using the following the steps:

1. **Surveillance on-chain:** The attacker monitors on-chain transactions, particularly token-related ones, and selects victims based on tokens recently sent.
2. **Address analysis:** The attacker ascertains the address the victim sent tokens to.
3. **Generating a spoof address:** The attacker generates a spoofed address that looks similar to the recipient of a transaction that the victim previously sent.
4. **Spoofed transaction generation:** The attacker generates a transaction to the spoofed address with the goal of putting the spoofed address in front of the victim, often through the user's wallet transaction history.
5. **Victims send to spoofed address:** The victim picks up a spoofed recipient address from a blockchain explorer or through their wallet and unwittingly pastes it into the recipient line when the user conducts a transaction.

Prevention

- Educate users on verifying website authenticity.
- Educate users on what a legitimate signature for a contract looks like and what permission granting actually means.
- Enable multi-factor authentication, not using SMS, whenever possible. This adds an extra layer of security, even if attackers manage to obtain login credentials.
- Encourage users to leverage browser security features such as website identity indicators, address books, and warnings. Wallet extensions often highlight secure connections and issue warnings for potentially deceptive sites.
- Encourage users to analyze the address they plan to send funds to and to make sure it is not spoofed.
- Stay updated on the latest phishing tactics and share relevant information with users. Awareness is a key defense against evolving threats.

In the beginning of 2023 alone, it was estimated that over $19 million was lost to these tactics.

Spearphishing

Definition and History

Spearphishing is an advanced form of phishing and social engineering in which scammers tailor their attacks to deceive individuals into disclosing sensitive information. While phishing traditionally involves creating fake webpages to lure in victims, spearphishing goes beyond by aiming at specific targets.

How It Operates

Similar to a more generalized phishing campaign, an attacker may create a targeted domain or file for victims to access to ultimately grant the attacker access to the victim's funds. Spearphishers will often target individuals involved in DeFi projects, crypto exchanges, or other businesses that spearphishers believe are close to the business's source of funds. Spearphishers may also simply target high-net-worth individuals in the space.

Case Study: Arthur0x

The founder of DeFiance Capital and the NFT project Azuki, Arthur Cheong, experienced a significant loss of approximately $1.7 million in popular NFTs, including CloneX and Azuki NFTs.

Despite being a sophisticated crypto user with five years of experience, Cheong fell victim to a spearphishing attack initiated through an email appearing to be from one of DeFiance Capital's portfolio companies. The attacker gained access to Cheong's hot wallet after he opened the deceptive email attachment.

The attacker immediately sold Cheong's NFTs for ETH. In total, the attacker made nearly 600 ETH from the theft. The incident highlights the vulnerability of having user funds in one wallet, and remaining vigilant against spearphishing attacks, even for the most experienced users.

Prevention

From a financial institution's perspective, spearphishing is not a new phenomenon. However, here are some core considerations we ask DeFi projects, crypto exchanges, and users of all sizes to internalize:

For users and businesses

(1) User Education:

  a) Awareness Training: Conduct regular training sessions to educate users about the risks and tactics associated with spearphishing. Make them aware of the importance of verifying communication authenticity.

  b) Funds partitioning: As a rule of thumb, NFT holders should partition their holdings among several addresses, and better yet wallets to avoid potential detrimental loss if they fall for a scheme.

  c) Hardware Wallets: Store valuable assets on a hardware wallet, otherwise known as cold storage. These tools keep private keys separate from a user's internet-connected devices so that a user cannot sign transactions without physically attaching the wallet hardware. Spearphishers are therefore prevented from conducting transactions even if they have full access to the user's computer.

(2) Email Security:

  a) Email Filtering: Implement advanced email filtering systems to identify and filter out suspicious emails. These systems can detect patterns and characteristics common to spearphishing attempts.

(3) Verify Sender Authenticity:

  a) Check Email Addresses: Encourage users to carefully examine email addresses, especially the sender's address. Be cautious of slight variations or misspellings in familiar email addresses.

(4) Multi-Factor Authentication (MFA):

a) Enable MFA: Require the use of multi-factor authentication for accessing sensitive systems or conducting transactions. Even if login credentials are compromised, an additional layer of verification enhances security. If possible, avoid MFA using SMS or text messaging which is a common attack vector for scammers.

(5) Communication Verification:

a) Verify Unexpected Requests: In case of unexpected or suspicious requests, users should verify the legitimacy of the communication through a separate, trusted channel before taking any action.

For projects and businesses:

(6) Limit Access to Information:

a) Need-to-Know Basis: Limit access to sensitive information on a need-to-know basis. This reduces the potential impact if an individual's account is compromised.

(7) Secure Communication Channels:

a) Use Encrypted Channels: Encourage the use of encrypted communication channels, especially for sharing sensitive information. This adds an extra layer of protection against eavesdropping.

(8) Endpoint Security:

a) Security Software: Ensure that all devices, including computers and mobile devices, have updated and effective security software to detect and prevent malware that may be used in spearphishing attacks.

(9) Incident Response Plan:

a) Develop a Response Plan: Have a well-defined incident response plan in place. In the event of a suspected spearphishing attack, there should be a clear process for reporting and addressing the incident promptly.

(10) Regular Updates and Patching:

a) Keep Software Updated: Regularly update and patch all software, including operating systems and applications, to address vulnerabilities that could be exploited in spearphishing attacks.

(11) Use Advanced Threat Protection:

a) Implement ATP Solutions: Advanced Threat Protection (ATP) solutions can provide an additional layer of defense against sophisticated attacks by analyzing patterns and behaviors associated with spearphishing.

(12) Collaboration and Reporting:

a) Promote Reporting: Create a culture where users feel comfortable reporting suspicious emails or activities. Establish clear channels for reporting and investigate reported incidents promptly.

(13) Simulated Phishing Exercises:
  a) Conduct Simulations: Periodically conduct simulated spearphishing exercises within the organization to assess user readiness and identify areas for improvement.

Ponzi Schemes

Definition and History

Ponzi and high-yield investment programs (HYIPs) promise high returns using funds from new investors to pay earlier investors. Similar to Multi-Level Marketing (MLM) schemes in the past, the new wave of crypto Ponzi schemes offers returns for recruitment and making contributions.

How They Operate

Crypto variants of MLMs and HYIPs attract participants with the promise of extraordinary returns. As more investors join, returns are paid from new contributions, leading to an inevitable collapse.

Case Study

HYIP turned Ponzi—PlusToken

PlusToken remains one of the most prolific examples of a HYIP-turned Ponzi scheme to date. Launched in 2018, it was advertised across Chinese and South Korean social media as a way to invest in crypto and earn a quick yield.

The scheme worked as follows: PlusTokens users were required to deposit a minimum of $500 in order to participate. Once deposited they could begin sharing their affiliate link that would allow them to begin recruiting other victims. The more affiliates they produced, the more yield they would earn. The scheme raised over $3b by early 2019.

However, in June 2019, users suddenly were having difficulty withdrawing funds. PlusToken stated that it was due to high transaction fee costs. However, soon after, funds from the PlusToken team's own wallet, which had been used to supply liquidity, began dissipating. In the crypto space, when a project suddenly goes quiet, funds become locked down or otherwise inaccessible, and the operators begin dissipating funds, this is known as a "rug pull." We will discuss rug pulls in detail further along in this chapter.

Prevention

Investors and financial institutions should conduct rigorous due diligence on a potential crypto investment opportunity, including the following:

- Whitepaper Analysis:
  - Existence of a Whitepaper: Legitimate projects often have a detailed whitepaper outlining their goals, technology, team, and roadmap. Lack of a whitepaper or an overly vague one is a red flag.
- Project Viability:
  - Purpose and Utility: Understand the project's purpose and how it solves real-world problems. Be skeptical of projects that promise high returns without a clear use case.

- Technology: Assess the technology behind the project. Is it innovative, scalable, and does it have a genuine need for blockchain technology? Or is it just speculative?

- Returns:
  - Questionable Promises: Ponzis often promise consistently high returns with little to no risk. Be highly skeptical of any investment that guarantees profits, as all investments carry some level of risk.
  - Realistic Timeframes: Ponzis may promise quick and substantial returns within a very short period. Evaluate whether the projected returns align with the usual market trends and whether they seem too good to be true.
  - Emphasis on Recruitment: Ponzis often rely heavily on referral programs, where existing investors are rewarded for bringing in new participants. This structure is unsustainable and resembles a pyramid scheme.
  - Consistent Payments: Some Ponzis may initially pay out to build trust among investors. However, they eventually collapse or stop payments altogether. Research the payment history and withdrawal experiences of other investors.
- Transparency:
  - Team Information: Verify the background and qualifications of the project team. A lack of information or a team with a history of failed projects can be concerning.
  - Open Communication: Legitimate projects maintain open communication with their community. Check for regular updates on social media channels, blogs, or forums.
- Community and Reviews:
  - Community Engagement: A strong and engaged community is often a positive sign. Look for genuine discussions and feedback from community members. However, as we'll see below this can at times be manipulated.
  - Reviews and Ratings: Check independent reviews, ratings, and opinions from reputable sources. Be cautious of overly positive reviews without substance. Similarly, as we'll see below this can at times be manipulated.
- Regulatory Compliance:
  - Legal Status: Ensure the project complies with relevant regulations. Lack of legal clarity or a history of regulatory issues could indicate potential problems.
- Tokenomics (if the project involves a token):
  - Token Distribution: Assess the token distribution model. A large portion of tokens held by the team or early investors may lead to price manipulation.
  - Inflation and Supply: Understand how the token supply changes over time. Excessive inflation or an uncapped supply could devalue the token.
- Audits and Security:
  - Smart Contract Audits: Check if the project's smart contracts have been audited by reputable third-party firms. This helps ensure the code is secure and free from vulnerabilities.

  - Security Measures: Assess the project's security measures, including those related to user data and funds.
- Roadmap and Milestones:
  - Realistic Roadmap: Evaluate the project's roadmap for achievable milestones. Unrealistic promises or an overly ambitious timeline may indicate a lack of understanding or potential deception.
- Use of Funds:
  - Clear Allocation: Understand how the project intends to use the funds raised. A lack of transparency regarding fund usage can be a warning sign.
- Other Red Flags:
  - Promises of Guaranteed Returns: Be skeptical of projects promising guaranteed or unrealistically high returns.
  - Lack of Clarity on Business Model: If it's unclear how the project generates revenue or sustains itself, that could be a red flag.

Romance Scams (Redefined)—Pig Butchering (Sha Zhu Pan)

Definition and History

Pig Butchering scams or, the Mandarin phrase, Sha Zhu Pan are investment scams coupled with traditional romance scam. Gaining popularity in China, their name derives from the Chinese culinary practice of fattening a pig for slaughter, with the victim's funds in this case being the pig being fattened.

How They Operate

A pig butchering scam involves finding a victim through social media or dating websites and developing a relationship with them. The attacker will use fraudulent photos and information in order to appear successful and good-looking.

Once rapport is established, the attacker will begin developing a deeper connection with the victim, such as texting the victim every morning and night. Eventually, the attacker will ask the victims to co-invest in a HYIP that they've apparently already made earnings from.

The victim may need to be coaxed into investing in the platform. Once the victim invests in the platform, they will observe their capital growing as they check back on their investment daily.

Eventually, the victim will want to withdraw funds and from there they will be provided with a range of excuses. The victim may confront the attackers but, more often than not, the funds have already disappeared.

Case Study: A Former Colleague's Father

Cases of pig butchering are common, but similar to traditional romance scams they are rarely discussed because victims often feel a sense of shame or embarrassment.

Several case studies can be found online, but we'll detail one that was shared by a former colleague's father.

Their father was divorced and downloaded a popular Chinese Karaoke app on their phone. They very quickly met the attacker, who we will refer to as Jane. Jane quickly moved the conversation off the app and to WhatsApp. Jane's WhatsApp profile was of a beautiful Chinese girl no older than twenty-five.

As the conversation unfolded, she delved into the victim's family and personal life. Within a day, she started sending the victim good morning and good night texts, seemingly showing genuine concern. In less than five days, she unexpectedly professed her love for the victim, who was taken aback given that Jane was about 40 years his junior. In an attempt to redirect her interest, the victim tried setting her up with his son but she showed no interest.

Over the next couple of days, Jane inquired about the victim's knowledge of cryptocurrency, an area the victim wasn't well-versed in, and suggested investing in a project that had supposedly yielded significant returns for her. After some persuasion, the victim reluctantly signed up for the platform and invested funds.

Despite harboring skepticism, the victim sought advice from friends who promptly warned that Jane and the investment platform were part of a scam. Upset by these revelations, the victim confronted Jane, questioning her involvement in the scam and the legitimacy of the website. Jane's responses were vague, prompting the victim to make a phone call to her. However, this attempt led to Jane becoming angry, accusing the victim of invading her personal space and nearly cutting off communication to him entirely.

Despite warnings from friends, the victim continued to invest more funds. When attempting to withdraw funds, the platform refused the request. Seeking assistance, the victim contacted tech support via Telegram, but to no avail. Jane did not appear willing to help either. This pattern repeated itself for weeks.

In the end, the victim suffered substantial losses, totaling around $500,000.

Prevention

1. Educate users on the prevalence of the scam itself, similar to how well known the Nigerian prince scam is.
2. Encourage users to scrutinize people they meet online who appear to be "too good to be true" and who suddenly pitch special investments with high returns.
3. Encourage users to leverage browser security features such as website identity indicators and warnings. Wallet extensions often highlight secure connections and issue warnings for potentially deceptive sites.
4. Stay updated on the latest phishing tactics and share relevant information with users. Awareness is a key defense against evolving threats.

The unfortunate truth is that the scammer with whom a victim may be chatting with is, sadly, often a victim of human trafficking or similar scams themselves.

Pump and Dumps

Definition and History

Pump and dump schemes are those in which a project artificially inflates asset prices through misinformation, before selling off holdings for profit. Pump and dumps are well-trodden and date back to the 19th century. The most common examples of pumps and dump schemes today are often penny stocks.

Crypto-specific pump and dumps often involve the launch of a new token whose value is entirely built on speculation. Historically, pump and dumps were spread via word of mouth and later internet forums, however, crypto pump and dumps often leverage Social Media Marketing (SMM) panels to amplify their impact. SMMs allow these projects to appear legitimate across several social media platforms at once.

How They Operate

A pump and dump will start with the speculation of the launch of a new token (or with the actual launch). The speculation and excitement around the launch of this token is built via various social media platforms, usually X (formerly Twitter), Telegram, and Discord. SMMs are used to cultivate and artificially inflame follower count, as well as artificially drum up excitement in Discord through the help of bots and outsourcing.

Once hype is built out and the token is launched. A pool will be created for the token on a Decentralized Exchanges (DEX), such as Uniswap. A pool consists of two assets, which can be traded for one another. The project team will usually fund the creation of the pool, which requires upfront capital for both the newly launched token as well as the backing token (often a token of value, such as USDC or ETH).

Trading on the DEX is determined by supply and demand between the newly launched token and the backing token. The more demand and the less the supply of one, the higher its value is when compared to the other. Pump and Dumps leverage this mechanism by inflating the value of their token rapidly through excitement.

Once the value of the new token is sufficiently large enough, the scammers dump it in exchange for the valuable token.

Case Study: Squidgame

Pump and dumps remain extremely common. While some aspects of the scheme have evolved over the years, the main scaffolding of the scheme remains.

In October 2021, at the hype of the Netflix TV show Squid Game, the token SquidGame was launched on the BSC network. The token, similar to the TV show, was supposedly an entry ticket into a series of battles with other ticket holders for the funds raised by ticket sales.

The token could only be bought on the DEX Pancakeswap via the Squid/BNB pool. Similar to the TV show, users were unable to sell their tokens. Excitement about the project was shared on social media, particularly Twitter and Telegram and investors flocked to the project.

With increased demand from the popularity of the token, investors' inability to physically sell the token compounded demand for it. The price of the SquidGame token grew from $0 to $2k overnight.

Once this price was reached, the creator of the project dumped their Squidcoin holdings on the Squid/BNB pool in exchange for BNB. This dropped the value of the token back to $0 again. At the same time, the SquidGame website and its corresponding social media profiles went dark.

Prevention

Similar to investments in HYIPs/Ponzis, due diligence is a must for users in order to prevent investment in a pump and dump. However, because pump and dumps in the crypto space are often fleeting, the timeframe for due diligence is shorter and needs to be much more targeted around social media analysis and contract analysis.

- Whitepaper Analysis:
  - Existence of a Whitepaper: Often for a pump and dump no whitepaper will exist.
- Project Viability:
  - Purpose and Utility: Understand the project's purpose and how it solves real-world problems. Be skeptical of projects that promise high returns without a clear use case.
  - Technology: Assess the technology behind the project. Is it innovative, scalable, and does it have a genuine need for blockchain technology? Or is it just speculative?
- Returns:
  - Questionable Promises: Pump and dumps often promise consistently high returns with little to no risk. Be highly skeptical of any investment that guarantees profits, as all investments carry some level of risk.
  - Realistic Timeframes: Pump and dumps may promise quick and substantial returns within a very short period. Evaluate whether the projected returns align with the usual market trends and whether they seem too good to be true.
  - Emphasis in the community around gains: Be wary of communities that seem overly focused on gains and making the "price go up." When interacting with others in the Discord or Telegram, look for signs that the community is excited about something other than profit.
- Transparency:
  - Team Information: Verify the background and qualifications of the project team. A lack of information or a team with a history of failed projects can be concerning.
  - Open Communication: Legitimate projects maintain open communication with their community. Check for regular updates on social media channels, blogs, or forums.
- Community and Reviews:
  - Community Engagement: A strong and engaged community is often a positive sign. Look for genuine discussions and feedback from community members. However, as we'll see below this can at times be manipulated.
  - Reviews and Ratings: Check independent reviews, ratings, and opinions from reputable sources. Be cautious of overly positive reviews without substance. Similarly, as we'll see below this can at times be manipulated.
- Tokenomics (if the project involves a token):
  - Token Distribution: Assess the token distribution model. A large portion of tokens held by the team or early investors may lead to price manipulation.
  - Inflation and Supply: Understand how the token supply can change over time and who can inflate/deflate it.

- Audits and Security:
  - Smart Contract Audits: Check if the project's smart contracts have been audited by reputable third-party firms. This helps ensure the code is secure and free from vulnerabilities.
  - Token lock/override features: Assess whether keys to the wallet providing liquidity have been burned. If the project team retains control of the wallet, they can drain the liquidity pool. Alternatively, assess if the project wallet is controlled by a wallet that requires multiple users to sign each transaction. This is called a "multi-sig" and can mitigate the risk of one rogue team member.
- Roadmap and Milestones:
  - Realistic Roadmap: Evaluate the project's roadmap for achievable milestones. Unrealistic promises or an overly ambitious timeline may indicate a lack of understanding or potential deception.

Rug Pulls or Exit Scams

Definition and History

A "rug pull" (often shortened to "rug") is when a project, either legitimate from the outset or illegitimate, terminates the project abruptly and absconds with the proceeds.

We use the term rug pull and exit scam here interchangeably.

There are as many styles of rug pulls as there are scammers, but rug pulls can generally be divided into two categories:

- Centralized Finance, or CeFi:
  - Lack of decentralization and controls allowing core developers and others' access to user funds.
- Decentralized Finance, or DeFi:
  - Before tokens are "minted" on the blockchain, a majority of them are already allocated to developers.
  - Smart contract backdoors:
- Special features of the tokens' smart contract cause artificial pumps of the price by limiting the ability to sell a token.
- Built-in backdoors to a project's token may allow the developers to reassign the majority token/fund ownership to themselves or otherwise ascribe themselves royalties.

How They Operate

Often, rug pulls will involve the shuttering of a project's activities, physically or virtually, and will always involve the rapid theft of the project's funds employing various tactics.

Case Studies Legitimate and Legitimate Seeming Projects

Illegitimate project from the outset: SquidGame

While we can't 100% say that the SquidGame token was launched maliciously, it ended as described above with the creators absconding with all of the funds and laundering them through various means.

In particular, this rug pull was conducted by artificially inflating the price of the token by not allowing buyers to sell it.

Of note is that the project was only live for about 2 weeks before the project's social media and website were shuttered and the token was dumped in exchange for BNB.

Prevention

We recommend that investors follow similar guidance for rug pulls as the guidance for HYIPs.

- Team:
  - Team Transparency: Investigate the project's team members. Legitimate projects have transparent and visible team members, even if they are pseudonymous. Make sure to check their individual transactional activity to assess former project involvement.
  - Project History: Research the history of the project and its team. Look for previous projects or any incidents that might indicate a pattern of fraudulent behavior.
- Product:
  - Whitepaper and Roadmap: Scrutinize the project's whitepaper and roadmap, if one exists. A well-detailed whitepaper outlines the project's goals, technology, use case, and plans for development. A clear and realistic roadmap indicates a thoughtful and strategic approach.
  - Prototype or MVP: Projects with a working prototype or minimum viable product (MVP) are more likely to be legitimate. A tangible product demonstrates that the team has made progress and can deliver on their promises.
- Community:
  - Community Reputation: Assess the project's reputation within the cryptocurrency community. Look for reviews, discussions, and feedback on social media, forums, and community platforms. A well-engaged and positive community is generally a good sign. However, be wary of overhyped fleeting investment opportunities.
  - Community Moderation: Evaluate the project's Telegram groups, Discord channels, or other community forums. Legitimate projects maintain active and well-moderated communities. Be wary if there's an absence of moderation or if the community seems disorganized or otherwise fake.
- Tokens/Smart Contracts:
  - Launch Protocol: Examine how the project was launched. Did it use a recognized launchpad that required the project found to provide their real identities or "doxx," for example? Modern projects also sometimes decentralized escrow protocols that only permit the project team to access funds when they meet predetermined milestones.
  - Tokenomics: Examine the tokenomics of the project. Understand the distribution of tokens, especially if a significant portion is held by the team. A disproportionate distribution can be a red flag. Assess if the team is following through with their tokenomics plan on the chain.

   - Smart Contract Audit: Look for evidence of a smart contract audit. Reputable projects undergo audits by third-party security firms to ensure the integrity and security of their smart contracts. The audit report should be publicly available.
- Use of Funds: Check if the project has a clear plan for using the funds raised. Transparency regarding how the funds will be allocated for development, marketing, operations, and other purposes is essential. Assess whether funds are being used as described.
- Legal Compliance: Assess the project's legal compliance. If the project claims to operate within certain jurisdictions, verify that it complies with relevant regulatory requirements.
- Other Red Flags: Be cautious of red flags such as unrealistic promises of high returns, pressure tactics, lack of transparency, and the absence of clear communication from the team.

Initial Coin Offerings (ICOs)

Definition and History

Initial Coin Offerings (ICOs) involve fundraising by issuing new cryptocurrencies or tokens. While popular in 2017, ICOs are rare now because of the significant challenges and risks they posed to investors. The initial excitement and momentum around ICOs led to a surge in token sales, but numerous fraudulent projects and instances of unfulfilled promises marred this trend. Many investors experienced losses as a result of scams, poorly executed projects, and outright failures.

Regulatory scrutiny also played a pivotal role in the decline of ICOs. As governments worldwide started to recognize the risks associated with these fundraising methods, they began implementing stricter regulations to protect investors and maintain market integrity.

As a result, the crypto industry has evolved toward more compliant and secure fundraising methods, such as Security Token Offerings (STOs) and Initial Exchange Offerings (IEOs) or, the decentralized variant, Initial DEX Offerings (IDOs). That said, many of the same scams are feasible with these new methods, so the lessons below may be applied equally.

How They Operate

Simply put: Investors contribute funds in exchange for newly issued tokens for a specific project or chain. However, the crypto space has seen ICO projects fail to deliver on their commitments time and time again. In fact, some research by Investopedia found that 80% of ICOs were scams.

A typical ICO usually follows the following steps:

1. Publishing a Whitepaper: The project team publishes a detailed document called a whitepaper, outlining the key aspects of their project. This includes the project's purpose, technology, team members, tokenomics (details about the cryptocurrency/token), and the problem it aims to solve.
2. Creating a token: The project team creates a new token to be sold during the ICO. These tokens often serve a specific purpose within the project's ecosystem, such as granting access to features or representing a stake in the project.

3. Pre-sale (Optional): Some projects conduct a pre-sale/seed round before the official ICO. During this phase, early investors can purchase tokens at a discounted rate. Pre-sales are often limited to a smaller group of investors and may require a minimum investment.
4. ICO Launch: The ICO is officially launched, and the project team sets a specific duration for the fundraising campaign. Participants can buy the project's tokens using established cryptocurrencies or in some cases, fiat currencies.
5. Token Distribution: After the ICO concludes, the project team distributes the purchased tokens to the investors based on the terms outlined in the smart contract. This distribution may be immediate or staged over time.
6. Listing on Exchanges: To provide liquidity and allow investors to trade their tokens, the project seeks to list its cryptocurrency on various cryptocurrency exchanges. This step allows the token to be bought and sold in the broader market.
7. Project Development: With the funds raised during the ICO, the project team begins development work on their platform, product, or service as outlined in the whitepaper. Regular updates are often provided to keep the community informed about progress. But this doesn't always happen.

Most fraudulent ICOs will follow through with their promises up until either the token distribution, listing on exchanges, and project development.

Case Study: PlexCoin

The PlexCoin ICO gained notoriety in 2017. The chain aimed to be a fast-settling payments chain that was modeled after Ethereum. The team also promised a 1,300% ROI within 29 days.

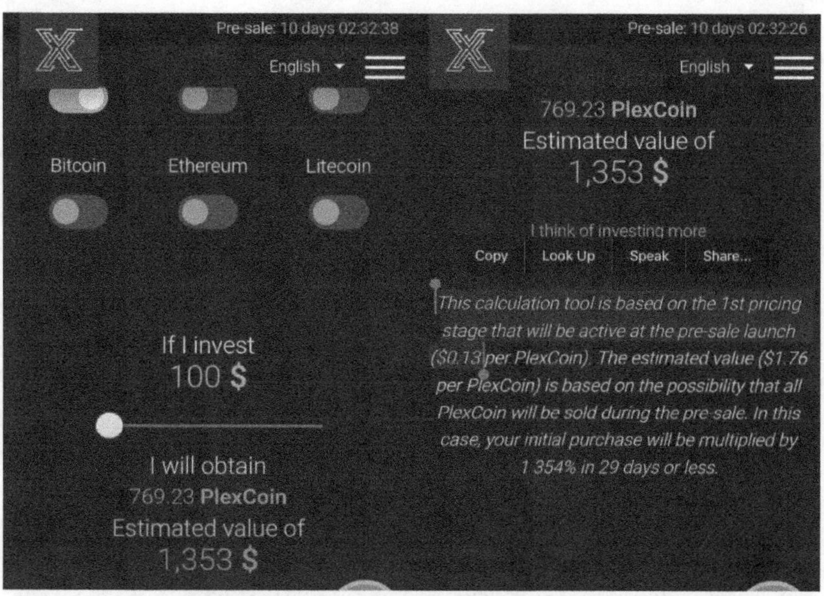

Although the team published a whitepaper,[1] it remains questionable what the specifics around this new chain was. Although the whitepaper also claims that the team consisted of several experts, SEC filings[2] allege that the ICO was conducted primarily through one person.

Prevention

Similar to investments in HYIPs/Ponzis, due diligence is a must for users in order to prevent investment in a fraudulent ICO. Some key factors to consider include:

- Whitepaper Quality:
  - Assesses a project's whitepaper and its existence of it. A legitimate ICO will have a comprehensive whitepaper that clearly explains the project's goals, technology, use case, tokenomics, team members, and roadmap. Be wary of vague, overly complex Whitepapers or Whitepapers with a lot of "padding."
- Transparent Team:
  - Verify the identities and backgrounds of the project's team members. Legitimate projects have a visible and experienced team with a track record in the relevant industry. Look for LinkedIn profiles and other professional details.
- Community Engagement:
  - Assess the level of community engagement. Legitimate projects often have active and responsive communities AND more importantly, team members, on social media channels, forums, and other platforms. Check for genuine discussions and feedback from community members.
- Tokenomics:
  - Understand the tokenomics of the project. Evaluate the purpose of the token, its utility within the ecosystem, and how it will be distributed. Be cautious if the tokenomics are unclear or if a large portion of tokens is concentrated in a few hands.
- Regulatory Compliance:
  - Check if the ICO is compliant with relevant regulatory requirements. A lack of transparency regarding compliance or statements claiming exemption from regulations is a red flag. Consider projects that are proactive about regulatory adherence.
- Smart Contract Security:
  - Assess the security of the smart contract. Smart contracts are crucial for ICOs, and vulnerabilities in the code can lead to security breaches. Look for projects that have undergone code audits by reputable third-party firms.
- Use of Funds:
  - Understand how the funds raised during the ICO will be used. Legitimate projects provide a clear breakdown of how the funds will be allocated for development, marketing, operations, and other expenses.

1. Citation to whitepaper: https://assets.bwbx.io/documents/users/iqjWHBFdfxIU/rwzk2_HjYOjw/v0.
2. Citation to SEC filings: https://www.sec.gov/files/litigation/complaints/2017/comp-pr2017-219.pdf.

- Partnerships and Advisors:
  - Investigate any claimed partnerships or advisors. Legitimate projects often have reputable partnerships and advisors who bring credibility to the project. Be cautious if there is a lack of information or if the partnerships seem dubious.
- Prototype or MVP:
  - Check if the project has a working prototype or minimum viable product (MVP). A tangible product or prototype demonstrates that the team is capable of delivering on their promises.
- Other Red Flags:
  - Be vigilant for common red flags such as unrealistic promises of high returns, pressure tactics, anonymous teams, and lack of communication. Stay informed about warning signs associated with fraudulent ICOs.
- Legal Opinion:
  - Seek legal advice if necessary. Consulting with legal professionals who specialize in blockchain and cryptocurrency, some of whom edited this volume, can provide insights into the legal status of the ICO and potential risks.

Chapter 10

Future Places, Regulated Spaces: CBDCs, DeFI, + NFTs, and New Markets

Daniel Payne

Future Regulation

At the federal level, the U.S. regulatory environment has been defined by enforcement actions rather than traditional rulemaking. This approach has had significant consequences. Investment in the industry has been warped by the threat of legal action with no clear mitigation techniques for private investment to insist on.

Many companies have decided that their best legal defense is to move fast and make enough money to defend themselves when the inevitable lawsuit arrives. Although that approach is likely riskier for the industry and consumers, it is a logical response to the alternative: move slowly and shut down when the inevitable lawsuit arrives. This appears to have been the strategy for both Ripple Labs and FTX, albeit with drastically different outcomes. Ripple had enough money on hand to go toe-to-toe with the SEC when it was sued in December 2020. It could afford to fight long enough to secure a valuable summary judgment victory in July 2023. FTX, on the other hand, appears to have moved too fast, ignoring basic corporate governance and basic risk management. Although it made significant money and could have afforded to fight an enforcement action, the lawsuits arrived after it crashed spectacularly in 2022. But contrast Ripple Labs and FTX with the dozens of companies that settled and closed down when the SEC or CFTC showed up. The options for companies in the U.S. are not attractive.

SEC Crypto-Related Alerts: A Comparison

SEC	Crypto Related	Total
Enforcement Actions	28	682
Investor Alerts	4	52
Rulemaking	7	226
Information and Guidance	3	86
News and Press Releases	58	944
Speeches and Statements	7	456

Additionally, regulation is not uniform across the country because the rulings in enforcement actions are not all the same. This causes headaches for companies trying to run businesses that span the U.S.; it is possible for a company to be compliant in one state and not in another.

Perhaps most significantly, the lack of crypto-specific regulation coupled with wave after wave of enforcement lawsuits has driven innovation offshore. Singapore, the EU, Switzerland, the UAE, and other jurisdictions have passed crypto-specific regulations that give businesses confidence that they can focus on their business rather than worrying about the government shutting them down.

Crypto-Friendly Jurisdictions

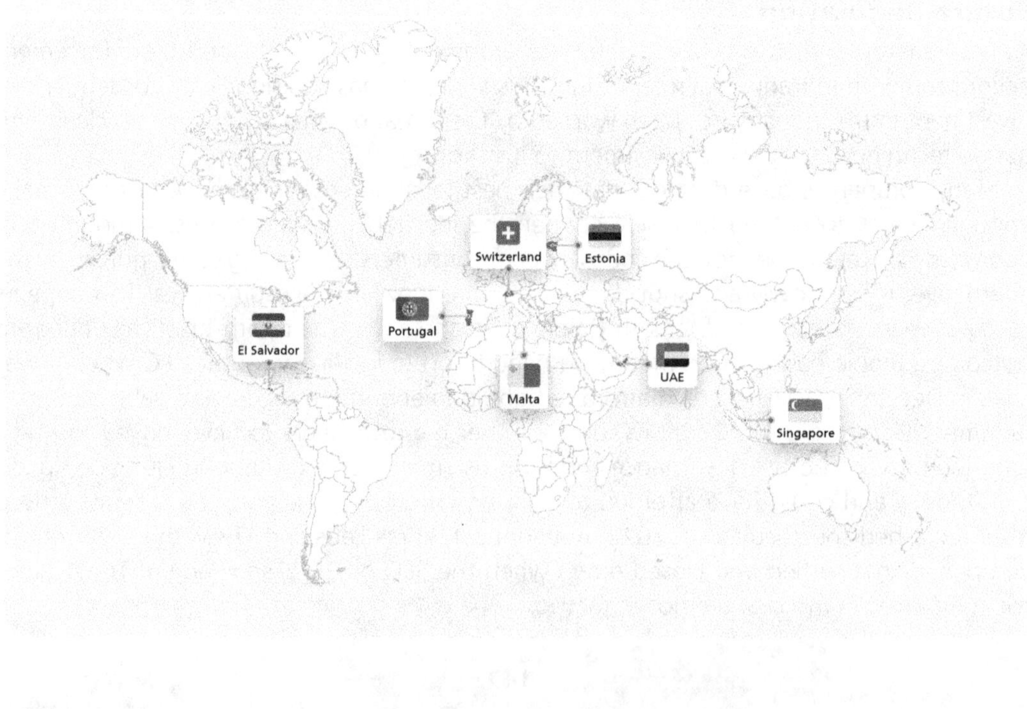

For businesses that stay in the U.S., they face a short-term reality that the blockchain industry continues to grow in the midst of an unclear regulatory regime. Many traditional companies that existed long before blockchain technology was invented are unlikely to move. But they face disruption and competition from blockchain technology and blockchain companies, so they will have to react to this reality. In the financial services industry, blockchain obviates the purpose of many financial intermediaries: trade settlement, transfer agents, escrow agents, etc. What strategy will they take in response? For example, will centralized stock and commodity exchanges prepare for competition from digital asset exchanges by introducing blockchain settlement of trades or offering trading in digital assets? Will escrow agents start slashing prices and handling escrow via smart contracts? Will credit card companies begin using blockchain as a supplemental settlement layer, as Visa has already begun?[1]

The nature of current U.S. blockchain regulation makes the future of regulation especially important to forecast. We hope that future regulation is created through new legislation and the traditional rulemaking process. One other important lesson for Congress as it eventually debates new blockchain legislation comes from FTX: a little bit of regulation can go a long way. The major misconduct at FTX involved improperly taking customer assets from FTX to fill a hole in the balance sheet at sister company Alameda Research. Would customer asset segregation with standard financial controls have prevented the stealing? What about multi-signature wallets requiring multiple people to be involved in moving customer assets anywhere except back to the customer? It is possible that the action needed from Congress to prevent more FTX-like crises is more manageable than creating a new regulator and regulatory regime.

What considerations are at play for the future regulation of crypto? Will there be a new crypto-specific regulator? Will multiple agencies continue to regulate different aspects of the crypto industry? Will a self-regulatory organization end up in control? We tackle all of that and more in three vital crypto areas: Central Bank Digital Currencies; Decentralized Finance; and Non-Fungible Tokens.

Central Bank Digital Currencies

The U.S. federal government has been studying a potential central bank digital currency (CBDC) in the U.S.[2] Meanwhile, China created the digital yuan in 2021 and began testing it in 2022,[3] and other countries are developing their own CBDCs. The U.S. Federal Reserve's patient approach to such a systemically critical decision is commendable. The dollar continues to be the reserve currency for the world, making the stakes higher for a digital dollar

1. Press Release, Visa, Visa expands stablecoin settlement capabilities to merchant acquirers (Sept. 5, 2023), https://usa.visa.com/about-visa/newsroom/press-releases.releaseId.19881.html.
2. Executive Order 14067 directed research into a potential design and deployment for a U.S. CBDC (Mar. 14, 2022) https://www.federalregister.gov/documents/2022/03/14/2022-05471/ensuring-responsible-development-of-digital-assets.
3. Amitoj Singh, Damanick Dantes, and James Rubin, *First Mover Asia: China to Widen Test of Digital Yuan as Russia Invasion Spotlights Crypto's Potential Role; Cryptos Decline*, CoinDesk (May 11, 2023), https://www.coindesk.com/markets/2022/03/03/first-mover-asia-china-to-widen-test-of-digital-yuan-as-russia-invasion-spotlights-cryptos-potential-role-cryptos-decline/.

than a digital yuan or digital pound. However, the private sector is already a decade ahead in providing the stable cryptocurrencies that a CBDC will compete with. The first question to be answered for a Digital Dollar, then, is whether one is even necessary.[4]

Governance

Clearly, the Federal Reserve will be the issuer and supervisor for a Digital Dollar: "The Federal Reserve does not intend to proceed with the issuance of a CBDC without clear support from the executive branch and from Congress, ideally in the form of a specific authorizing law."[5] Although the Federal Reserve's relative independence may be a benefit in managing a CBDC, the Federal Reserve remains part of the Executive Branch subject to the authority of the President and the oversight of Congress.

Thus, the biggest risk is that the government will be able to exert enormous leverage over its policy goals by implementing them through the money supply. For example, the Biden administration has made the transition from fossil to renewable energy a central policy objective. The Biden Administration unsurprisingly has called for a Digital Dollar to be "sustainable, avoiding the environmental concerns raised by some privately-issued digital assets."[6] Could an administration put sustainability concerns over security concerns? Some other policy areas that a future Congress or President could support through manipulation of the Digital Dollar include:

- Law enforcement: compelling a transfer of a convicted defendant's dollars to pay a fine or restitution.
- Free speech and association: identifying participants in unfavored groups based on contributions.
- Free markets: compelling an institution to lend or refrain from lending to specific individuals or groups.
- Favored industries: making it cheaper and/or easier to pay for things in favored industries than unfavored industries.

Technology

A CBDC requires the authority of the central bank to control the distribution of the digital currency. Thus, it is hard to conceive of a CBDC that would be distributed using a permissionless blockchain. The U.S. Office of Science and Technology Policy reported that "a permissionless approach does not make sense for a system that has at least one trusted

4. There is a constituency for a federal ban on a Digital Dollar. Florida Governance Ron DeSantis, who is currently running for President, took action to prevent Florida from issuing a digital currency. Press Release, Florida Govt., Governor Ron Desantis signs first-in-the-nation legislation to protect against government surveillance of personal finances (May 12, 2023), https://www.flgov.com/2023/05/12/governor-ron-desantis-signs-first-in-the-nation-legislation-to-protect-against-government-surveillance-of-personal-finances/.

5. Fed. Rsrv. *Money and Payments: The U.S. Dollar in the Age of Digital Transformation* 7 (Jan. 2022), https://www.federalreserve.gov/publications/files/money-and-payments-20220120.pdf.

6. Dr. Alondra Nelson, Alexander Macgillivray, and Nik Marda, *Technical Possibilities for a U.S. Central Bank Digital Currency*, The White House (Sept. 16, 2022), https://www.whitehouse.gov/ostp/news-updates/2022/09/16/technical-possibilities-for-a-u-s-central-bank-digital-currency/.

entity (i.e. the central bank)."[7] Within a permissioned environment there is still a spectrum of potential mediation among the issuance of dollars by the central bank and the transfer of dollars between Americans and businesses. Will Americans be able to send Digital Dollars peer-to-peer or will they need to go through an intermediary (and is that intermediary private or public)? Where are Digital Dollars custodied? Who maintains customer accounts and is there a limit on how many accounts someone can have? What role will banks play in mediating and settling transfers? Though some blockchains have begun developing tools to exert permissioned control over tokens on a permissionless ledger, the technology is far from widespread.[8]

The White House's Office of Science and Technology (OSTP) Report identifies the factors that will need to be considered when determining how intermediated the blockchain should be. A less intermediated blockchain "could improve the privacy of sensitive financial data...; could hamper compliance with AML/CFT requirements...; [and] could affect the improvement of payment systems." A more intermediated blockchain "may provide traditional financial and digital protections...; could provide additional benefits and mitigate risks for consumers, investors, and businesses...; could advance [or negatively affect] financial inclusion and equity...; and may reduce security of CBDC system."

Another significant technological question is how interoperable the CBDC system will be with the private crypto sector. Will the CBDC system attempt to interoperate with popular chains like Bitcoin and Ethereum? Will it require private projects to request permission to plug in or interoperate with the CBDC system? Again, the OSPT identifies the trade-offers: a less interoperable system may be more functional because there will be fewer challenges with governance and standards across borders, but a more interoperable system could be faster, more resilient, and more efficient within the U.S.

Learning from the Digital Yuan

The Chinese Communist Party deployed a digital yuan in 2021, seven years after beginning work on it.[9] Perhaps unsurprisingly as one of the first CBDCs in the world, the digital yuan is not a fully realized digital currency. Although the system relies in part on distributed ledger technology (DLT), pure DLT was abandoned in favor of a hybrid system.[10]

The use cases are slowly rolling out two years later. For example, in early 2023, a Chinese city began paying government staff in digital yuan.[11] Then, the digital yuan was used to settle a large oil purchase for a Chinese oil company in October 2023.[12] But the digital yuan has yet to make a dent in world capital markets.

---

7. *Technical Design Choices for a U.S. Central Bank Digital Currency System*, The White House (Sept. 2022), https://www.whitehouse.gov/wp-content/uploads/2022/09/09-2022-Technical-Design-Choices-US-CBDC-System.pdf (hereinafter "OSTP Report").
8. *Token Extensions*, Solana, https://solana.com/solutions/token-extensions.
9. Sam Reynolds, *Analysis: What Exactly is China's CBDC?*, Blockworks (May 3, 2021), https://blockworks.co/news/analysis-what-exactly-is-chinas-cbdc.
10. *Id.*
11. Shalini Nagarajan, *Chinese City To Pay Government Staff in CBDC*, Blockworks (Apr. 24, 2023), https://blockworks.co/news/china-cbdc-government-salaries.
12. Katherine Ross, *Digital Yuan Used to Settle Crude Oil Trade for Chinese Oil Company: Report*, Blockworks (Oct. 23, 2023), https://blockworks.co/news/china-digital-yuan-oil.

Thus, there are at least three important lessons to be learned from the digital yuan:

1. Balancing a true blockchain-based CBDC with the needs of a central bank is difficult. China was forced to forego pure DLT to roll out the digital yuan. If the goal of the United States is a true CBDC, then it will have to spend the additional time necessary to overcome this challenge.
2. The demand for a CBDC does not yet exist. China's rollout has been rather slow since the digital yuan was released in 2021. And private stablecoins continue to perform very well, meeting the current demand for stable cryptocurrencies to enable decentralized finance.
3. Private stablecoins can compete with CBDCs. Whether private stablecoins like Tether and USDC can compete with a Digital Dollar remains to be seen, but the digital yuan had little effect on their market capitalizations. If the U.S. decides to roll out a CBDC, it should carefully contemplate the role of private stablecoins and avoid unfair competition with them.

Privacy Concerns

Perhaps the biggest concern for a U.S. CBDC is privacy. Fortunately, the current chair of the U.S. Federal Reserve Bank recognizes this concern. Chair Jerome Powell told an audience at a monetary conference in 2022: "We would not want a world in which the government sees, in real-time, every money transfer that anyone makes with a CBDC." Of course, if the government controls a blockchain with a ledger of every CBDC transaction, it would require significant controls to prevent such snooping. This is reminiscent of the NSA spying scandal of 2013, when it was discovered that the controls to prevent the government from listening to Americans' phone calls had failed.[13]

Congress is concerned enough about privacy issues related to CBDCs that it held hearings in September 2023. Representatives argued whether a "wrongly-structured system of money is 'perhaps the biggest existential threat to Western civilization,'" or whether such privacy concerns are "'fear mongering'... [that] can shut down discussions."[14] One witness told the committee that central banks will always prioritize identity verification over privacy given governmental national security concerns, while another cautioned that a CBDC would "place all financial transactions either in a government database or leave them a keystroke away."[15] Another witness warned that considering the privacy tradeoffs for a CBDC requires understanding the baseline: how is privacy protected (or not) in today's financial system.[16]

---

13. *See, e.g.*, Tessa Berenson, *New Snowden Documents Reveal Obama Administration Expanded NSA Spying*, Time (Jun. 4, 2015), https://time.com/3909293/edward-snowden-obama-nsa-spying/.
14. Ben Strack, *Privacy Remains Sticking Point in America's Ongoing CBDC Debate*, Blockworks (Sept. 14, 2023), https://blockworks.co/news/congress-cbdc-privacy-concerns (quoting Rep. Warren Davidson and Rep. Stephen Lynch, respectively).
15. *Id.*
16. *Id.*

DeFi

Decentralized Finance, or "DeFi," is an entirely new financial ecosystem built on blockchain technology. The central feature is disintermediation: the blockchain can replace the bankers, brokers, escrow agents, transfer agents, and other intermediaries that run the TradFi (Traditional Finance) system. But regulation of TradFi has traditionally focused on regulating these intermediaries—requiring banking charters, broker licenses, money transmitter licenses, etc. Removing the intermediaries in DeFi saves costs and improves efficiencies, but it has had the related effect of sidestepping traditional regulation of common financial transactions.

One of the early and important DeFi cases is *Risley v. Universal Inc.*[17] In August 2023, the court granted the defendants' motion to dismiss in a highly instructive opinion. The class action lawsuit accused the developers and venture capital backers of Uniswap of securities fraud for permitting "rampant fraud on the exchange." Uniswap is one of the most well-known decentralized exchanges in which a blockchain-based apparatus is available for anyone to create liquidity pools for digital assets to be traded via smart contracts. Its defining feature is that there is no centralized person or entity with the authority or governance rights to control trading on the exchange. That structure led the court to dismiss the action. Importantly, the court held:

- Decentralization = real protection. The judge ruled that "[d]ue to the Protocol's decentralized nature, the identities of the scam Token issuers are basically unknown and unknowable, leaving Plaintiffs with an identifiable injury but no identifiable defendant." The court would not countenance holding the developers liable for the actions of the users of the Protocol. This was an enormous win for developers. Though the SEC[18] and Department of Treasury[19] have indicated resistance to this view, if the precedent holds up in the future, truly decentralized finance platforms will have the ability to grow and innovate. Consumer protection will need to come from new regulations.
- Crypto assets are not (yet) securities. The court found that there has yet to be a "definitive determination" that crypto assets are securities, undermining the claim that Uniswap offered and sold unregistered securities. This is in stark opposition to the SEC's aggressive claim that essentially all non-bitcoin digital tokens are securities, which has led to dozens of lawsuits over the past few years. The opinion is an invitation to Congress to act to define the characteristics that make a crypto asset a security instead of permitting the SEC to continue to push its unsupported view of broad jurisdiction over essentially all crypto assets.

17. *Risley v. Universal Inc.*, Case No. 1:22-cv-02780 (S.D.N.Y. 2023).
18. Press Release, SEC, BarnBridge DAO agrees to stop unregistered offer and sale of structured finance crypto product (Dec. 22, 2023), https://www.sec.gov/news/press-release/2023-258 (indicating that a decentralized asset pool could be an "investment company" within the meaning of Section 7(a) of the Securities Act).
19. Press Release, Dept. of Treasury, U.S. Treasury sanctions notorious virtual currency mixer Tornado Cash (Aug. 8, 2023), https://home.treasury.gov/news/press-releases/jy0916 (indicating that an ostensibly decentralized mixing protocol could be a SDN).

- Current regulations do not squarely cover innovations like DeFi. While regulators like the SEC, CFTC, OCC, the Fed, and others have claimed that existing regulations give them sufficient authority to police the crypto space, the court clearly rejected that view. The court held that it "declines to stretch the federal securities laws to cover the conduct alleged and concludes that the plaintiff's concerns are better addressed to Congress than to this court."

Taking the *Uniswap* opinion as a reasonable starting point, regulation of DeFi will require new laws from Congress. Let's consider four areas of traditional regulation and assess what questions future regulations will have to answer:

1. AML/KYC: who is responsible for conducting Know-Your-Customer and Anti-Money Laundering processes? If issuers or sellers of financial products are anonymous, what mechanism will enforcement authorities use to require them to implement such processes? How will KYC work for anonymous or pseudonymous customers? Will Congress permit DeFi to have anonymous users?
2. Consumer protection: how can consumers be protected if the DeFi platform is not liable? Is caveat emptor strong enough? Will DeFi platforms be required to conduct any diligence or verifications for their users?
3. Market stability: centralized exchanges are tightly regulated to control potential market manipulation. If there is no centralized authority to monitor manipulation on a DeFi platform, can an outside party be given that authority?
4. Tax: who will be required to report transactions to the IRS? How sophisticated is the IRS' capacity for reading the blockchain to determine which wallets have taxable profits? Will the IRS be given the authority to ensure such wallets are ultimately paying their required taxes?

Andreeson Horowitz was named as a defendant in the *Uniswap* lawsuit as an investor in the protocol. Prevailing on the motion to dismiss is likely to further buoy it and other venture capital firms who have been investing heavily in DeFi. DeFi saw a 41x increase in venture capital investment in 2022 compared with 2020.[20] Continued interest from venture capital firms is a strong indication that DeFi has a strong strategy for disrupting TradFi if it can be properly regulated. Indeed, some venture capital firms are specifically focused on funding DeFi projects with a solid regulatory strategy.[21]

Non-Fungible Tokens and Digital Collectibles

Can NFTs recognize their enormous potential if the SEC is able to regulate them as securities? Likely not, although the SEC's appetite for NFT enforcement has been tame compared to the number of cases it has brought against fungible token projects and digital asset

---

20. Bessie Liu, *Crypto Funding: DeFi Replaces CeFi as VC Favorite*, Blockworks (Mar. 5, 2023), https://blockworks.co/news/defi-new-favorite-vc-funding.

21. Jacquelyn Melinek, *6 Crypto Investors Talk About DeFi and the Road Ahead for Adoption in 2023*, TechCrunch (Jan. 10, 2023), https://techcrunch.com/2023/01/10/six-crypto-investors-talk-about-defi-and-the-road-ahead-for-adoption-in-2023/.

exchanges. One of the first indications that the SEC will not remain hands-off with NFTs, though, is *In re Impact Theory, LLC* (Admin. Pro. 3-21585). This was a settled order with no decision from a court; it therefore has no precedential value, but it highlights the SEC's current view of NFTs.

The *Impact Theory* case involved an allegation by the SEC that the defendant's $30 million NFT collection sale constituted an unregistered securities offering.[22] Of particular concern to the SEC was repeated statements by the seller that the fortunes of NFT purchasers were linked to the fortunes of the seller and that the seller would undertake to increase the value of the NFTs.[23] The SEC also determined that the royalties on secondary market sales (a 10 percent payment via smart contract to the seller upon each secondary market sale) was relevant for establish the common enterprise element of the *Howey* test. The settlement order did not contain any discussion of the nature of NFTs and how their non-fungibility and lack of equity or income rights mitigated their appearance as securities.

The danger is that the SEC's approach to NFTs starts to look like its approach to fungible tokens. The SEC's enforcement playbook started with crypto assets that looked most like a security and/or were part of an obvious fraud (e.g., a rug pull). But it has gradually expended its playbook to cases that do not involve fraud, and, more frustratingly, do not involve crypto assets that look like securities.[24]

Ultimately, if the SEC becomes the dominant regulator for NFTs, certain regulatory areas like consumer protection and exchange registration are easier to predict. The SEC will require registration of NFT offerings and consumers will be afforded the protection of the disclosures therein. Consumers can also bring private actions if sellers are involved in fakes, pumps, or fraud. Likewise, NFT marketplaces will be forced to register as securities exchanges. But such registration would likely be prohibitively expensive for most if not all, NFT projects and secondary marketplaces, effectively snuffing out the NFT ecosystem in the U.S.

But if Congress steps in to define NFTs outside of the SEC's jurisdiction, or if the courts are unwilling to bless the SEC's view of NFTs as securities, then those regulatory areas will have to be addressed differently. Certainly, if Congress undertakes to define NFTs, it can create a regulatory framework to protect consumers from seller misconduct. More interesting to consider is whether there would be a need for regulation of NFT marketplaces. Congress or the courts may decide that blockchain technology creates a framework in need of little regulation, where non-securities transactions can take place without a regulator's heavy hand and watchful eye.

---

22. *In re* Impact Theory, LLC, Admin File Release No. 3-21585 (2023).

23. *Id.*

24. See, e.g., SEC Commissioner Hester M. Price, Statement on dissent on LBRY (Oct. 27, 2023), available at https://www.sec.gov/news/statement/peirce-statement-lbry-102723 (recognizing that the LBRY case was brought despite the blockchain being functional and the token having recognized utility at the time of the token sale).

Chapter 11
The Government's Role in Crypto Bankruptcies

Joseph B. Evans, Darren Azman, Grayson Williams, and Joseph Aminov

The crypto industry has seen a significant number of major market participants filing for bankruptcy across the United States. These bankruptcy cases have presented unique challenges which were met with creative solutions, such as in-kind crypto distributions to creditors and complex claim valuation issues. Also unique in these bankruptcy cases is the out-sized role that U.S. government law enforcement and regulatory bodies have played. While the U.S. Trustee plays a major role in all cases, the broader Department of Justice, the Securities and Exchange Commission, and various state regulators have engaged in significant objections, cross-examined witnesses at confirmation hearings, and otherwise asserted themselves in those proceedings. This chapter examines whether the government's involvement has provided benefits to creditors. This chapter also calls into question whether the government's aggressive participation in crypto bankruptcy cases has been driven by protecting ancillary regulatory and litigation positions as opposed to maximizing the efficient distribution to crypto creditors.

Developments in Crypto Enforcement

Recently, there has been a demonstrated effort by the SEC to increase enforcement within the crypto industry. SEC Chairman Gary Gensler has made numerous comments in line with the proposition that "many tokens may be unregistered securities, without required disclosures or market oversight."[1]

In the past few years, the SEC's Division of Enforcement has brought enforcement actions against high-profile cryptocurrency companies in the United States—including those against Kik, Telegram Group Inc. in 2019 and Ripple Labs Inc. in 2020—asserting that certain cryptocurrencies and associated fundraising efforts constituted the unregistered sale of securities. More recently, in June 2023, the SEC brought actions against Binance Holdings Ltd. and Coinbase Global Inc.,[2] alleging that both were operating as unregistered securities exchanges, unlicensed brokers, and clearing agents. The SEC has also brough an action against Terraform.

While Chairman Gensler has not specified which cryptocurrencies constitute a security, he has very publicly maintained his position that many cryptocurrencies fit into the SEC's jurisdiction.[3] Such actions by the SEC evidence a trend toward further reaching—and more inclusive—enforcement of the securities laws against cryptocurrencies. Likewise, it sets a foundational understanding of how regulators are seeking to close gaps in rulemaking and establish authoritative boundaries.

Even after the SEC's recent approval of spot Bitcoin Exchange-Traded Products, Chairman Gensler reiterated that the approval "should in no way signal the Commission's willingness to approve listing standards for crypto asset securities" and that "the vast majority of crypto assets are investment contracts and thus subject to the federal securities laws."[4] While claiming that the Commission is "merit neutral" with regard to crypto, many of the SEC's enforcement actions and public statements make clear that crypto enforcement actions are a high priority on the SEC's agenda.[5]

With these developments and objectives in mind, the recent spur in crypto bankruptcies has incentivized the SEC to take a more aggressive interventionist position in bankruptcy proceedings.

---

1. U.S. Securities and Exchange Commission, *Chair Gary Gensler's Remarks before the Aspen Security Forum* (Aug. 3, 2021), https://www.sec.gov/news/public-statement/gensler-aspen-security-forum-2021-08-03.
2. See *SEC v. Telegram Group Inc.*, 448 F. Supp. 3d 352 (S.D.N.Y. 2019); *SEC v. Ripple Labs Inc. et al.*, No. 20-cv-10832, ECF No. 4 (S.D.N.Y Dec. 22, 2020); *SEC v. Binance Holdings Limited et al.*, No. 1:23-cv-01599 (U.S. D.D.C. 2023); See *SEC v. Coinbase, Inc. and Coinbase Global, Inc.*, No. 1:23-cv-04738 (U.S. D.D.C. 2023).
3. See, e.g., U.S. Securities and Exchange Commission, *Chair Gary Gensler's Remarks before the Aspen Security Forum* (Aug. 3, 2021), https://www.sec.gov/news/public-statement/gensler-aspen-security-forum-2021-08-03 ("I believe we have a crypto market now where many tokens may be unregistered securities, without required disclosures or market oversight."); Wall St. J., *SEC Chairman on New Regulations on Cryptocurrencies and Climate Risk* (Dec. 12, 2021), https://www.wsj.com/articles/sec-chairman-on-regulations-on-cryptocurrency-and-climate-risk-11639165931?mod=itp_wsj&yptr=yahoo ("With regard to these digital currencies, if you're still raising money from the public, that still comes under the securities laws.").
4. U.S. Securities and Exchange Commission, *Chair Gary Gensler's Statement on the Approval of Spot Bitcoin Exchange-Traded Products* (Jan. 10, 2024), https://www.sec.gov/news/statement/gensler-statement-spot-bitcoin-011023.
5. *Id.*

Government Crypto Bankruptcy Intervention

Voyager

In the *Voyager Digital* bankruptcy proceedings, the Debtors sought to make the first in-kind distribution of crypto to crypto-creditors. This means that if a creditor was holding a particular crypto on Voyager, the Debtors sought to distribute recoveries to that creditor in whatever crypto that customer was holding. In a questionnaire distributed to Voyager crypto creditors, the overwhelming majority opted to receive crypto distributions as opposed to fiat distributions. In order to facilitate that distribution and to otherwise maximize recoveries to crypto creditors, the Debtors sought to engage BAM Trading Services Inc. (Binance. US) as a liquidation agent. Debtors argued that the transaction would maximize in kind distributions to crypto account holders, and would "limit the amount of cryptocurrency sales that the Debtors would have to make … thereby [] reduc[ing] the extent to which sales … might adversely affect market prices."[6] While the Debtors and the Official Committee of Unsecured Creditors (Voyager UCC) were supportive of this distribution plan, the government was the key party that strongly objected.

The SEC objected to such provisions in the Chapter 11 plan on grounds including that the Debtors needed to prove that any transaction may involve the distribution of unregistered securities and that Binance.US may have been operating as an unlicensed securities broker.[7] The SEC contended that the "the transactions in crypto assets necessary to effectuate the rebalancing [including the VGX token] … may violate the prohibition in Section 5 of the Securities Act of 1933 against the unregistered offer, sale, or delivery after sale of securities," and that the disclosure statement did not adequately address this possibility.[8] Notably, this was prior to the SEC bringing its case against Binance or alleging that the cryptocurrencies to be distributed were unregistered securities. Other than VGX, the SEC did not identify any particular cryptocurrency that it was alleging was an unregistered security.

The SEC and the DOJ submitted objections and cross-examined witnesses at the confirmation hearing. However, neither the SEC or the DOJ submitted any admissible evidence concerning whether any of the cryptocurrencies to be distributed to creditors were unregistered securities.

Judge Wiles of the U.S. Bankruptcy Court for the Southern District of New York rejected the SEC's objection. In particular, Judge Wiles rejected the notion that Debtors were responsible for figuring out what aspects of their own transaction, or what activities of Binance. US, could raise registration issues.[9] Judge Wiles stated in his decision the following: "The plain fact is, however, that the SEC has not actually made any objection. It has only vaguely

---

6. *Decision Regarding (1) Approval of The Debtors' Disclosure Statement, (2) Confirmation of the Debtors' Plan of Reorganization, (3) Motions Seeking the Appointment of a Trustee, (4) Motions Requesting Full Customer Access to Account Holdings, and (5) Related Matters, In re Voyager Digital Holdings, Inc., et al.*, Case No. 22-10943 (Bankr. S.D.N.Y. Feb. 22, 2023), ECF No. 1170, p. 5. ("Decision").

7. *Objection of the U.S. Securities and Exchange Commission to Final Approval of the Adequacy of the Debtors' Disclosure Statement and Confirmation of the Chapter 11 Plan, In re Voyager Digital Holdings, Inc., et al.*, Case No. 22-10943 (Bankr. S.D.N.Y. Feb. 22, 2023), ECF No. 1047 ("Objection").

8. Objection, at ¶ 4.

9. See Decision, at 10.

hinted at possible issues that have not even been described in a manner that would permit the Court or the parties to address them."[10]

Further, the court acknowledged that customers and creditors deserve a resolution of the case, which could not be put into an "indeterminate and expensive deep freeze while regulators figure out whether they do or do not think there is any problem with the transactions that are being proposed."[11] The bankruptcy court noted that the SEC was aware of Voyager's platform and the VGX token for years while Voyager was in business prior to bringing their objection. The bankruptcy court stated that the SEC had put it "in the unenviable position of having to make a ruling about the proposed transaction in the face of hearsay accusations of potential wrongdoing, in an industry where other firms have apparently engaged in real wrongdoing, while having absolutely no evidence indicating that there is any good basis for the [] that have been raised."[12] Judge Wiles stated that he expected that "a regulator [] tell [the court] that it has an actual objection (as opposed to saying that there "might" be an issue), and also to tell [the court] what the issue is and why it is an issue, so that other parties may address it and so that [the court] may make a proper and well-considered ruling."[13]

The government also objected to the "exculpation" clause. The exculpation clause is routinely granted in each bankruptcy case. It means that the court appointed professionals—financial advisors, law firms, accountants—cannot be sued for work done in connection with the bankruptcy cases. In this case, the government sought to object to the exculpation clause with respect to future regulatory or other enforcement concerning the distribution to creditors. Conversely, this crypto distribution was court-ordered pursuant to the Plan. This means that the professionals *shall* distribute crypto as required by the Plan. Judge Wiles rejected this position stating that the government cannot lay in wait and watch professionals act pursuant to a court ordered plan and later pursue a regulatory action. That issue is still being appealed by the government. The Voyager professionals opted to distribute crypto to creditors while the exculpation clause appeal is ongoing.

It appears that the government was fearful that if they don't object to crypto distributions than they may have been conceding that certain cryptocurrencies were not securities. But there was no such finding by any court.

In Voyager, government objections and appeals cause the estate to spend millions of dollars and delayed distributions to creditors. Ultimately, distributions to most creditors were made in crypto as originally contemplated by the Plan.

Celsius

Similarly, SEC intervention in the *Celsius* bankruptcy proceedings demonstrates a concerted effort to reserve authority with regard to contested regulatory and enforcement issues. In *Celsius*, the SEC objected to the proposed Chapter 11 plan proffered by debtors, which

10. See *id.* at 13 ("The plain fact is, however, that the SEC has not actually made any objection. It has only vaguely hinted at possible issues that have not even been described in a manner that would permit the Court or the parties to address them").

11. *Id.*

12. *Id.* at 8.

13. *Id.* at 10–11.

proposed to engage Coinbase as distribution agent for international customers.[14] The SEC filed a limited objection and reservation of rights, based on certain of the documents filed as part of the plan supplement, which they claimed were inconsistent and raised concerns under federal securities laws.[15] The SEC specifically argued that the "Coinbase Agreements go far beyond the services of a distribution agent, contemplating brokerage services and master trading services that implicate many of the concerns raised in the SEC's District Court action against Coinbase."[16] In its action against Coinbase, the SEC alleged that, among other things, Coinbase "has acted as an exchange, a broker, and a clearing agency, without registering as an exchange, broker, or clearing agency."[17]

The SEC argued that the bankruptcy court should not approve a deal where the material terms are missing and inconsistent, and the SEC reserved rights to object if the Debtors did not adequately address Coinbase's role in the confirmation order and in an amended agreement that was made available for review.[18] Notably, the SEC had already alleged that the CEL Token was offered and sold as a security, and that Celsius and its CEO raised billions of dollars through the unregistered and fraudulent offer and sale of securities.

Like in *Voyager*, the SEC sought to have the bankruptcy court interject into deciding on whether a security exists, and to do so for the purposes of making distributions under the plan.[19] However, there are marked differences in the circumstances surrounding Voyager, including the SEC's prior investigations into the platform and its executives and determination of the existence of violations of securities laws. Unlike in *Voyager*, the SEC had already filed a complaint against Celsius Network Limited and its former CEO, Alexander Mashinsky, alleging that the defendants raised billions of dollars from investors through the sale of unregistered crypto asset securities.[20] This demonstrates that the intervention included a level of ripeness that was otherwise non-existent in *Voyager*.

After the Chapter 11 plan confirmation, the *Celsius* Debtors ultimately decided to pivot estate resources toward a Bitcoin mining operation, which it is working with the SEC to register as a publicly traded company that will be owned by Celsius customers. The company, previously described in the plan as Fahrenheit NewCo will be called Mining NewCo. Based on the SEC's feedback on regulatory requirements, the Debtors determined that certain of the assets transferred to Fahrenheit NewCo must be retained by Debtors' estates to be administered and monetized for the benefit of creditors, which Debtors acknowledged would likely entitle them to greater in-kind recoveries of liquid cryptocurrency.[21]

---

14. See *Limited Objection and Reservation of Rights of the U.S. Securities and Exchange Commission to Debtors' Chapter 11 Plan, In re Celsius Network LLC, et al.*, Case No. 22-10964 (Bankr. S.D.N.Y. Sep. 22, 2023), ECF No. 3522 ("Limited Objection").
15. See *id.*
16. *Id.* at ¶ 9.
17. *SEC v. Coinbase, Inc.*, Case No. 1:23-cv-04738 (S.D.N.Y.).
18. See Limited Objection, at ¶ 10.
19. See *id.* at ¶ 11.
20. See *SEC v. Celsius Network Ltd.*, No. 1:23-cv-06005 (Bankr. S.D.N.Y.)
21. *Notice of Press Release, In re Celsius Network LLC, et al.*, Case No. 22-10964 (Bankr. S.D.N.Y. Nov. 20, 2023), ECF No. 4017, Ex. A.

BlockFi

Prior to BlockFi Lending LLC's (together with its affiliates, BlockFi) bankruptcy filing in November of 2022, the SEC charged BlockFi for failing to register the offers and sales of its crypto lending products, known as BlockFi Interest Accounts (BIAs). The SEC initially charged BlockFi with a $100 million penalty in February of 2022 ($50 million to the SEC and $50 million to 32 states), noting that "[t]hrough BIAs, investors lent crypto assets to BlockFi in exchange for the company's promise to provide a variable monthly interest payment," the SEC said in its press release.[22] Between February and November 2022, BlockFi paid approximately $20 million of the fine owed to the SEC, leaving a balance of $30.28 million.

During the bankruptcy proceedings, BlockFi filed a proposed plan of reorganization that sought to subordinate the SEC's penalty claim behind the payment of general unsecured creditors and other claims. The SEC objected to such proposed treatment, and asserted that its penalty claim should be treated *pari passu* with other general unsecured creditors. Following extensive negotiations, BlockFi and the SEC filed a stipulation and agreed order that permitted the SEC's claim to be subordinated under the plan of reorganization.[23]

In the Stipulation, BlockFi maintained the position that subordination is proper since the Bankruptcy Code allows for the subordination of penalties and the SEC's claim involves such penalties. The stipulation provides that the SEC's claim "will be re-classified as a general unsecured claim in new Class 15" and will not receive any distributions under the plan "until payment in full of all other Allowed Claims in Classes 1, 2, 3, 4 and 11," which are the classes for secured tax claims, priority claims, account claims, general unsecured claims, and intercompany claims, respectively.[24]

According to the Stipulation, the SEC maintains its disagreement with the previously proposed plan treatment and "asserts that its claims are general unsecured claims entitled to participate *pari passu* with other general unsecured creditors."[25] However "due to the specific facts" of the case and "in order to maximize the amount that may be distributed to investors and avoid delay in such distribution," the SEC has "agreed to forego participating in any distributions under the Plan or requiring any cash reserve in connection with such distributions, on account of any claims that may be or become Allowed Claims based on the Commission POC until all other allowed claims in Classes 1, 2, 3, 4, and 11 (as defined in the Plan) are paid in full."[26]

Finally, it is worth noting the ongoing saga of the FTX bankruptcy. That case hit the industry like a wrecking ball in November of 2022, with statements from new and court-appointed FTX CEO John J. Ray, III, that there was a complete absence of corporate controls and reliable financial information at FTX, and stating that the lapses in oversight, security

---

22. See Press Release, U.S. Securities and Exchange Commission, *BlockFi Agrees to Pay $100 Million in Penalties and Pursue Registration of its Crypto Lending Product* (Feb. 14, 2022), https://www.sec.gov/news/press-release/2022-26.
23. See *Stipulation and Agreed Order Between U.S. Securities and Exchange Commission and Debtors to Forego Receiving Distribution from Debtors' Bankruptcy Estates*, Case No. 22-19361 (Bankr. D. N.J. June 22, 2023), ECF No. 1099 (the "Stipulation").
24. *Id.* at ¶ 2.
25. *Id.*
26. *Id.*

and corporate governance were the worst he had ever seen in a 40 year career (and Ray had managed the Enron bankruptcy).

There was significant maneuvering within the bankruptcy, including disputes over who should serve as counsel for the FTX estate, an issue ultimately resolved in favor of Sullivan & Cromwell, which previously had served as one of FTX' s corporate counsel. There also was a motion by the U.S. Bankruptcy Trustee (the government watchdog in Chapter 11 re-organizations) for the appointment of an Independent Examiner. The Trustee's argument was that the allegations of unprecedented fraud leading to the FTX collapse should be reviewed by a disinterested person, and not left to an internal investigation. That request was denied by Bankruptcy Judge John Dorsey in February 2023. He agreed with FTX, and its Official Committee of Unsecured Creditors, that an Independent Examiner would be too costly and duplicative of existing investigations already underway by FTX's new leadership, by the Creditors Committee, and by several Federal agencies. However, on January 22, 2024, the Third Circuit Court of Appeals reversed Judge Downey and ordered the appointment of an Independent Examiner, ruling that the Bankruptcy Code mandates such an appointment, and stating that an Examiner should be able to provide "much needed elucidation" as well as ensuring that the Bankruptcy Court "will have the opportunity to consider the greater public interest when approving the FTX Group's reorganization plan."

Notably, this ruling came after FTX's submission of its re-organization plan, which proposed that creditors receive approximately $0.90 on the dollar, based on the lower dollar value of their holdings of cryptocurrencies when FTX filed for bankruptcy in November 2022. For example, that would cause account holders to recover the value of FTX-held Bitcoin assets at a price of $16,871 as opposed to today's price of over $65,000. Not surprisingly, numerous creditors object to that valuation methodology. Moreover, open questions remain as to what the true customer losses were, which had been estimated at approximately $8 billion. An additional open question is what the value is of some of the assets in which Bankman-Fried invested, such as AI firm Anthropic, which, based on current valuations, could add roughly $2.5 billion to the FTX estate, on top of the $6.7 billion reported in September by Mr. Ray. Moreover there are other assets that the Ray team did not count, such as an investment in Genesis Digital Assets (a leading bitcoin miner), and numerous other token holdings, which may or may not be liquid. However, some of those are Solana tokens, which have enjoyed a fivefold in market value in 2023, as well other holdings which taken together, could add another billion dollars to FTX assets.

Whether the Independent Examiner will give any comfort to the objecting creditors remains to be seen. Moreover, FTX claims that it is owed billions of dollars and has filed a dozen or so lawsuits in an effort to claw back those funds. Thus, we can be reasonably sure of two things. First, the FTX bankruptcy will continue to go on at least through the remainder of 2024. Second, the net outcome will be far from a total loss for investors, and there is a reasonable expectation (dependent on market conditions) that at least some may see a return of all or substantially all of their underlying investment.

Implications

Bankruptcies are a unique battlefield for regulatory disputes. While many defendants in enforcement actions complain of unfair advantages given to federal regulators, the bankruptcy bench seems to treat government regulators on an even playing field with other litigants. The bankruptcy bench is laser-focused on creditor recoveries and compliance with the bankruptcy code and has little patience for regulatory agenda-based litigation positions. As a result, federal regulators may find venues other than bankruptcy court to be safer battlefields for crypto-related regulatory litigation in the future.

Chapter 12
International Impact

Maneesha Gupta

Introduction

The international legal framework for blockchain is characterized by a patchwork of regulations, varying from proactive and accommodating approaches to cautious and restrictive measures. Against evolving issues of privacy, security, and jurisdiction, a nuanced understanding of the evolving legal terrain becomes imperative for policymakers, legal practitioners, and businesses navigating this revolutionary landscape. This chapter delves into the jurisdictional challenges arising from blockchain technology, examining the implications for legal enforcement and regulatory oversight.

Depending on the application of a particular business model and its connection to global markets, trading, lending, and other activities involving crypto contracts may be subject to various legal requirements worldwide. These requirements extend beyond the scope of this chapter but should be taken into account. They may include the potential application of international banking legislation, regulations governing loans and trusts in different jurisdictions, consumer protection laws, privacy regulations, proposed new legislation on retail payments globally, trade and economic sanctions imposed by different nations, compliance with business registration requirements across jurisdictions, adherence to advertising and marketing laws internationally, compliance with anti-spam laws, and consideration of language laws in relevant jurisdictions.

Global Context: Territoriality

In the context of public, permissionless blockchains, such as Bitcoin, the absence of a fixed geographical base complicates where and how jurisdictions assign legal responsibility. The decentralized architecture allows individuals, irrespective of their physical location, to operate a node if they possess the requisite hardware and technical knowledge. This decentralization poses a challenge in terms of legal accountability, as the absence of a specific location makes it intricate to assign legal responsibility.

There is no central authority overseeing the distributed ledgers in the network, adding further complexity. Unlike traditional systems with a single governing body, each participant in the blockchain network might have to follow different legal rules. Consequently, each network node may be subject to diverse legal requirements, contributing to a decentralized approach to jurisdictional application. This absence of a central authority raises significant questions regarding the application of legal frameworks and regulations, as the distributed nature of blockchains counters traditional notions of territoriality and regulatory oversight.

The nature of blockchains introduces challenges when trying to identify the country where damage occurs due to activities on these networks. This conduct may, in certain circumstances, transect different areas of law including non-contractual disputes and tort liability. In a global landscape, determining which laws apply and where the damage occurred becomes a significant challenge. The issue here is that legal regulations frequently refer to the location of damage. It might not be entirely evident in which country the damage occurs concerning actions on distributed ledgers. For example, in the European Union (EU), the Rome II Regulation, which concerns the selection of applicable laws governing disputes within the EU, focuses on the location or potential occurrence of damage.[1] This serves as a basis for establishing the relevant legal framework concerning non-contractual disputes. When addressing cyberspace issues, considering the location of damage might necessitate considering an approach rooted in negligence and tort liability, as indicated by authoritative judicial principles.[2]

Comparable difficulties arise when examining the territorial jurisdiction of the courts. When identifying a suitable court for tortious liability under the EU Brussels I regime, the general guideline is to consider the location where the harmful events have taken place or may take place.[3] When employing the relevant legal criteria to determine jurisdiction over a dispute, the Court of Justice of the EU has, in certain instances, considered the place of the causal event to be equated with the domicile or establishment of the pertinent information society service provider.[4] One potential step toward achieving clarity regarding the legal frameworks is leveraging current regulatory instruments. Rome II offers helpful provisions on how to determine governing law and the jurisdiction of the courts, allowing parties to opt for governing law and determine the courts with jurisdiction over any disputes.[5]

1. Article 4, Regulation (EC) No 864/2007 of the European Parliament and of the Council of 11 July 2007 on the law applicable to non-contractual obligations (Rome II).
2. See, for example, Case C-170/12, Peter Pinckney ECLI:EU:C:2013:635; Case C-523/10, Wintersteiger ECLI:EU:C:2012:220.
3. Article 7(3), Regulation (EU) 1215/2012 of the European Parliament and of the Council of 12 December 2012 on jurisdiction and the recognition and enforcement of judgments in civil and commercial matters (recast) (Brussels I Recast).
4. Case C-441/13 Hejduk ECLI:EU:C:2015:28; C-360/12 Coty Germany ECLI:EU:C:2014:1318; C-523/10 Wintersteiger ECLI:EU:C:2012:220.
5. Article 14, REGULATION (EC) No 864/2007 OF THE EUROPEAN PARLIAMENT AND OF THE COUNCIL of 11 July 2007 on the law applicable to non-contractual obligations (Rome II).

Enforceability

For laws to have practical effect, they must be enforceable through penalties or sanctions imposed on those who break them. Achieving this enforcement requires the law's ability to identify the violators, a task that proves challenging within a blockchain platform. The potential for pseudonymity and, in certain scenarios, complete anonymity on blockchains has led to the perception in certain circles that they can function as lawless zones advantageous to criminals. While this is possible, in private or corporate permissioned blockchains, where participants are known, it is not difficult to identify the responsibility of key actors. As blockchain platforms continue to evolve, some private blockchains are employed by bad actors as they provide true anonymity. However, more widely used platforms do not support anonymity.

Governments and regulatory bodies are actively working to prevent anonymity and adapt existing legal frameworks to address these challenges. For example, *Anti-Money Laundering* (AML) and *Know Your Customer* (KYC) regulations are being extended to cryptocurrency exchanges to regulate transactions and identify users. These rules aim to monitor and regulate the intersection between digital currencies and traditional currencies. Even if law enforcement or regulators cannot directly oversee each data point, information, and transaction on a blockchain, that does not make it impossible to regulate blockchains. There are many "access points" that authorities can utilize for enforceability, including Internet Service Providers and mining pools.[6]

The existing frameworks predate the emergence of blockchain and were conceived within an understanding of traditional, centralized data processing. Legislation, such as the *General Data Protection Regulation* (GDPR), which protects the personal data rights of citizens of the European Union, provides a clear example of the tensions between blockchains, anonymity, data processing, and regulations. See *Chapter 8—Privacy and Cybersecurity in Blockchain* for further implications of private international law. The evolution of the blockchain necessitates collaboration among regulators and lawmakers on an international scale to synchronize legal, technological, and regulatory frameworks while mitigating potential risks.

Singapore's Progressive Approach to Blockchain Regulation

Key Legal Developments

Singapore has embraced a progressive approach to blockchain regulation, fostering a conducive environment for innovation. Introduced in 2019, the *Payment Services Act* (PSA) regulates digital payment token services, providing clarity on cryptocurrency-related activities. The act categorizes digital payment tokens and requires service providers to adhere to AML and counter-terrorist financing (CTF) regulations. Singapore's regulatory sandbox allows fintech and blockchain companies to test their products and services in a controlled environment. This approach promotes innovation while maintaining regulatory oversight. Further, the Monetary Authority of Singapore (MAS) issued guidelines on digital token offerings, providing a framework for companies conducting initial coin offerings (ICOs) to comply with securities laws.

---

6. Michéle Finck, *Blockchain Regulation and Governance in Europe*, Cambridge, 2019.

Implications

Singapore continues to prioritize innovation in blockchain and fintech, with regulatory efforts geared toward balancing innovation with risk management. The regulatory landscape in Singapore is evolving to provide enhanced consumer protection measures, ensuring the responsible development of blockchain applications and services. Singapore is also actively collaborating with international counterparts to establish common standards and frameworks for blockchain technology, fostering cross-border innovation.

China's Blockchain Regulation and Legal Developments

Key Legal Developments

China has demonstrated a dual approach to blockchain, restricting certain aspects like cryptocurrency trading while actively promoting the technology's use in various industries. The significance of blockchain regulation in China lies in its potential to shape the country's digital future, drive technological advancements, and enhance regulatory oversight. Introduced in 2019, the Blockchain Information Service Management Regulations mandate that blockchain service providers must register with the Cyberspace Administration of China (CAC). The rules aim to ensure the legitimate use of blockchain technology while maintaining regulatory control. China has imposed restrictions on cryptocurrency trading, prohibiting Initial Coin Offerings (ICOs) and shutting down domestic cryptocurrency exchanges. This approach reflects the government's concerns about financial stability and speculative activities. Further, China has invested significantly in developing a national blockchain infrastructure, aiming to enhance the efficiency and transparency of various sectors, including supply chain management, healthcare, and public services.

Implications

The Chinese government plays a pivotal role in driving blockchain innovation, emphasizing its strategic importance in various sectors. China is actively developing its digital currency, the Digital Currency Electronic Payment (DCEP), aiming to establish a central bank digital currency (CBDC). This initiative reflects China's commitment to exploring new forms of currency and payment systems. China actively participates in international efforts to standardize blockchain technology, contributing to the development of global frameworks.

Insights from Canada: A Deeper Dive

As the acceptance of cryptocurrency gained traction in society, the Canadian government sought to address the anticipated legal complexities of blockchains. In 2014, Canada made history by amending the Proceeds of Crime and Terrorist Financing Act (PCA), marking the first instance globally where a nation implemented laws exclusively addressing individuals and entities engaged in cryptocurrency transactions.[7]

---

7. Mark J. Krone, et al., *Tales from the Crypt: Cryptocurrency Is Here-How Will Crime Insurers Respond?*, 24 Fidelity L. J. 1, 31 (2018).

Government View

Similar to numerous countries, the oversight of cryptocurrencies in Canada is distributed among different tiers of government and administrative bodies, contingent upon the specific nature of the undertaken activities. Despite these jurisdictional complexities, regulators in Canada typically maintain an open-minded and forward-thinking stance toward regulation. Notably, they have demonstrated this approach by approving cryptocurrency-based exchange-traded funds (ETFs) and constructing a practical regulatory oversight and compliance framework within the context of provincial securities regulation.

Regulation of Cryptocurrency in Canada

The primary regulatory framework for digital assets in Canada is established through provincial securities and derivatives regulations. In Canada, federal oversight is also exerted through anti-money laundering legislation, compelling the registration of specific virtual currency exchange or transfer services as money services businesses (MSBs).

Regulation of cryptocurrency in Canada primarily falls under securities regulation, overseeing the distribution and trading of securities and derivatives. This encompasses the enforcement of prospectus requirements, obligations for registration as dealers, advisers, and investment fund managers, and specific mandates for entities operating exchanges, alternative trading facilities, or other marketplaces facilitating trading activities. Additionally, this regulatory framework encompasses associated reporting and disclosure obligations.

The Canadian Securities Administrators (CSA) serves as an overarching body encompassing provincial and territorial securities regulators in Canada. When a virtual currency falls under the classification of a security or derivative, it becomes subject to securities regulations administered by the CSA. Although no specific rules or regulations pertain to digital assets, the CSA has issued guidance through various staff notices. These notices aim to navigate the dynamic landscape of retail crypto markets and adapt the existing regulatory framework to encompass digital assets.

In collaboration with the Canadian Industry Regulatory Organization (CIRO), the CSA delineates its framework and proposed approach for regulating this asset class in Staff Notice 21-329—Guidance for crypto asset Trading Platforms: Compliance with Regulatory Requirements (Staff Notice 21-329).[8] Staff Notice 21-329 presented a practical roadmap, expanding on prior guidance, which included the 2019 Consultation Paper 21-402—Proposed Framework for crypto asset Trading Platforms (the Consultation Paper).[9] Canadian provincial securities and derivatives laws might apply to virtual currencies if they are deemed to be securities or derivatives under these laws. The definition of a security under these laws encompasses various forms, including investment contracts.

8. Canadian Securities Administrators, Staff Notice 21-329—Guidance for crypto asset Trading Platforms: Compliance with Regulatory Requirements (Canadian Securities Administrators, 2021) (Staff Notice 21-329).

9. Canadian Securities Administrators and Investment Industry Regulatory Organization of Canada, Consultation Paper 21-402—*Proposed Framework for Crypto Asset Trading Platforms* (Canadian Securities Administrators and Investment Industry Regulatory Organization of Canada, 2019) (the Consultation Paper).

Pacific Coin Test for Investment Contracts

The Pacific Coin Test for investment contracts emerges as a crucial factor within the Canadian regulatory framework, particularly concerning the intersection of virtual currencies and blockchains. This test, rooted in securities and derivatives laws, plays a pivotal role in evaluating whether a virtual currency qualifies as an investment contract, thereby subjecting it to provincial securities and derivatives regulations. In the context of blockchains, the Pacific Coin Test becomes especially relevant as it addresses the dynamics of decentralized systems and their associated tokens.

The four-part test articulated in the Supreme Court of Canada's decision in *Pacific Coast Coin Exchange v. Ontario (Securities Commission)* is used to determine whether an investment contract exists.[10] The elements of the test are:

1. **Investment of Money:** The first prong considers whether the arrangement involves an investment of money.
2. **Common Enterprise:** The second prong examines whether the investment is part of a common enterprise, where the investor's fortunes are interlinked with those of others.
3. **Expectation of Profit:** The third prong assesses whether investors anticipate profits from their investment, emphasizing the significance of their expectations.
4. **Management by Others:** The final prong considers whether the success of the investment relies significantly on the efforts of individuals or entities other than the investor.

The significance of this test to blockchain law lies in its application to determine whether certain token offerings or transactions within the blockchain space fall under the definition of securities. If a particular blockchain-based investment meets the criteria of the Pacific Coast Coin Exchange test, it could be deemed an investment contract and consequently subject to securities regulations. This has implications for Initial Coin Offerings (ICOs) and token sales, requiring careful examination to ensure compliance with securities laws and regulations. The test provides a legal framework for regulators and market participants to navigate the evolving landscape of blockchain investments within the context of securities regulation.

As per the Staff Notice, each ICO is distinct and necessitates an evaluation based on its individual characteristics. Should a cryptocurrency offering be categorized as a securities offering, the entity conducting the offering is obligated to adhere to prospectus, registration, and/or marketplace requirements.

Complexities in Applying the Pacific Coin Test

The application of the Pacific Coin test to virtual currencies is often complex. Industry stakeholders argue that utility tokens, possessing specific functions or utilities beyond a mere

10. *Pacific Coast Coin Exchange v. Ontario (Securities Commission)* [1978] 2 SCR 112, which is itself based on the better known "*Howey* Test" set out by the Supreme Court of the United States in *SEC v. W.J. Howey Co.*, 328 U.S. 293 (1946).

profit expectation (such as enabling the acquisition of products or services), should not be categorized as securities. This standpoint seems to have gained general acceptance from the CSA and CIRO. The Consultation Paper from the CSA and CIRO also acknowledges the widespread belief that certain well-established virtual currency assets, serving as decentralized network payment methods (e.g., BTC), are presently not considered securities or derivatives. These assets exhibit features analogous to commodities like currencies and precious metals.

When determining if a specific virtual currency falls under Canadian securities laws, the CSA typically employs a comprehensive, multi-factor approach. The focus is on assessing the existence of an investment contract by delving into the substance rather than the form of the virtual currency.

If a particular virtual currency satisfies the Pacific Coin test criteria or exhibits certain characteristics outlined in the CSA guidance, it may be appropriately classified as an investment contract and consequently considered a security, subject to Canadian securities laws. This broad methodology is anticipated to be similarly applied in the examination of non-fungible tokens (NFTs). Factors considered include the presence of capital-raising or investment elements, the correlation between the number of tokens issued and their original purpose, and the anticipation of token trading on secondary markets.

In recent developments, the CSA has extended its regulatory approach to encompass arrangements deemed securities or derivatives due to being categorized as crypto contracts. The implications of such classification include adherence to distribution-related (prospectus) requirements and obligations to register as a dealer and/or marketplace.

CSA Guidance on Facilitating Cryptoasset Transactions

The guidance provided in Staff Notice 21-327 clarifies the conditions under which the CSA will deem "any entity facilitating transactions involving cryptoassets" to be subject to securities legislation requirements related to platform recognition and dealer registration.[11] Specifically, the CSA has emphasized that securities legislation may also be applicable to platforms facilitating the buying and selling of cryptoassets, even those categorized as commodities. This is because the user's contractual entitlement to the cryptoasset may itself be considered a derivative. This is generally the case when the platform is determined to be offering users a contractual right or claim to an underlying cryptoasset, rather than an immediate delivery of the cryptoasset.[12]

While regulators will assess all terms within the relevant contract or instrument, the CSA holds the perspective that if there is no instant delivery of the cryptoasset, securities legislation will generally be applicable. In this context, immediate delivery is considered to have taken place if: (a) there is an instantaneous transfer of ownership, possession, and control of the cryptoasset, allowing the user to freely use or deal with the cryptoasset without

11. Canadian Securities Administrators, Staff Notice 21-327—*Guidance on the Application of Securities Legislation to Entities Facilitating the Trading of Crypto Assets* (Canadian Securities Administrators, 2020) (Staff Notice 21-327).

12. Canadian Securities Administrators and Investment Industry Regulatory Organization of Canada, Consultation Paper 21-402—*Proposed Framework for Crypto Asset Trading Platforms* (Canadian Securities Administrators and Investment Industry Regulatory Organization of Canada, 2019) (the Consultation Paper).

further involvement or reliance on the platform or its affiliates. Furthermore, the platform or any affiliate should not retain any security interest or other legal right to the cryptoasset; and (b) subsequent to immediate delivery, the user is not exposed to insolvency risk (credit risk), fraud risk, performance risk, or proficiency risk from the platform.

Additional factors that should be taken into account include: (a) the contractual agreements between the platform and the user; (b) the presence of immediate settlement in the transaction; (c) the existence of margin and leverage trading; (d) prevailing commercial practices related to immediate delivery; (e) whether there is an instant transfer to a user's wallet; and (f) the party with ownership, possession, or control over the transferred cryptoasset.

Prospectus Requirements for Virtual Currencies

If a virtual currency is considered a security, the issuance or distribution of that security to the public is typically subject to prospectus requirements. The CSA mandates that a prospectus, a formal document providing details about the investment, be filed and approved before the virtual currency can be offered to the public. The CSA provides certain exemptions from prospectus requirements for specific types of transactions. Entities may seek exemptions to conduct private placements or exempt distributions, allowing them to distribute securities without a full prospectus, subject to certain conditions. Various alternatives exist for distributing securities in Canada on a prospectus-exempt basis, commonly known as exempt distributions or private placements. The majority of these exemptions are streamlined under National Instrument 45-106 Prospectus Exemptions. The CSA has communicated that individuals seeking to distribute virtual currencies can opt for these exemptions.[13]

Registration Requirements

Individuals or entities involved in trading or advising on securities and, in specific Canadian jurisdictions, derivatives, are required to register as a dealer or adviser. Alternatively, they may carry out these activities under an exemption provided by the relevant securities or derivatives laws. If an individual or entity oversees the business, operations, and affairs of an investment fund as defined by applicable laws, compliance with the investment fund manager registration requirement is necessary, or an exemption must be obtained. In the context of blockchain regulations, this emphasizes the need for entities involved in blockchain-based securities or derivatives trading and advisory services to adhere to registration requirements.

In the Canadian regulatory landscape, the obligation to register as a dealer or adviser is activated when an individual or entity engages in trading or advising activities related to securities or derivatives for business purposes. The mere indication, whether direct or indirect, of a willingness to partake in the business of trading securities may necessitate dealer registration. Determining the need for registration involves evaluating various factors, such

---

13. Canadian Securities Administrators, Staff Notice 46-307—Cryptocurrency Offerings (Canadian Securities Administrators, 2017) (Staff Notice 46-307).

as engaging in activities akin to a registrant, acting as an intermediary, and anticipating remuneration or compensation.

When applied to the context of virtual currency distributions, the Canadian Securities Administrators (CSA) has identified additional criteria to ascertain whether an individual or entity is conducting securities trading for business purposes. These include: (a) actively soliciting a diverse set of investors, including retail investors; (b) utilizing the internet to reach a broad audience of potential investors; (c) participating in public events to actively promote the sale of virtual currency; and (d) raising a substantial amount of capital from a large pool of investors. This acknowledgment of specific factors by the CSA aims to provide clarity within the evolving realm of blockchain regulations in Canada.

Promotion and Marketing

The Joint Staff Notice 21-330, titled "Guidance for Crypto-Trading Platforms; Requirements relating to Advertising, Marketing and Social Media Use," was issued by the CSA and CIRO on September 23, 2021. This comprehensive notice addresses various aspects of promotional activities for crypto-trading platforms under Canadian securities legislation. It encompasses requirements, best practices, and illustrative examples pertaining to advertising, marketing, social media engagement, fee disclosure, and other compliance considerations. For technologies operating within the crypto-trading space, this notice shows the importance of compliance with advertising, marketing, and social media use requirements. It aims to provide clear directives and standards to ensure that promotional activities within the evolving cryptocurrency sector are conducted in accordance with regulatory expectations. Regulatory frameworks like these play a crucial role in establishing guidelines that foster transparency, investor protection, and the responsible promotion of crypto-trading platforms within the Canadian market.

In addition to guidance on promotional activities, the CSA has introduced a regulatory sandbox initiative aimed at supporting fintech businesses seeking to introduce innovative products, services, and applications in the Canadian market. This initiative provides a streamlined process, allowing firms to register and/or obtain exemptive relief from securities law requirements more swiftly and flexibly than the standard application process. The goal is to facilitate the testing of products, services, and applications in the Canadian market on a time-limited basis. Several initiatives by provincial securities regulators in Canada provide additional avenues for blockchain businesses to navigate regulatory requirements and contribute to the overall growth of the fintech ecosystem in Canada. By creating an environment that fosters innovation through regulatory support and streamlined processes, these initiatives play a crucial role in positioning Canada as a hub for blockchain development. They provide opportunities for blockchain startups to thrive, contributing to a dynamic and innovative fintech ecosystem that benefits both industry participants and the broader Canadian economy.

Registration for Financial Entities

According to the federal Proceeds of Crime (Money Laundering) and Terrorist Financing Act (Canada) (the PCMLTFA), any entity involved in foreign exchange dealing, remitting or transmitting funds, issuing or redeeming money orders or similar instruments, dealing in virtual currency, or offering crowdfunding platform services must register in Canada as an MSB. Guidance from the Financial Transactions and Reports Analysis Centre of Canada (FINTRAC)[14] stipulates those entities holding permits, licenses, or registrations for these services, advertising their engagement in such services, or reporting income from these services as a separate business must also register as an MSB. Additionally, entities without a physical presence in Canada, directing any of the mentioned services at, and providing them to, individuals or entities in Canada, must register as a Foreign Money Services Business (FMSB). Both domestic and foreign MSBs are required to establish a compliance program to implement measures such as know-your-customer, reporting, record-keeping, travel rule, and other compliance requirements under the PCMLTFA.

In Canada, the legislation lacks a specific definition for activities categorized as dealing in virtual currency. However, FINTRAC has interpreted that these activities encompass virtual currency exchange services and virtual currency transfer services, primarily targeting entities like virtual currency exchanges. It does not extend to individuals or businesses employing virtual currency for purchasing and selling goods or services. In this context, a virtual currency exchange transaction is outlined as the exchange, upon request from another person or entity, of virtual currency for funds, funds for virtual currency, or one virtual currency for another. Virtual currency transfer services involve the transfer of virtual currency at a client's request or receiving a virtual currency transfer for remittance to a beneficiary. Entities registered as the equivalent of a MSB and/or engaging in any of these covered services may also be obligated to register as a FMSB in Canada.

Foreign Property

The Canada Revenue Agency (CRA) has clarified that virtual currencies located, deposited, or held outside of Canada are considered specified foreign property, as outlined in the Income Tax Act (ITA).[15] In this regard, Canadian residents are required to inform the CRA when the cumulative value of virtual currencies situated, deposited, or held outside Canada surpasses C$100,000 at any point during the year.[16]

Crypto and ESG

An important challenge facing cryptocurrencies in the realm of ESG (environmental, social, and governance) is the growing unease regarding the energy consumption associated with certain cryptocurrency activities, particularly the mining of specific cryptocurrencies.[17] The annual energy consumption of Bitcoin, in particular, has gained notoriety for rivalling or surpassing that of entire countries, such as the Netherlands or Argentina.

---

14. The Financial Transactions and Reports Analysis Centre of Canada (the FINTRAC) is Canada's financial intelligence unit and is responsible for monitoring compliance, enforcement and registration under the PCMLTFA. The FINTRAC guidance can be found here: https://www.fintrac-canafe.gc.ca/msb-esm/intro-eng.

15. Canada Revenue Agency, Document No. 2014-0561061E5, April 16, 2015.

16. Canada Revenue Agency, Document No. 2022-0936241C6, October 7, 2022.

17. Manitoba Hydro, "Province Directs Manitoba Hydro to Pause New Cryptocurrency Connections," November 28, 2022 and Government of British Columbia, "Province hits pause on electrical connections for cryptocurrency mining," December 21, 2022.

While some argue that the benefits of cryptocurrencies could outweigh this energy consumption issue, citing the potential social advantages they offer, others point to alternative cryptocurrencies that employ different technologies, potentially using less energy. For instance, proponents argue that cryptocurrencies contribute to social advantages by democratizing financial markets, eliminating intermediaries, or reducing the cost of remittance corridors between wealthier and less affluent countries. This is especially pertinent for migrant workers who can send funds home to their families more affordably.

The industry is actively grappling with this dilemma, and various approaches are being explored to address concerns about energy consumption.

Some initiatives involve the launch of new products designed to mitigate environmental impact, such as purchasing emission offsets or associating cryptocurrencies with carbon credits to trade as a unified asset. Government intervention can also shape the trajectory of this area, as demonstrated by the provincial government of Inner Mongolia's decision in March 2021 to ban all cryptocurrency mining operations, particularly in pursuit of carbon reduction targets set by the central government. As the fields of ESG and cryptocurrencies evolve, it remains intriguing to observe how the market will respond to these concerns and how they will inform the development of blockchain law.

As the cryptocurrency and digital assets sector advances, it will persist in confronting both existing and emerging challenges. These challenges encompass reconciling the distinctions between crypto securities and crypto commodities, exploring the potential emergence of central bank digital currencies (CBDCs), and grappling with the complexities of jurisdictional concerns for an intangible product operating across borders. It is evident that regulators consider this industry a pivotal focus, and the resolution of the distinctive issues it raises will remain an ongoing priority well into the future. Enforcing laws on blockchain platforms is hindered by pseudonymity and anonymity, necessitating efforts to adapt legal frameworks, including AML and KYC regulations. From jurisdictional challenges to reshaping contractual relationships and redefining privacy norms, blockchain's influence reverberates across diverse legal domains.

Singapore embraces innovation while providing a robust regulatory framework, fostering a vibrant blockchain ecosystem. Meanwhile, China seeks to harness blockchain's potential for economic development while maintaining strict control over certain aspects. Both countries contribute significantly to the global evolution of blockchain law, shaping the trajectory of this transformative technology. As blockchain continues to transcend borders, Canada's regulatory approach serves as a noteworthy reference point for other nations grappling with the challenges of legal frameworks, anti-money laundering measures, and the broader implications of decentralized technologies. As nations grapple with these changes, the collaboration between regulators, industry stakeholders, and innovative fintech businesses in Canada sets a precedent for fostering cross-border innovation and harmonizing global standards in the evolving realm of blockchain law.

Chapter 13
[Not] The Conclusion

Sumeet H. Chugani

Welcome to the blockchain
Things are about to change
Open up the gates
Systems get replaced
Bitcoin
Decentralize the trust
Security, transparency
The network's run by us …

—DECAP feat. Toby—Welcome to the Blockchain

We stand at the crossroads of traditional banking and innovation. Blockchain is ushering in a new era of decentralization and transparency—forcing traditional financial institutions to adapt and adopt new technologies. The future will undoubtedly bring more clarity to blockchain's rules of the road—introducing new governance while allowing innovation to flourish. Successful Banking [on] Blockchain will involve a mix of market awareness, prudent risk management, and updated regulations, balancing caution with openness to the opportunities of innovation.

The transformation is in full flight. On January 11, 2024, the SEC approved the first U.S.-listed exchange-traded funds (ETFs) to track bitcoin, in a watershed for the world's largest cryptocurrency and the broader crypto industry. Until now, the vast majority of regulated financial entities and the banking system overall were precluded from investing in Bitcoin. With ETF approval, IRAs, pension funds, and prominent institutional players have gained the ability to invest in Bitcoin, and opened the door for mass crypto adoption in financial services.

This is just the beginning. The benefits of blockchain implementation in the financial services industry will ultimately be shared by all stakeholders, including financial institutions and the general public. By creating trust between third-party entities and facilitating information transfer through means that did not previously exist, blockchain will unlock collaboration between financial institutions and strengthen the banking industry's role as a trusted intermediary.

The time is now for the age-old banking industry to modernize by incorporating both public and private blockchains in financial services. If we fail to build, we risk stifling innovation and forfeiting America's leadership in leading world-changing technologies. With appropriate governmental regulation, the banking industry will soon validate and reap the fruits of its big bet: Banking [on] Blockchain.

WAGM[L]: We're All Gonna Make [Law]

Afterword

Norman Reed

Driving a Future of Efficiency and Innovation

As this book comes to an initial close (the incredible pace of change suggests future additions), it is obvious that digital asset and blockchain technology—particularly as it relates to banking and other TradFi—is in a state of "becoming." We should end with a note of confidence and optimism about what the future will look like—considerably more efficient, reliable, and less expensive. A problem that has vexed banking since the days merchants in Florence, Venice and Genoa, is the complexity of the flow of funds and tracking. Banks have responded admirably over time with more complex technology, attempting to manage ever more complex transactions. With complexity, however, comes added intermediaries, processes, expense, delay, and uncertainty. As financial services continue to democratize, move faster and ignore national borders, that state of affairs must change.

The good news: blockchain is an effective solution. As adoption increases through its power to simplify operations as well as through accelerating market acceptance, much of the fear, uncertainty and doubt surrounding the interplay between blockchain and banking will dissipate. Blockchain technology or distributed ledger technology (DLT) is more than cryptocurrencies. While there are any number of uses for this technology, it can be used for any transaction, allowing for reliable recordkeeping and transparency.

During my years at The Depository Trust & Clearing Corporation (DTCC), as counsel to its institutional trade processing business, we only analyzed DLT for post-trade execution processing of securities. However, a DLT bonus includes the virtual elimination of Madoff style fraud, since DLT removes the ability to falsify records and allows for close scrutiny of transactions by all interested parties.

The Securities and Exchange Commission (SEC or Commission) should encourage DLT use by financial intermediaries to better protect investors, lower fees and increase the efficiency of security transactions. In doing so, the Commission would be complying with

Congress' instructions when it enacted Section 17A of the Securities Exchange Act of 1934 and urged the SEC to facilitate "new data processing and communications techniques [to] create the opportunity for more efficient, efficient and safe procedures for clearance and settlement." [See "Concept Release Securities Transactions Settlement" Release No. 33-8398; 34-49405; IC-26384; Federal Register Vol. 69 No.53 (March 18, 2004 at page 12922. (Concept Release)]

DLT Should Be Used to Clear and Settle Securities

Applying DLT to clearance and settlement could dramatically shorten the current settlement cycle. While this period will soon be reduced to trade date + one day, one may wonder why securities transactions are not being processed in seconds today. The current system for processing securities is complicated, involves actions by a number of different parties, and takes too much time and money. Today, post-trade execution of securities up to final settlement (where title to the securities passes from seller to buyer and the seller is paid by the buyer for the securities) requires the involvement of many different parties who must work together to finalize a transaction: (i) broker-dealers, (ii) their investment adviser customers (at least for institutional trades), (iii) transfer agents (responsible for maintaining record ownership of securities), (iv) custodians (responsible for maintaining custody of securities), (v) clearing houses like the NSCC or FICC (where trade obligations are compared, guaranteed and often netted), and finally (vi) central security depositories (CSDs) (where street name settlement occurs, i.e., when beneficial ownership of the relevant securities is transferred and payment is made). If corporate actions like shareholder votes and distributions are involved, then proxy solicitation firms are also required to be involved.

The results of such a step-by-step reactive process are often (i) delay, (ii) the redundant flow of non-essential data, and (iii) error as the same data is re-entered into different systems. As the SEC has repeatedly noted, "time equals risk."

DLTs would make the processing of securities transactions simpler, easier, faster, cheaper and safer. Assuming that securities are tokenized (i.e., transformed into digital tokens that can be represented on and processed by blockchains), securities, or digital representations of securities, could "live" on DLTs that would be available to the network of financial intermediaries involved in the trading, processing, and the clearing and settlement of securities, as well as offering a direct means of communication between security issuers and security owners. There would be no need for entities whose primary purpose is to maintain "golden copies" of the ownership of a particular issue or securities, such as transfer agents and CSDs. Broker-dealers, investment advisors and custodians would be able to reduce the size and complexity of their back-office operations. Intercompany friction and securities processing costs would be further reduced by utilizing smart contracts, essentially code that automatically executes and enforces contractual provisions on a blockchain.

Distributed Ledger Technology Serves the Regulatory Mission + Benefits the TradFi Industry

Disclosure, the close cousin of transparency, has long been the basis of security laws in the United States. This principle of transparency lies at the heart of our securities laws. And, the lack of transparency is seen as fundamentally unfair and the basis of many enforcement actions brought by the SEC—e.g., insider information.

Blockchains publicly display all transactions that have occurred on the blockchain, and make information easily available to financial intermediaries, investors, regulators and law enforcement and are immutable. If records of financial transactions cannot be altered and are publicly available ,fraudsters have a very steep mountain to climb.

In light of the above, it is surprising to witness the zeal with which the SEC and other US regulatory agencies attack DLT. A disinterested observer may question why the SEC is not encouraging the adoption of this technology—a technology that aligns with disclosure and fairness at the foundation of our securities laws, and a technology that puts the SEC's goal of immediate, accurate processing of securities transactions in reach. If US regulators step back and examine the big picture, they should realize the DLT is a tool that can be used to accomplish their ends and strengthen the US financial market. The SEC's current stance on this technology simply inconsistent with its mission I am confident that over time those views will change.

Glossary

A

- **Address**: A string of letters and numbers where crypto can be sent to and from
- **AIFMD**: The respective EU and UK versions of Directive 2011/61/EU of the European Parliament and the Council of 8 June 2011 on Alternative Investment Fund Managers, as amended (as applicable)
- **Airdrop**: Distribution of tokens or coins to an audience, often as part of marketing campaigns
- **Algorithm**: Process or set of rules followed in performing calculations or problem-solving
- **Altcoin**: Alternative coin to Bitcoin
- **AML**: Anti-Money Laundering, legal and regulatory procedures to minimize and prevent funds generated by illegal activities
- **APIs**: Application Programming Interfaces, sets of protocols and tools for building software applications

B

- **Balance Sheet**: A list of a cryptocurrency exchange's assets and liabilities
- **Bitcoin**: a particular type of decentralized cryptocurrency
- **Block**: Foundational component of a blockchain, containing multiple transactions
- **Block Explorer**: Website that displays details about transactions and blocks on a blockchain
- **Block Height**: Number assigned to each block in a blockchain, indicating its position relative to the genesis block
- **Block Reward**: Amount of cryptocurrency given to miners for successfully adding a new block to the blockchain
- **Blockchain**: A system of records that are connected using cryptography to protect data

C

- **CBDC**: A central bank digital currency, which is a digital form of money established by government regulation
- **CFTC**: U.S. Commodity Futures Trading Commission
- **Cold Storage**: Method of storing cryptocurrency offline, away from the Internet, reducing the risk of hacks
- **Confirmation**: Verification of a transaction by inclusion in a block on the blockchain
- **Consensus**: Agreement among participants in a blockchain regarding the validity of transactions and the addition of new blocks
- **Consortium Chain**: Type of blockchain managed by a predetermined group of organizations
- **Contract Address**: Unique identifier associated with a smart contract deployed on a blockchain
- **Contract Code**: Source code defining the functionality of a smart contract
- **Crypto Assets**: These are assets issued or transferred using distributed ledger or blockchain technology (also called digital assets)
- **Cryptocurrency**: Form of digital asset secured by cryptography, controlling the creation of additional units and verifying transactions
- **Cryptography**: The conversion of data into private code using encryption algorithms, typically for transmission over a public network

D

- **Decentralized**: A system that has no single authority or administrator
- **DeFi (Decentralized Finance)**: which is a category of financial services, such as borrowing and lending, operating via applications on decentralized public blockchain networks and that do not involve intermediaries, such as banks
- **Deterministic Wallet**: Wallet generating addresses deterministically from a seed phrase
- **Difficulty Adjustment**: Mechanism adjusting the difficulty level of finding a new block according to the current rate of block production
- **Disintermediation**: Removal of intermediaries in a transactional process due to the adoption of blockchain technology

E

- **ERC-20**: Technical standard used for smart contracts on the Ethereum blockchain ensuring compatibility across various tokens
- **ERC-721**: Standard for non-fungible tokens (NFTs) on the Ethereum blockchain
- **Ether**: the name of the cryptocurrency tokens used for payment on the Ethereum network

- **Ethereum**: a blockchain network that is similar to Bitcoin. It has its own cryptocurrency, called Ether or ETH, and can be used to build, publish, and monetize decentralized digital applications on the network
- **Ethereum Virtual Machine (EVM)**: Software environment enabling the execution of smart contracts on the Ethereum blockchain
- **Etherscan**: Popular website displaying details about transactions and blocks on the Ethereum blockchain

F

- **Fiat currency**: a government-issued currency that is not backed by a commodity, like oil or gold, but rather by the issuing government itself, such as the U.S. dollar or the Euro
- **Fork**: Change to the protocol of a blockchain resulting in two branches
- **Fractional Reserve Banking**: System allowing banks to lend more money than they physically possess
- **Full Node**: Complete version of a blockchain client capable of downloading and validating the entire blockchain

G

- **Genesis Block**: First block in a blockchain, used as the foundation of the entire network
- **Governance**: Management of a blockchain platform by its stakeholders

H

- **Halving**: Reduction of reward received by miners for adding a new block to the blockchain
- **Hard Fork**: Irreversible change to the protocol of a blockchain, creating a new branch
- **Hash**: Encoded representation of data used to confirm the integrity of a block
- **Hashrate**: Measure of computational power per second used when mining
- **HD Wallet**: Wallet utilizing hierarchical deterministic algorithms to generate addresses

I

- **ICO Scam**: Fraudulent initial coin offerings aimed at defrauding investors
- **Immutability**: Property of blockchain records preventing alteration or deletion
- **Inflation**: Increase in the quantity of money circulating in an economy over time
- **Initial Coin Offering (ICO)**: Fundraising technique involving issuing cryptocurrency tokens in exchange for fiat currencies or other established cryptocurrencies
- **Initial Exchange Offering (IEO)**: Fundraising technique conducted via cryptocurrency exchanges
- **ISO**: the International Organization for Standardization **ISO27001** the international standard for information security

K

- **Keystore File**: JSON-formatted file containing the private key of a wallet
- **Know Your Customer (KYC)**: Legal requirement for businesses to verify the identity of customers

L

- **Ledger**: Digital recordkeeping system tracking cryptocurrency transactions
- **Lightning Network**: Second-layer solution increasing transaction speeds and volumes on blockchains
- **Linear Feedback Shift Register (LFSR)**: Sequential generator used in cryptocurrency mining
- **Linux**: Open-source operating system widely adopted in blockchain development

M

- **Mainnet**: Operational blockchain network supporting real-world usage
- **Malleability**: Property of blockchain transactions permitting changes without invalidating the overall block
- **Market Capitalization**: Total monetary value of all outstanding shares of a company or cryptocurrency
- **Masternode**: Special full node providing extra services, including instant payments and privacy protection
- **Merkle Tree**: Data structure used in blockchain verification processes
- **Metadata**: Information describing other data
- **Microtransaction**: Small payment for a service or good
- **Miners**: People creating new cryptocurrency through the process of solving computational problems that validate transaction blocks and work to maintain the blockchain ledger
- **MPC**: Multi-party computation

N

- **NFT**: A non-fungible token that represents ownership of a unique item, such as digital-only artwork, music, or games. This means that the token cannot be interchanged with something else
- **Nodes**: Computers connected to the blockchain network, helping to validate transactions
- **Nonce**: Random number used during proof-of-work mining to ensure uniqueness of a block
- **Notary Service**: Third-party validation of documents or transactions

O

- **Oracle**: External source supplying real-world data to smart contracts
- **Overcollateralization**: Providing more collateral than needed to borrow a loan

P

- **Paper Wallet**: Printout containing a cryptocurrency address and private key, used for cold storage
- **Pay-Per-Last N Shares (PPLNS)**: System that pays miners after the pool discovers a block
- **Pay-per-Share (PPS)**: Miners compensated for each valid share contributed
- **Peer-to-Peer**: Communication protocol not requiring a central hub
- **Pegged Asset**: Cryptocurrency whose value is tied to another asset, such as fiat currency or precious metal
- **Permissioned Blockchain**: Private blockchain where nodes must be authorized by a central entity
- **Poisson Distribution**: Mathematical model used to analyze block arrival times in blockchain systems
- **Polygon (MATIC)**: Scaling solution for the Ethereum blockchain
- **Ponzi Scheme**: Investment scheme paying existing investors with funds from new investors
- **Pool Mining**: Group mining approach increasing chances of earning a block reward
- **Portfolio**: Collection of all current crypto holdings in one place
- **Pre-sale**: Exclusive token sale event preceding a public ICO
- **Premined Coins**: Tokens created prior to launching a blockchain project
- **Privacy Coins**: Cryptocurrencies designed for transaction anonymity and user privacy
- **Privacy Coins**: Cryptocurrencies emphasizing enhanced privacy and anonymity
- **Private key**: The secret access to encrypted digital information that is paired with a public key and shared by the encoder with an authorized party to enable access to the information
- **Private Keys**: Alphanumeric string enabling transactions from a cryptocurrency address
- **Proof of Authority (PoA)**: Consensus algorithm assigning block validation based on identity and reputation
- **Proof-of-Burn (PoB)**: Consensus algorithm assigning block validation based on coins/tokens burned by the validator
- **Proof-of-stake (PoS)**: A non-mining platform where participants commit a stake of their private or collective capital to the platform in the form of the platform's native tokens, which are locked up for a given period of time
- **Proof-of-work (PoW)**: A blockchain protocol that involves miners solving complex mathematical problems/algorithms in order to place a block of transactions on the chain

Q

- **Quantitative Easing**: Monetary policy increasing money supply to stimulate the economy

R

- **Rekt**: Slang term for significant financial loss in trading or investment
- **Resistance Level**: Price point at which an asset tends to stop rising due to selling pressure

S

- **Satoshi**: The smallest unit of Bitcoin, named after its pseudonymous creator
- **Scalability**: Ability of a blockchain network to handle increasing transaction volumes
- **Security Token Offering (STO)**: Fundraising method involving issuing security tokens backed by real-world assets
- **Sharding**: Technique dividing the blockchain into smaller parts to improve scalability
- **Smart Contract**: Self-executing contract with terms directly written into code on the blockchain

T

- **Tokenomics**: Economics of a token, including its creation, distribution, and value proposition
- **Transaction Fee**: Amount paid for processing transactions on a blockchain network

U

- **Unbanked**: Refers to individuals who are either unable to access banking services or choose not to
- **Uncle Block (Ommer Block)**: Refers to the discarded block in the phenomenon when two blocks are simultaneously created, resulting in one block being omitted from the blockchain
- **Unconfirmed**: A state in which a transaction has not been appended to the blockchain
- **Unhosted Wallet**: A wallet held by the user
- **UNI Token**: A native governance token of Uniswap, the largest decentralized exchange at the time of writing
- **Uniswap**: Decentralized exchange protocol allowing users to swap various cryptocurrencies without an intermediary
- **Unit of Account**: A standardized unit of measurement used in accounting to record and track financial transactions.
- **United States House Committee on Financial Services**: A committee of the United States House of Representatives that oversees all components of the US's financial and housing services

- **Unpermissioned Ledger**: A public ledger that is open to anyone, without being controlled by a single owner
- **Unrealized Profit & Loss**: Unrealized profit and loss occur when you have a position open in a security that has appreciated or depreciated in value
- **Unregulated**: Something that isn't controlled by a centralized authority or a governing intuition
- **Unspent Transaction Output (UTXO)**: A transaction that is left unspent after being completed, similar to leftover change after making a purchase
- **Unstoppable Domains**: A San Francisco-based company that provides blockchain-based domain names to users
- **US Office of Foreign Assets Control (OFAC)**: A financial intelligence and enforcement agency of the US Treasury Department
- **Use Case**: A description of the interactions between an actor (human or system) and a system that leads to an event
- **User Interface**: The user's interaction with a website or application using a digital device
- **UTC Time**: Coordinated Universal Time
- **Utility Mining**: A mechanism that allows for the distribution of tokens based on user activity and active participation
- **Utility Token**: Tokens that are designed specifically to be able to help people use something

V

- **Validator**: On a proof-of-stake (PoS) blockchain, a participant responsible for validating blocks and receiving rewards
- **Vanity Address**: A customizable cryptocurrency public address chosen by its owner
- **Vaporware**: An unreleased cryptocurrency project that does not exist beyond promotional materials
- **VASP**: Virtual Asset Service Provider
- **Verification Code**: A security measure used to protect against automated bot attacks
- **Vesting Period**: Restrictions placed on the release of tokens following an initial coin offering (ICO)
- **Virgin Bitcoin**: Bitcoins that have never been spent
- **Virtual Automated Market Makers (vAMMs)**: Systems that allow traders to trade synthetic assets without holding actual ones
- **Virtual Commodity Association (VCA)**: A proposed self-regulating body for the U.S. virtual currency industry
- **Virtual Private Network (VPN)**: Technology that secures internet connections by establishing a secure tunnel between devices and servers
- **Virtual Reality (VR)**: Simulated environments experienced through specialized equipment

- **Virus**: Malicious programs installed on computers to steal sensitive information or cause damage
- **Vitalik Buterin**: One of the founders of Ethereum, the second-largest cryptocurrency
- **Volatility**: The degree of variability in the price of an asset over time
- **Volume**: The total amount of cryptocurrency traded over a specific period

W

- **Wallet**: An application or device for storing the private keys providing access to the digital asset
- **Wallstreetbets (WSB)**: A popular Reddit community focused on discussing stocks and options trading
- **WannaCry Ransomware**: A widespread cyberattack that targeted vulnerable computers running Microsoft Windows
- **Wasabi Wallet**: A privacy-centric Bitcoin wallet
- **Wash Trade**: Manipulative practice where buyers and sellers artificially inflate trading volume
- **Watchdog Organization**: Independent groups monitoring government activities on behalf of the public
- **Watcher (OMG Foundation)**: A computer that ensures correctness of transactions and confirms network operations
- **Watchlist**: A personalized list of cryptocurrencies followed by individual users
- **Weak Hands**: Investors susceptible to panicking and selling during periods of volatility
- **Web 1.0**: The earliest stage of the World Wide Web
- **Web 2.0**: The modern iteration of the web featuring interactive content and social media platforms
- **Web 3.0**: the next evolution of the internet that provides a more decentralized method of user-content generation and allows users to interact via peer-to-peer networks
- **When Lambo**: Phrase asking when cryptocurrency investments will reach levels sufficient to buy luxury cars
- **When Moon**: Term used to express anticipation of dramatic increases in cryptocurrency values
- **White Hat Computer Hacker**: Skilled professionals who identify and report security flaws to improve safety
- **White Label**: Customizable products sold under different brand names
- **White Label Staking**: A staking service offered by a third-party provider on behalf of clients
- **White Swan Event**: Predictable events based on current information.
- **Whitelist**: List of approved participants in an initial coin offering

X

- **XRP Ledger**: Open-source blockchain protocol for digital payments developed by Ripple

Y

- **Yield Curve**: Graph showing relationships between bond yields and maturity dates
- **Yield Farming**: Strategy in DeFi where users provide liquidity to earn rewards and fees
- **Yield Sensitivity**: How much a fixed-income asset's price changes due to fluctuations in interest rates
- **YTD**: Acronym for Year To Date

Z

- **Zero Confirmation Transaction**: Transactions that haven't been fully processed and confirmed on the blockchain
- **Zero Knowledge Rollup**: A layer 2 scaling solution leveraging zero-knowledge proofs to perform computations and storage off-chain while keeping funds locked in smart contracts
- **Zero-Knowledge Proof**: Method allowing one party to prove knowledge of information without revealing the information itself
- **zkApps**: Applications built upon zero-knowledge rollups
- **zkOracles**: Trustless sources of data passing through zero-knowledge proofs
- **zkSharding**: Concept of sharding blockchains using zero-knowledge proofs

Index

Note: 'n' note has been given to entries taken from footnote.

C

E

F

J

K

L

M

N

O

P

T

U

V

W

About the Editors

Sumeet H. Chugani

General Counsel at Cloaked, Ex-Coinbase, Citizens Bank, Apple Bank; Ex-Litigator

Sumeet H. Chugani is currently General Counsel + Chief Compliance Officer at Cloaked. He was previously an Associate General Counsel at Coinbase, Deputy General Counsel at Apple Bank, and VP, Senior Counsel at Citizens Bank. Prior to his in-house roles, Sumeet was a regulatory consultant at PwC, and a consumer financial services litigator at Akerman LLP and Diaz, Reus & Targ LLP.

Sumeet has been in the trenches building state-of-the-art banking, blockchain, and de-identification technology, including acting as lead counsel for Coinbase's Multi-Party Computation wallet, Native Decentralized Exchange (DEX), Retail Advanced Trade, and International Exchange. He also led Citizen's build of the iPhone Upgrade Program, Microsoft Xbox All Access Program, and other Citizens Pay Buy-Now-Pay-Later solutions. As General Counsel at Cloaked, Sumeet launched Cloaked and Cloaked Pay, allowing users to create secure, instant identities to protect their personal identifiable information and payment details against identity theft, breach, and privacy exposure.

Stephen T. Gannon

Partner, Davis Wright Tremaine LLP

Stephen T. Gannon is a financial services industry leader with over 40 years of experience in private practice and in-house counsel positions. He began his career at Hunton & Williams (now Hunton Andrews Kurth) focusing on securities litigation and went on to establish securities practices at other firms.

Steve previously served as the General Counsel of Citizens Financial Group, the nation's 12th-largest retail and commercial bank. In this position, he served on the Executive Committee and was responsible for all legal, corporate governance, corporate transactions, government relations, regulatory relations, and litigation functions. Prior to Citizens, he served as Head of the Legal Department at Capital One Financial Corporation as well as General Counsel for Wachovia Securities (now Wells Fargo Advisors). He is now a partner at Davis Wright Tremaine LLC.

During the course of his career, Steve has held significant leadership positions in several financial industry organizations including the Securities Industry and Financial Markets Association (SIFMA) (Advisory Council, Co-Chair of Bank Regulation Sub-Committee); Bank Policy Institute (General Counsel's Forum); The Clearinghouse Association (Chair, Managing Board); and The Financial Services Roundtable. Steve has spent the last two decades as a senior advisor at the highest levels of strategic decision-making for several of the country's largest financial institutions. He advises the banking industry on regulatory and strategic matters ranging from public policy and corporate governance to litigation, regulatory compliance, and administrative actions. He also focuses on helping the industry stay abreast of burgeoning fintech and blockchain/digital asset spaces, about which he is a frequent writer and speaker.

About the Contributors

Joseph Aminov

Law Clerk, McDermott Will & Emery

Joseph Aminov focuses his practice exclusively on cryptocurrency and blockchain, with a specific emphasis on cryptocurrency-related litigation, regulatory advice, bankruptcies, and government investigations.

Mark M. Attar

Partner, Davis Wright Tremaine LLP

Mark, a former lawyer at the Securities and Exchange Commission for 12 years and co-lead of the firm's securities regulatory business line of the Banking and Financial Services practice group, has extensive experience counseling domestic and international participants in the financial markets, with a particular focus on federal securities laws and market regulation issues. He has advised a wide range of market participants, including broker-dealers, investment advisers, digital asset firms, trading platforms, institutional investors, clearing organizations, and credit-rating agencies. His practice includes the representation of clients in examinations and enforcement proceedings, with a particular focus on SEC and FINRA financial and operational rules, including rules relating to net capital, custody, margin, books and records, reporting, and risk assessment. He assists clients with broker-dealer formation, SEC registration, and FINRA membership and helps firms satisfy their independent consultant undertakings with regulators.

During his tenure at the SEC, Mark served as branch chief and senior special counsel in the Division of Trading and Markets. In those roles, he managed attorneys responsible for numerous rulemaking initiatives, including mandated rulemaking under the Dodd-Frank Act relating to security-based swap dealer capital, margin, and segregation, statutory and regulatory credit rating reference removal, and broker-dealer reporting, audit, and notification requirements. He handled numerous interpretive issues and provided formal guidance in the form of no-action and interpretive letters. He acted as a primary liaison on enforcement and examination matters involving broker-dealer financial responsibility rules, and represented the SEC on several international initiatives, including as a member of Joint Forum and IOSCO working groups.

Mark was a shareholder at McGonigle, P.C., before the firm combined with Davis Wright Tremaine.

Patrick Austin

Cybersecurity & Data Privacy Counsel, Woods Rogers Vandeventer Black | Ex-DWT

Patrick Austin is Of Counsel in the Cybersecurity and Data Privacy practice group of Woods Rogers Vandeventer Black. Patrick works in the Richmond, Virginia office of Woods Rogers advising clients on breach response, data privacy, information security, and regulatory compliance related to domestic and international privacy laws, including the General Data Protection Regulation (GDPR), California Consumer Privacy Act (CCPA), Virginia Consumer Data Protection Act (VCDPA), Health Insurance Portability and Accountability Act (HIPAA), and the Freedom of Information Act (FOIA).

Patrick is a Certified Information Privacy Professional with expertise in both U.S. and European law (CIPP/US & CIPP/E) by the International Association of Privacy Professionals (IAPP) and Co-Chair of the IAPP's Richmond KnowledgeNet Chapter.

Patrick obtained his Juris Doctorate from the George Mason University School of Law where he served as Editor-in-Chief of the National Security Law Journal.

Darren Azman

Partner, McDermott Will & Emery

Darren Azman is a member of the firm-wide Management Committee and a partner in the Business Restructuring group. Darren's practice focuses on corporate restructurings, creditors' rights, and distressed acquisitions. His clients include troubled companies, official creditors' committees, private equity sponsors, financial and strategic purchasers of distressed assets, and others in connection with in-court and out-of-court restructurings.

Darren has distinct restructuring experience in the fields of energy, manufacturing, healthcare, blockchain and cryptocurrency, technology, maritime and transportation, and cross-border restructurings, including insolvency proceedings involving Canada, British Virgin Islands, Brazil, Germany, Japan, South Korea, and other countries. He routinely litigates matters in US Bankruptcy Courts.

Darren is a recognized leader in the cryptocurrency space, having led the representation of the official committee of unsecured creditors in the first-ever crypto Chapter 11 case, Cred. Inc. His efforts in Cred have led to the development of novel case law that has generated millions of dollars of recoveries for creditors, including obtaining a court order requiring Cred's former chief capital officer to return more than $6 million of stolen cryptocurrency within 30 minutes after the court hearing concluded. Darren subsequently led the representation of the official committee of unsecured creditors in the Chapter 11 case of Voyager Digital, a crypto exchange with more than 1 million customers. He also represented the official committee of unsecured creditors in the first crypto mining Chapter 11 case,

Compute North. Darren is currently representing Prime Trust, a leader in the crypto space with more than $3.8 billion of crypto and fiat under custody at its peak, in its Chapter 11 bankruptcy case. Darren is frequently asked to speak around the country on the intersection of bankruptcy and cryptocurrency and regularly publishes articles on that topic, including in the American Bankruptcy Institute Journal, the Journal of Corporate Renewal, and Law360.

Michael T. Borgia

Partner, Davis Wright Tremaine LLP

Mike Borgia leads DWT's information security group in the technology, communications, and privacy and security practice. He advises clients on data breach prevention, readiness and response, complex internal investigations, and compliance with global security laws and regulations. Mike draws on his years of experience as outside counsel, cybersecurity consultant, in-house counsel at a global technology consultancy, and implementation project manager at a major software firm to help clients identify and tackle their toughest information security problems.

Mike's practice spans every phase of the information security lifecycle. He advises clients on compliance with global security, privacy, and information technology laws, frameworks, and standards. He works with clients of all sectors and sizes to assess and improve their incident readiness and security posture.

A veteran incident response professional, Mike has led investigations of and responses to hundreds of security incidents, from ransomware attacks to trade secret theft to sophisticated nation-state hacking campaigns. After incidents occur and threats are contained, Mike works closely with his clients to identify root causes and incorporate lessons learned into their information security programs.

Madison Breshears

Associate, Davis Wright Tremaine LLP

Madison Breshears obtained her juris doctorate with a concentration in the regulation of financial services from George Mason University, Antonin Scalia Law School, where she was the 2019 F.A. Hayek Law and Economics Scholarship recipient.

Prior to joining DWTs financial services practice group, Madison served as a legal intern to Commissioner Hester Peirce at the Securities Exchange Commission as well as a research assistant at the Cato Institute, where she assisted legal and policy scholars within the Center for Monetary and Financial Alternatives.

Madison has worked closely on academic and legal matters pertaining to digital assets and blockchain technology, securities enforcement actions and defense, as well as banking law and legal issues faced by various regulated financial intermediaries.

Mike Carter

Senior Managing Director, FTI Technology

Mike Carter is an expert in digital assets, regulatory compliance, and financial crimes investigations. Mr. Carter has extensive experience providing advisory and investigative services for financial crime matters globally, including leading complex engagements for financial institutions, digital asset service providers, financial technology and payments companies, and gaming companies to address risk and compliance concerns.

Mr. Carter most recently served as the Chief Compliance Officer (CCO) from 2020 to 2023 at a major digital asset exchange where he led the scaling and redesign of the global compliance program addressing issues related to money laundering, sanctions, fraud, data privacy and protection, market surveillance, product risks, licensing, and regulatory examinations.

In addition to his experience as CCO, Mr. Carter has led numerous compliance and regulatory projects at global consulting firms, including addressing regulatory risks at numerous digital asset companies during startup and growth phases, supporting government-appointed monitors, conducting sensitive investigations for high-profile matters, building executable compliance roadmaps and implementing data models to assess risk.

Mr. Carter served as the Anti-Money Laundering (AML)/Bank Secrecy Act (BSA) Committee Chair for the Virtual Commodity Association from 2019 to 2020 and on the AML Committee for TRUST Travel Rule from 2020 to 2023. He authored the digital assets section of the Committee of Sponsoring Organizations of the Treadway Commission (COSO) and the Association of Certified Fraud Examiners (ACFE) 2023 Fraud Risk Management Guide.

Mr. Carter is a United States Army combat veteran and served in Operation Enduring Freedom. He also serves as a board member of The Ability Experience and a board member of the Association for Women in Cryptocurrency. He holds PMP, CFE, CAMS, and CGSS certifications, and earned his MBA from George Mason University.

Jason M. Covert

Partner, Taft Stettinius & Hollister

Jason is a partner in Taft's Compliance, Investigations, and White Collar Defense group. He counsels clients through a wide range of matters, from evaluating the efficacy of compliance programs to defending regulatory and criminal investigations and litigating complex civil disputes. His clients include financial institutions, payment companies, private equity funds, and manufacturers in highly regulated industries. Jason leverages his experience and knowledge as a trusted advisor and a former prosecutor to provide clients with the guidance they need to navigate the ever-increasing complexity of the federal regulatory and criminal justice systems.

Prior to joining Taft, Jason spent more than a decade with the federal government, serving the last six years as a white-collar prosecutor with the U.S. Department of Justice's (DOJ) Criminal Division, Fraud Section, and before that, as an enforcement attorney with the Office of the Comptroller of the Currency (OCC). At the DOJ, he served as a prosecutor in the Market Integrity and Major Frauds unit, where he investigated and prosecuted individuals and corporations engaged in complex white-collar matters, including securities fraud, accounting fraud, investment fraud, bank fraud, environmental fraud, insider trading, FCPA violations, and money laundering. At the OCC, he investigated nationally chartered banks and thrifts and institution-affiliated parties (IAPs) and negotiated institutional and individual administrative enforcement actions. His experience at the OCC included matters related to unsafe and unsound banking activities, compliance with the Bank Secrecy Act, and violations of other federal regulations and statutes.

Jason is an active member of the American Bar Association and currently serves on the ABA's Banking Law Committee as the vice-chair of the Enforcement, Insider Liability, and Troubled Banks subcommittee. He also maintains a robust pro bono practice that includes representing clients in immigration and asylum proceedings and providing training to attorneys and judges in the Maldives.

Joseph B. Evans

Partner, McDermott Will & Emery

Joseph (Joe) B. Evans is the co-head of the FinTech & Blockchain Practice and head of Crypto Litigation and Regulatory Defense at McDermott. He is widely recognized as a leader in the crypto industry. The American Lawyer recognized Joe as a "Trailblazer" for his progressive work in crypto and he is one of the few individuals that Chambers ranked in Crypto-Asset Disputes. Joe runs the industry's only crypto-exclusive team whose members spend 100% of their time serving the crypto industry. That team is one of the few Chambers ranked in crypto-asset disputes.

Since 2013, Joe has been representing companies and individuals in all aspects of crypto and blockchain-related legal matters, spanning from defending government investigations, pursuing cutting-edge crypto litigation, obtaining money transmitter and other state licenses, and advising on initial coin offerings. Joe leads a team of crypto lawyers who are devoted exclusively to working on crypto and blockchain matters.

Joe has been recognized for his success in crypto-related litigation. Joe has demonstrated success in pioneering first-of-its-kind crypto litigation, including crypto trading, decentralized autonomous organization (DAO) litigation, and pursuing actions against fictitious entities and anonymous founders. Joe's in-court successes include a series of wins in connection with the crypto industry's largest bankruptcy cases in the United States and intellectual property litigation between competing crypto companies. Joe has qualified crypto tracing experts in federal court and obtained immediate recovery of stolen crypto. Joe also obtained emergency relief in intellectual property litigation against competitors using the same and similar names for competing crypto. Joe has defended crypto exchanges and other market participants in federal and state investigations. With regularity, Joe successfully defends these crypto regulatory investigations without penalties, fines, enforcement actions, or media attention of any kind.

Joe regularly rolls out crypto exchanges and other technology companies nationwide by obtaining state-by-state money transmitter and similar licenses and seeking no-action relief. Joe specializes in banking regulations, money transmitter laws, and securities regulations as they pertain to crypto and other FinTech companies. Joe and others from McDermott obtained a first-of-its-kind determination by the Wyoming Division of Banking holding that a particular Wyoming trust company is permitted to custody crypto as a qualified custodian under the Investment Advisers Act of 1940. Joe also advises crypto companies and other digital payment platforms on anti-money laundering, regulatory, sanctions, and other compliance issues.

For many years Joe has been publishing crypto-related articles and performing at speaking engagements. Joe was recently called upon to provide a training program on crypto tracing to a federal law enforcement agency.

Joe has defended government officials and senior executives in some of the nation's most high-profile government investigations and criminal jury trials. Joe represents clients in complex litigation matters and appeals in state and federal courts, with a primary focus on fraud-related litigation. Joe also defends public figures, senior executives, and corporate defendants in a variety of state felony and misdemeanor matters.

Joe is a Certified Fraud Examiner and a member of the Association of Certified Fraud Examiners.

Josh Garcia

Partner at Ketsal PLLC

Joshua has worked closely with developers, funds, exchanges, NFT platforms, and investors in the fintech and blockchain space for nearly a decade. His counsel draws from experience at tech-forward international law firms Cooley, White & Case, and Goodwin Procter. Joshua has been recognized as a thought leader by CoinDesk, Coin Center, Bitcoin Magazine, and others. He has counseled and presented to the Money Transmitter Regulators Association, the New York City Bar Association, congressional hill staffers, the Israel Securities Authority, the State Bank of Pakistan, and at various international industry events. He focuses on advocating sound crypto policy and advising clients on strategies for managing regulatory risk. His legal expertise focuses on securities, commodities, lending, consumer protection, and payments laws.

Michael Glotz

CEO, SRA Consulting and Co-Founder

Mr. Glotz is the Chief Executive Officer and Co-founder of Strategic Risk Associates (SRA) Consulting and is the firm's practice leader for risk management, governance, capital management, and digital assets activities. He has led numerous risk management and capital planning engagement efforts for national, regional, and community organizations. Mr. Glotz served as Senior Vice President and Strategic Financial Officer for Crestar Bank and later SunTrust Bank through acquisition.

During his tenure with SunTrust Bank, he held various senior financial positions including Strategic Financial Officer and head of Strategic Cost Management. Immediately before SRA's founding, Mr. Glotz was a Managing Vice President with Capital One Financial Corporation. Mr. Glotz held a number of senior positions with Capital One including Managing Vice President of Corporate Audit and Credit Review Services for Capital One Bank, which included the oversight and development of over 100 audit and risk professionals.

Mr. Glotz also supported the implementation of Enterprise Risk Management and led independent assessments of bank acquisition and integration activities for large-scale mergers. Mr. Glotz is Risk-Reward Co-Chair of the American Association of Bank Directors and is a faculty member of the Institute of Bank Director Education. Mr. Glotz was a Faculty Professor of the Virginia Bankers School at the University of Virginia where he taught Risk Governance and ERM. He has delivered Bank Director training for many State Banking Association, and individually for a number of Boards.

Mr. Glotz received a BBA Degree in Business from the University of Wisconsin, an MBA from the University of Richmond, and completed the Executive Development Program at Wharton, University of Pennsylvania. He is a Certified Risk Professional.

Andrew W. Grant

Partner at Runway LLP

Andrew is a seasoned attorney who specializes in providing regulatory, compliance, and transactional guidance to financial institutions and fintech companies. He has extensive experience advising banks, non-bank lenders, money transmitters, blockchain technology firms, and other entities involved in financial services on a variety of issues, with a particular focus on eCommerce, payments, and digital assets.

His legal practice involves counseling both bank and non-bank financial services companies on a wide range of regulatory and transactional issues, including federal consumer protection laws such as the Truth-in-Lending Act (TILA); the Equal Credit Opportunity Act (ECOA); Unfair, Deceptive, or Abusive Acts or Practices (UDA(A)P); the Fair Debt Collection Practices Act (FDCPA); the Fair Credit Reporting Act (FCRA); the Consumer Leasing Act (CLA); and the Electronic Fund Transfer Act (EFTA). Relatedly, Andrew advises clients on federal and state laws and payment network rules related to payments, including credit cards, prepaid cards or other forms of stored value, and other payment methods. In addition, he is knowledgeable about and has advised on various articles of the Uniform Commercial Code, including Articles 2A, 3, 4A, 9, and 12, as well as state laws, including state lending laws and loan brokering laws. Andrew is also proficient in state money transmitter laws and their application to digital currency companies and has expertise in virtual currency specific issues including issues and obligations surrounding stablecoin issuance and custody arrangements and agreements.

For transactional and contracting experience, Andrew has assisted banks and fintechs in all aspects of their relationships. For transactional work, Andrew represented clients in negotiating bank partnership agreements, "banking-as-a-service" agreements, card network program agreements, and other related matters. For consumer-facing contracts, Andrew has assisted clients with drafting loan agreements (credit cards, open-end credit, and closed-end credit), user agreements, terms of service, and other customer-facing materials.

Andrew has experience analyzing electronic signature and record platforms for compliance with all relevant laws and regulations, including the Electronic Signatures in Global and National Commerce Act (ESIGN) and state Uniform Electronic Transactions Acts. He also counsels non-bank marketplace lenders and banks on "Madden" and True Lender concerns, and assists clients with privacy and data security matters, including compliance with the Gramm-Leach-Bliley Act, the Telephone Consumer Protection Act, and the CAN-SPAM Act.

Before joining Runway, Andrew worked at a boutique fintech practices firm, a top 10 law firm, and a boutique financial services firm in Washington, D.C. In his free time, he enjoys outdoor activities with his partner Lisa, caring for his small zoo (cats, snakes, and fish), gardening, and reading or listening to any kind of espionage or cyberpunk novel.

Andrew also publishes his newsletter, Legal-tender: Your fin-tastic guide to crypto & fintech, which covers the latest legal developments in the fintech and virtual asset space.

Maneesha Gupta

Group Counsel—Banking, Vencora, a part of Constellation Software Inc.

Esha is Group Counsel—Banking at Vencora, a part of Constellation Software Inc (TSX: CSU) where she advises a global portfolio of financial services software companies across the United States, Canada, South America, and Europe. In this role, Esha is responsible for overseeing the company's legal functions around the world, including regulatory affairs, mergers and acquisitions, corporate formation and structuring, reorganizations, corporate governance, litigation, ethics and compliance, contracts, all aspects of employment, privacy, cybersecurity incident response, and intellectual property.

Prior to her current role, Esha worked at Baker & McKenzie LLP, Norton Rose Fulbright LLP, and Counsel—Wealth at a top-four Canadian bank. Esha received Osgoode Hall Law School's Gold Key Award as the "One-to-Watch" for exceptional leadership, professionalism, and compassion not only in her career, but in her dedication to promoting mental health and opportunity for racialized lawyers, women, youth, and people with disabilities. She was also honored as a TEDx Speaker, 50 Under 50 Indo-Canadians, and the Top 25 Most Influential Lawyers by Canadian Lawyer Magazine.

Aside from practicing law, she is also a speaker and has given lectures at universities and colleges across Ontario, and presented in panel events at the Law Society of Ontario and Toronto Region Board of Trade. Esha judges various national advocacy competitions and lectured at her alma mater, Osgoode Hall Law School, and the Ted Rogers School of Management. She regularly writes and presents cases involving privacy and cyber risks associated with AI adoption.

Esha is the owner of Mindful Lawyer Canada where she teaches meditation and mindfulness to legal professionals. The group was founded to tackle psychological distress, anxiety, and depression across all areas of the legal fraternity.

Eric Cheung Hall

Associate, DLA Piper LLP (US)—Litigation

Eric is a blockchain- and web3-focused litigator whose clients have included major centralized and decentralized exchanges in litigation, as well as foreign token issuers, DeFi protocols, NFT projects, and other virtual asset service providers. To these clients, Eric brings his experience navigating commercial disputes, regulatory investigations and enforcement actions, and consumer class actions across multiple jurisdictions. Eric also serves as an editor on DLA Piper's Blockchain and Digital Asset News and Trends newsletter. Outside of his work for DLA Piper, Eric is a bona fide Web3 citizen. He participates in DAO governance, collects digital art, and experiments enthusiastically with DeFi.

Emily J. Honsa Hicks

Senior Financial Regulatory Attorney, DLA Piper

Emily Honsa Hicks is a Senior Financial Regulatory Attorney with DLA Piper, with over ten years of legal experience largely centered in consumer financial services regulation, electronic signature compliance, and other risk management needs, including federal and state compliance, construction and review of robust compliance management systems, review of electronic transaction systems, secured and unsecured lending, and blockchain and cryptocurrency/virtual currency.

Prior to joining DLA Piper, Emily served as underwriting counsel assisting title insurance agents in their resolution of complex real estate legal issues on behalf of a leading real property title insurance underwriter; performing consumer regulatory audits, supporting multiple lines of business to ensure regulatory, bankruptcy, and foreclosure compliance, and handling compliance review of escalated regulatory complaints and complaint reporting, trending, and analysis at a national bank, her breadth of experience informs her practice—her uniquely practical perspective allows her to tailor advice for the operational reality her clients face. In multiple roles, she has interpreted supervisory guidance and actions to assist clients in reviewing and developing compliant policies, procedures, risks, and controls. She has also served as a court mediator, aiding homeowners and financial institutions in reaching resolutions in one of the markets hardest hit by the foreclosure crisis.

Emily is a graduate of Hiram College and holds an Executive Certificate in Negotiation and a Certificate in Strategies for Conflict Management from the University of Notre Dame's Mendoza College of Business. She earned her J.D. at Cleveland-Marshall College of Law (now Cleveland State University College of Law), where she received the Steven J. Werber Collegial Integrity Award and the Joseph M. Perry, Jr Award for Parliamentary Advocacy among other recognitions. While attending law school, she interned at the U.S. Attorney's Office for the Northern District of Ohio and the Naval Criminal Investigative Service (NCIS) in Washington, D.C., handling immigration and criminal matters at the U.S. Attorney's Office and administrative labor law and criminal matters at NCIS.

Emily enjoys pro bono legal work and is qualified for recognition on the D.C. District Court's Capital Pro Bono Honor Roll. In her free time, she enjoys spending time with family and engaging in community service, as well as various artistic and creative pursuits.

Samridhi Jain

Designer and Project Manager, Banking [on] Blockchain

Samridhi Jain is a freelance legal writer and content marketer. She works with independent legal professionals, legal technology companies, law firms, and consultants around the world to help them with their content requirements. She has over four years of experience building and executing marketing strategies from scratch, writing website copy such as sales and landing pages, and creating content assets for websites such as articles, eBooks, Whitepapers, and case studies. She has written for clients in CLM, document automation, contract review, matter management, eDiscovery, intake, eBilling, productivity, low-code/no-code, cryptocurrency, finance, commercial law, mergers and acquisitions, technology law, and contracting. For her law firm clientele, she has written case summaries, case wins, partner profiles, and practice area pages, and has also designed brochures, infographics, and decks.

Alongside her freelance business, Samridhi has served as a legal intern at multiple legal consultancy firms. She's currently pursuing her law degree from India and started her freelance business back in 2020 by creating helpful content for the legal community on LinkedIn. Samridhi has worked closely on numerous legal design projects that involve the simplification of privacy policies, terms and conditions, standard NDAs, and MSAs.

Samridhi enjoys empowering the legal community to create content on social media platforms and has authored chapters and articles on personal branding for legal professionals in various books and on multiple platforms.

Jenny Leung

Partner at Ketsal PLLC

An Associate at Ketsal PLLC, Jenny advises on a range of regulatory and legal issues specific to blockchain, cryptocurrencies, and fintech. She focuses on issues related to U.S. securities laws, state money transmitter laws, data protection laws, and payments regulatory matters. Prior to joining Ketsal, Jenny was a regulatory attorney at the Australian Securities and Investments Commission (ASIC). In her capacity there, she oversaw the ASX's attempted implementation of distributed ledger technology (DLT), worked closely with fintech startups that came through the Innovation Hub, and drafted ASIC's first piece of regulatory guidance regarding DLT. Jenny was also a Key Contributor to Australia's National Blockchain Roadmap RegTech Working Group. She also consulted on GDPR, CCPA, and other data privacy issues at PwC.

Jenny is a regular publisher and speaker on blockchain and crypto regulation. She enjoys discussing and questioning dystopian ideas involving technology, 90's music, and hanging out with her two dogs.

Bobby Lowe

Senior Director, FTI Technology

Bobby Lowe is the former compliance governance lead for a prominent digital asset exchange and compliance professional with a focus on FinTech and digital assets. Mr. Lowe focuses on regulatory risk, financial regulatory compliance, safety and soundness, and financial crime risks across various industries. In addition to his regulatory work, he has conducted financial due diligence and compliance investigations in the United States, Europe, Middle East, and Asia and developed models to assess risk for firms with global footprints across multiple industries. Mr. Lowe possesses a strong understanding of how examiners and third-parties evaluate internal compliance, financial, and operational controls related to regulatory obligations.

In his role as the compliance governance lead for a prominent digital asset exchange, Mr. Lowe's regulatory duties included maintaining the firm's state money transmitter license posture which involved leading numerous state examinations with examiners, reporting to and communicating with regulators, and licensure applications with various regulatory bodies including the NYDFS. Mr. Lowe's efforts directly led to improved relationships with previously adverse regulators and multiple positive Reports of Examination. Mr. Lowe's governance duties involved, but were not limited to, leading the reporting function between internal audit and compliance, maintaining the compliance training program and compliance policies and procedures, and assisting with the maintenance of the exchange's external banking and third-party vendor relationships.

Prior to his time in the digital assets industry, Mr. Lowe led workstreams surveying regulatory risks and conducting investigations into potential fraud and other financial crime matters for a global consulting firm. Mr. Lowe is also experienced in assisting government-appointed monitors and preparing expert witnesses. Mr. Lowe earned his Bachelor's Degree from the University of Florida and J.D. from Stetson University College of Law.

Ciaran McMullan

Ciaran has held multiple CEO roles in the U.S. community and regional banking market and has extensive international experience at multinational banking organizations, financial technology companies, and advisory firms.

He was most recently President and CEO of Suncrest Bank in California (prior to its sale in 2022) leading the bank through a period of significant growth. Suncrest was the fastest growing publicly traded bank in the U.S. between 2013 and 2018, receiving multiple awards and nominations including Top 100 Performing Community Banks (S&P Global), Top 200 Healthiest Banks (DepositAccounts.com); Best Banks to Work For (American Banker Magazine); and Best Small Cap IR (Investor Relations Magazine).

Since the sale of the bank, Ciaran has been consulting with financial technology companies, banks, and industry associations advising on topics including market entry strategy, acquisitions, capital raising, business planning, financial technology, decentralized finance (defi), and regulatory strategy.

Previous senior roles include Chief Executive Officer of National Australia Bank's US Regional Bank, based in Chicago, where he led multiple acquisitions including the Great Western Bank; Chairman of the Great Western Bancorporation based in Sioux Falls, SD; Senior Advisor with Cappello Capital, a boutique investment bank in Los Angeles; Banking Partner with Cap Gemini Ernst & Young in Melbourne, Australia, leading advisory projects ranging from strategy development through to financial technology deployment.

He has also served on the Board of Directors of the Greater Sacramento Economic Council and was one of the founders of the region's Fintech Consortium. Ciaran began his career as a Market Analyst with Abbey National Bank in London.

He is a graduate of both Stirling University and Sheffield Hallam University in the UK and has attended Harvard Business School's Executive Education Programs in both FinTech and Agribusiness. He recently completed a certification in Decentralized Finance (defi) at Duke University.

Ciaran was born and raised in Northern Ireland and has lived and worked on five continents. An avid mountaineer when he was younger, he has climbed four of the seven summits and multiple other high-altitude peaks around the world.

Daniel M. Payne

Securities and Crypto Attorney, Blockade United, PLLC

Mr. Payne has developed an expertise in advising crypto companies in the myriad issues they face in the current unsettled U.S. regulatory environment. Mr. Payne currently serves as counsel and strategic advisor to a dozen companies disrupting various industries (financial services, health and wellness, gold mining, marketing, etc.) by incorporating blockchain technology and cryptocurrency. Mr. Payne has architected the decentralization strategy and legal risk mitigation efforts at these companies. The architecture involves multi-stage decentralization, DAO-like governance, and a Swiss-based company called Node Governance.

Mr. Payne was previously a shareholder at the law firm of Murphy & McGonigle, the Securities Regulation Law Firm of the Year in 2021 and 2022. Murphy & McGonigle was acquired by Davis Wright Tremaine in 2022.

Norman Reed

Norman Reed is currently Interim CEO of Binance.US. He is a graduate of Columbia Law School and has worked for the Federal Reserve Bank of New York and the Division of Trading and Markets at the Securities and Exchange Commission. He also served as General Counsel for Ripple Labs. He spent eight years as the General Counsel of Omgeo LLC, which at that time was a joint venture of The Depository Trust & Clearing Corporation and Thomson Reuters. Given the US Financial Systems Reliance on decades old technology and the subsequent cost and risk to investors, Mr. Reed now works in San Francisco where he hopes new technologies will pave the way for a better, fairer, cheaper financial infrastructure that will benefit all Americans.

David Stier

Partner, DLA Piper LLP (US)—Global Investigations & Compliance, White Collar Defense

David is a litigator, trial attorney, and strategic advisor leading global compliance and advisory matters and investigations involving anti-money laundering (AML), anti-fraud, anti-corruption, sanctions, and export controls, and securities laws and regulatory issues. He counsels clients in highly regulated industries, including financial institutions and financial services and advisory companies, digital asset and blockchain-based companies, chemicals and precious metals companies, and others.

With more than twenty years of experience in both government and private practice, David has a proven record of successfully leading teams through complex investigations, litigations, and prosecutions, including navigating historic challenges in the aftermath of the 2008-2009 global financial crisis, and through the global COVID-19 pandemic. As a skilled strategic advisor, David assists clients in the design, implementation, and improvement of thoughtful, risk-based compliance controls designed to avoid, or mitigate the impact of, costly litigation and investigations.

Prior to joining DLA Piper, David served in various government positions, including at the U.S. Department of Justice (DOJ) and the U.S. Treasury Department.

During his time at the DOJ, David was a prosecutor in the Money Laundering and Asset Recovery Section's (MLARS) Bank Integrity Unit and the DOJ Fraud Section's Market Integrity and Major Frauds Unit where he investigated and prosecuted individuals and corporations in connection with complex white collar matters, including financial fraud, securities fraud, investment fraud, accounting fraud, bank fraud, insider trading, BSA and FCPA violations, and money laundering. David was also a member of an interagency law enforcement group providing guidance to the Treasury Department and the Financial Action Task Force (FATF) on emerging anti-money laundering regulatory issues.

While at the U.S. Treasury Department, David served in senior roles as an investigator and compliance advisor for the Office of Financial Stability, as the Assistant Chief Investigative Counsel, and in other roles for the Office of the Special Inspector General for the Troubled Asset Relief Program (SIGTARP). David led nationwide investigations involving complex securities fraud, bank fraud, and government program fraud, and liaised with the U.S. Attorney's Offices, the Securities and Exchange Commission, and financial regulators throughout the country. David further created and administered compliance and audit review policies and procedures for Treasury Department financial agents, including those involved in mortgage-backed securities trading and housing finance.

David is an active member of the American Bar Association and serves on the ABA's Banking Law Committee as the Vice Chair for the Bank Secrecy Act and Anti-Money Laundering subcommittee. He is also a member of DLA Piper's Corporate Transparency Act Working Group helping advise the firm and its clients on the implementation of the historic AML legislation involving the creation of a beneficial ownership database.

Heidi Wilder

Lead Blockchain Security Researcher Coinbase Unit 0x Team

Heidi Wilder is a Lead Blockchain Security Researcher on Unit 0x at Coinbase. Her work focuses on identifying and mitigating potential blockchain security threats both internally and externally.

Before starting work on the Security side, Heidi was a Manager for Special Investigations at Coinbase. Her work primarily concentrated on combating terror funding campaigns, sanctions evasion, and large-scale money laundering networks, among other major risk areas.

Prior to joining Coinbase, Heidi led a Crypto Intelligence team at the blockchain intelligence company Elliptic in London. While at Elliptic, she oversaw the team responsible for collecting, assessing, and analyzing data that sustained the Elliptic suite of tools. Before entering the cryptocurrency space, Heidi was an Associate at PwC's Global Intelligence practice where she worked on numerous private and public sector engagements.

Heidi received a master's degree in public policy and a bachelor's degree in economics from the University of Virginia.

Grayson Williams

Associate, McDermott Will & Emery

Grayson Williams focuses his practice on restructuring and insolvency, emphasizing bankruptcy, corporate restructuring, workouts, creditors' rights, and commercial litigation. Grayson also teaches Bankruptcy Law in the Paralegal Studies Department at Collin College.

Following law school, Grayson served as a term clerk to the Honorable Harlin D. Hale for the US Bankruptcy Court for the Northern District of Texas.

Chen Xu

Counsel, Debevoise & Plimpton

Chen Xu is a corporate counsel and a member of the firm's Financial Institutions and Special Situations Groups. In addition, he is an active thought leader on emerging issues in the bank regulatory space. Mr. Xu's insights have appeared in the Reuters and the American Banker and he has authored articles on a wide range of bank regulatory topics, including in Lexology: Getting the Deal Through.

Mr. Xu is recognized as an up and coming lawyer by Chambers USA (2023), where clients say he is "responsive, intelligent and pragmatic," "a model of efficiency" and "an industry leader in the US regulatory capital space." He is also said to provide "consistently high-quality advice" and is "a great resource for his clients." In previous editions of the guide, sources note that he is "just exceptional at working through the real technical nuances of capital rules and the other quantitative aspects of technical regulations." Mr. Xu is also noted as a Rising Star by IFLR1000 (2022).

Mr. Xu joined the firm in 2013. He received a J.D. in 2013 from Columbia Law School, where he was a Harlan Fiske Stone Scholar. Mr. Xu received a B.A. with High Honors from the University of California, Berkeley in 2010, where he was elected to Phi Beta Kappa.